# THE ELEMENTS OF PHILOSOPHY

# THE ELEMENTS OF
# PHILOSOPHY

## A Compendium for
## Philosophers and Theologians

### WILLIAM A. WALLACE, O.P.

WIPF & STOCK · Eugene, Oregon

Wipf and Stock Publishers
199 W 8th Ave, Suite 3
Eugene, OR 97401

The Elements of Philosophy
A Compendium for Philosophers and Theologians
By Wallace, William, OP
Copyright©1977 Alba House
ISBN 13: 978-1-62032-308-3
Publication date 5/1/2011
Previously published by Alba House, 1977

# ACKNOWLEDGMENT

The Catholic University of America has extended permission for the incorporation into the text of this book of parts of copyrighted articles from the *New Catholic Encyclopedia* (15 vols. and Supplement, New York: McGraw-Hill Publishing Co., 1967, Supplement, 1974).

# PREFACE

Philosophy is among the oldest of intellectual disciplines, and it has undergone extensive development throughout the ages. So extensive has this development been, considering only its growth in the West, that it is exceedingly difficult to summarize in a systematic and historical way its knowledge content. Yet there would seem to be common agreement that certain elements go to make up philosophical knowledge, just as there would seem to be broad consensus that certain persons have figured most prominently in its articulation. This book assumes that these premises are correct and addresses itself to the task of making a précis of such knowledge and its development, of presenting the content of philosophy and its history in concise and organized fashion.

The work is projected to meet a twofold need and so is addressed to a twofold audience. The first need is that of philosophers and of students of philosophy, who require a comprehensive view of the entire scope of their discipline and its history, but who frequently, because of specialization and the limited number of course offerings to which they have access, are unable to attain it. This need has always existed, but it has been exacerbated in recent years because of various factors that have affected both Catholic and non-Catholic education alike. In the case of the former, the years following Vatican II have seen a steady decline in the number and quality of philosophy courses taught in Catholic colleges and seminaries. In many institutions the abandonment of a philosophy requirement has forced philosophy departments to resort to a variety of methods to attract students. Unfortunately such methods, based as they are on the pragmatism of relevance, result in a dilution of course content and a lowering of the level of instruction. As a consequence difficult material is not being taught, nor are students expected to gain a comprehension of matters that previously would have been regarded as *scientia debita* in their discipline. A matching situation exists in non-Catholic institutions, except that here the inroads of analytical philosophy, preoccupied as it is with the piecemeal solution of problems tractable by its methods, have caused whole areas of systematic and historical knowledge to be dropped from the philosophy curriculum. In very few institutions, as a consequence, can a student now obtain a complete education in philosophy, and one might even venture to say that the philosophical community at large is currently in danger of losing its considerable heritage from times past.

Although fascinating in its own right, philosophy has been cultivated for centuries in the Western World because of the unique service it can render to Christian theology. Just as mathematics is regarded as the "handmaiden of the sciences," so philosophy is rightfully called the "handmaiden of theology." It is for this reason that the Church has insisted that candidates for the priesthood have a substantial foundation in philosophy before beginning their theological studies. In recent years, however, seminarians have encountered difficulties similar to those of philosophy majors in their attempts to secure this requisite knowledge. In neither case is the situation desirable, but for seminarians it has been made even less so by two factors that complicate theological education in the U.S. The first is the present tendency to relegate the philosophical education of future theologians to the four years of college that precede their entrance into a seminary. For many students this means that the philosophy credits they bring to the seminary will not be from a Catholic college, incomplete as the instruction even there may be. Now philosophy in our day is a very diversified discipline, pursued in a variety of ways by its many practitioners. While throughout the centuries, moreover, philosophy has come to be regarded as the "handmaiden of theology," not all recent philosophy can be so regarded. Indeed many types of philosophy that have come to predominate in non-Catholic institutions in the U.S. would be more a hindrance than a help for the study of Christian theology. A person might even have earned a Ph.D. in this discipline and still be poorly prepared philosophically to begin his theological studies.

The other complicating factor is the more recent expectation that seminarians have a broad base of preparation in the behavioral and social sciences as part of their training for the priesthood. Although these sciences may have ministerial value, not infrequently they are taught in such a way as to impart a world-view that works against traditional philosophical positions of special importance for theology. The curriculum of a college student is limited, and the more time he devotes to psychology and sociology, say, the less time he inevitably has for philosophy. Add to this the distinct possibility that greater numbers of students may soon be coming to seminaries with undergraduate majors in the behavioral and social sciences than with majors in philosophy. In such circumstances the theology professors who address incoming students may well wonder what they can rightfully expect by way of previous philosophical preparation, or what remedial courses should be provided to make up for deficiencies that are clearly known to exist.

This book is designed as a practical expedient to meet the needs of both situations just outlined, those respectively of the philosophy major and the prospective theologian. It is simply a primer, an elementary presentation of the main teachings of philosophy that can promote a competent grasp of that discipline, either for its own sake or as a preparation for theology. Beyond this it pretends to be little more than a syllabus, i.e., a listing of the more important matters on which students may be expected to have some convictions, or at least informed opinions, by the time they complete their studies. It is directed to students themselves, for use either while studying philosophy in a formal way or while otherwise engaged, perhaps already studying theology, in making up deficiencies in their previous formation. Hopefully it will be useful also to teachers and to administrators charged with providing courses for philosophy majors or for pre-theology students, by way of suggesting topics to be covered in lectures and in other teaching situations, and even for structuring examinations, either as philosophy comprehensives or to test a student's achievement level before beginning theology.

A syllabus, of course, supplies a mere skeleton or outline of knowledge. To put flesh on that skeleton or to fill out the outline it is necessary to refer the user to other reading materials and teaching aids. The author has sought to do this in the present work by relying on his long experience as editor and member of the editorial board of the *New Catholic Encyclopedia*. This encyclopedia is widely available in the U.S., and it is relatively up-to-date: the first fifteen volumes were published in 1967, and a sixteenth supplementary volume was issued in 1974. More important, it contains an extensive and authoritative treatment of all aspects of philosophy, its history, and its relations to other disciplines, written by acknowledged experts in their fields and with the needs of Catholic scholarship explicitly in mind. Most articles include a bibliography that features works in English, at an elementary level when available, where the student can find further exposition of the subject matter in which he is interested. Teachers may supplement these bibliographies with their own preferred readings, to be sure, but it may be observed that, with the decline of Catholic publishing during the post-Vatican II period, relatively few new textbooks have appeared, and thus such readings will generally have to be found in the periodical literature.

References to fuller treatments in the *New Catholic Encyclopedia* of materials discussed herein are given by parenthetical entries of the type (11:292c). Here the first number (11) is that of the volume, the second number (292) that of the page, and the letter (c) that of the quadrant on the page where the treatment begins (a, b, c, and d indicate respectively the upper and lower halves of the left and right columns of the page). Usually only beginning references are given, although in some cases both beginning and ending references are indicated to specify a particular passage of interest. The user should refer to these referenced articles and passages for a fuller explanation of the statement here given. Generally he will find that the statement itself has been extracted from the fuller exposition in the encyclopedia, and in many instances he will discover not only how the matter of interest fits into the synthesis here proposed, but also how it relates to other, often diverse, systems of thought. After that he may wish to consult the bibliography and continue on with books or articles that are more expository in character, until he has answered all his questions or otherwise satisfied his curiosity. A teacher, it goes without saying, can be of inestimable help in this process, and a structured classroom situation will generally facilitate his acquisition of knowledge better than directed reading alone. Should either of these aids be lacking, however, the situation is by no means hopeless, particularly for the student who is properly motivated and who sees his task as one of essential preparation for his life's work.

Apart from these references to the encyclopedia, the book also contains internal or cross references to materials treated elsewhere in its pages. This has been thought desirable because the fields into which philosophy is divided are interrelated, and one field frequently makes use of concepts developed in others. A system of cross reference also eliminates the need to repeat material that has been, or will be, explained better in other contexts. To facilitate such internal reference the chapters of the book have been divided into sections that are consecutively numbered from beginning to end; the paragraphs within each section are also numbered with Arabic numerals, beginning with the number one in each section. Cross references are inserted directly into the text and enclosed in square brackets. A typical reference would be [§19.6]; this refers the reader to section 19 (the subdivision of Chapter 3 that deals with place and time) and to the sixth numbered paragraph within that section, which treats of individuation.

The author is aware that the style he has here adopted is terse, even dense, and that his summary is so packed as to contain far more information than the average student can master in, say, two years of study. Such depth and range, however, actually give the resulting product a special flexibility as a pedagogical aid, particularly in view of its being keyed to the *New Catholic Encyclopedia*. With a minimum of guidance from a teacher it can prove helpful for general inquiry into the subject matter of philosophy and its history, and at the same time it contains enough material to engage the serious student, and to serve as a reference guide against which he can check his comprehension of this difficult discipline as he advances in its mastery.

Philosophy, of course, is an intriguing and life-long study. It cannot be reduced to a finite number of propositions or concepts, nor can it be circumscribed by any philosophical system. But one can surely be introduced to its study by focusing on its knowledge content as expressed in more or less systematic form. This has always been the ideal behind the notion of the *philosophia perennis* that has successfully been used by the Church to prepare its philosophers and theologians over the centuries. It is hoped that this simple compendium may serve a similar function in the decades that lie ahead, or at least until something better comes along that can meet the specific needs of philosophy majors and of students preparing for theology.

The author claims no originality for this work, aware that he is more its redactor than its composer. As already noted, he has summarized many of the articles contained in the *New Catholic Encyclopedia,* and in so doing has had no scruples over incorporating verbatim into the text passages that suited his needs. The book has been constructed, in this fashion, largely from the work of others. The user can readily verify this by consulting the references given to the encyclopedia, where, at the end of each article cited, he will discover the name of the original contributor. This feature should make the presentation more authoritative, involving as it does the collaboration of hundreds of authors with recognized expertise on the topics treated. Still, the work of the redactor has been more than editorial, for to him must be ascribed the overall synthesis, the shades of interpretation involved in reshaping its components, and, unhappily, any errors that may have insinuated themselves in the process. He is deeply aware, of course, of his indebtedness to many colleagues and friends, particularly the collaborators just mentioned. He must express special debts of gratitude, finally, to Norman H. Fenton for his careful reading of the manuscript, and to The Catholic University of America, holder of the copyright of the encyclopedia, for permission to use materials that have already appeared in its pages.

William A. Wallace

Washington, D. C.

# ANALYTICAL TABLE OF CONTENTS

Preface . . . . . . . . . . . . . . . . . . . . . . . . . . . . . . . . . . . . vii

Chapter 1. Introduction . . . . . . . . . . . . . . . . . . . . . . . 3
§1. *Introduction to Philosophy:* 1 notion, 2 as science, 3 unity, 4 branches, 5 speculative, 6 practical, 7 new disciplines, 8 Christian philosophy, 9 scholastic philosophy, 10 philosophy and science, 11 philosophical pluralism, 12 division, 13 pre-theology requirements.

PART I. SYSTEMATIC PHILOSOPHY: BASIC
DISCIPLINES

Chapter 2. Logic . . . . . . . . . . . . . . . . . . . . . . . . . . . . . 13
§2. *Aristotelian Logic:* 1 as an art, 2 as a science, 3 three acts of mind, 4 formal, material.

Formal Logic . . . . . . . . . . . . . . . . . . . . . . . . . . . . . . . . 14
§3. *Simple Apprehension:* 1 notion, 2 concept, 3 term, 4 sign, 5 comprehension, 6 definition, 7 nominal, real, 8 division. §4. *Judgment:* 1 judgment, 2 subject, predicate, 3 existence, 4 truth, falsity, 5 proposition, 6 its modifications, 7 compound propositions, 8 square of opposition. §5. *Reasoning:* 1 reasoning, 2 consequence, 3 argumentation, 4 inductive, deductive, 5 syllogism, 6 categorical, 7 principles, 8 laws, 9 variations, 10 hypothetical, 11 induction, 12 fallacies.

Material Logic . . . . . . . . . . . . . . . . . . . . . . . . . . . . . . . 23
§6. *Material Logic:* notion. §7. *Universals:* 1 notion, 2 kinds, 3 ontological status, 4 abstraction, 5 phantasm, 6 intelligibles. §8. *Predicables:* 1 notion, 2 kinds, 3 definitions, 4 order.

§9. *Categories:* 1 notion, 2 modes of being and knowing, 3 kinds, 4 substance, 5 quantity, 6 quality, 7 relation, 8 action and passion, 9 time, 10 location, situation, vestition. §10. *Kinds of Distinction:* 1 notion, 2 formal, material, 3 real, 4 absolute, modal, 5 separability, 6 rational, 7 reason reasoning, 8 reason reasoned about. §11. *First Principles:* 1 second act of mind, 2 first principles, 3 proper, 4 common, 5 comparison, 6 other distinctions. §12. *Demonstration:* 1 third act of mind, 2 demonstration, 3 kinds, 4 *propter quid*, 5 *quia.* §13. *Science:* 1 notion, 2 kinds, 3 speculative, 4 orders of abstraction, 5 mixed, 6 practical. §14. *Nature of Logic:* 1 as an art, 2 as a science, 3 as an instrument.

Chapter 3. Natural Philosophy ....................... 41
§15. *Philosophy of Nature:* 1 notion, 2 subject, 3 procedure. §16. *Matter and Form:* 1 change, 2 kinds, 3 matter, 4 form, 5 privation, 6 final cause, nature, 7 principles, causes. §17. *Nature:* 1 notion, 2 matter as nature, 3 form as nature, 4 nature and end, 5 chance, 6 violence, 7 mathematics, 8 demonstrations, 9 properties. §18. *Motion:* 1 notion, 2 kinds, 3 local motion, 4 alteration, 5 augmentation, 6 action, passion, 7 continuum, 8 infinity. §19. *Place and Time:* 1 measures, 2 place, 3 space, 4 time, 5 the instant, 6 individuation. §20. *The First Unmoved Mover:* 1 the problem, 2 motor causality principle, 3 conditions for motion, 4 existence of the first cause, 5 its nature, 6 prelude to metaphysics.

Chapter 4. Psychology ........................... 59
§21. *Philosophical Psychology:* notion. §22. *Life and Soul:* 1 life, 2 soul, 3 first actuality, 4 organized body, 5 formal effects, 6 kinds, 7 powers, 8 power parts. §23. *Cognition:* 1 knowledge, 2 cognition, 3 immateriality, 4 intentionality, 5 intentional species, 6 types. §24. *Sensation and Perception:* 1 sensation, 2 knowledge of object, 3 senses, 4 external, 5 sensibles, 6 internal, 7 central, 8 imagination, 9 cogitative, 10 memory, 11 perception, 12 unified knowledge. §25. *Intellection:* 1 intellect, 2 abstractive process, 3 concept forma-

tion, 4 object, 5 immateriality, 6 reflection. §26. *Appetition:* 1 appetite, 2 kinds, 3 elicited, 4 sense and will. §27. *Sensitive Appetites:* 1 notion, 2 kinds, 3 emotions. §28. *Volition:* 1 will, 2 free will, 3 its object, 4 as related to other powers, 5 its acts, 6 other influences. §29. *Man:* 1 philosophical anthropology, 2 man, 3 human soul, 4 its immortality, 5 its origin, 6 person, 7 subsistence, 8 individual differences.

Chapter 5. Metaphysics ........................... 85
§30. *Metaphysics:* 1 notion, 2 subject, 3 being in general. §31. *Being:* 1 common, 2 real, 3 categories, 4 without a genus, 5 analogy, 6 kinds. §32. *Transcendentals:* 1 notion, 2 extension, 3 properties of being, 4 unity, truth, goodness, 5 beauty, thing, otherness, 6 first principles. §33. *Principles of Being:* 1 notion, 2 potency and act, 3 real distinction, 4 priority and limitation, 5 essence and existence, 6 really distinct. §34. *Substance and Subsistence:* 1 substance, 2 finite substance, 3 accident, 4 subsistence, 5 nature, supposit, existence, 6 mode. §35. *Causality:* 1 notion, 2 kinds, 3 condition, 4 occasion, 5 form, 6 formal causality, 7 material, 8 efficient, 9 instrumental, 10 final, 11 exemplary, 12 participation. §36. *Wisdom:* 1 wisdom, 2 understanding.

Chapter 6. Epistemology ........................... 109
§37. *Epistemology:* 1 notion, 2 reflection, 3 four questions. §38. *Knowledge:* 1 notion, subject and object, 2 interiority and exteriority, 3 consciousness, 4 kinds of knowledge. §39. *Truth and Falsity:* 1 truth, 2 material truth, 3 formal truth, 4 validity of judgment, 5 falsity, 6 other theories of truth. §40. *Evidence and Certitude:* 1 evidence, 2 kinds, 3 certitude, 4 doubt, wonder, aporia.

Chapter 7. Natural Theology ....................... 121
§41. *Natural Theology:* 1 notion, 2 relation to metaphysics, 3 non-philosophical assumptions, 4 other positions. §42. *Participation and the Act of Being:* 1 common being, 2 being and participation, 3 proper proportionality, 4 intrinsic attri-

bution. §43. *Proofs of God's Existence:* 1 argument from *esse*, 2 naming God, 3 the five ways, 4 modern proofs, 5 confirmatory arguments. §44. *God's Essence and Attributes:* 1 ways of knowing God, 2 negation, 3 eminence, 4 divine attributes, 5 rationally distinct, 6 divine essence, 7 aseity. §45. *Entitative Attributes:* 1 simplicity, immutability, 2 unicity, 3 infinity, perfection, 4 eternity, immensity. §46. *Operative Attributes:* 1 intelligence, 2 thought thinking itself, 3 possibles, future contingents. 4 will of God, 5 objects of divine will, 6 divine freedom, 7 providence, 8 omnipotence. §47. *Divine Causality:* 1 divine causality, 2 creation, 3 creation and revelation, 4 conservation, 5 creatures as causes, 6 primary and secondary causes, 7 premotion, concurrence. §48. *The Problem of Evil:* 1 problem of evil, 2 notion of evil, 3 kinds, 4 subject, 5 physical evil, 6 moral evil, 7 cause of moral evil, 8 providence and evil, 9 mystery.

Chapter 8. Ethics ............................149
§49. *Moral Philosophy:* 1 ethics, 2 subject, 3 order as normative, 4 Christian ethics, 5 division. §50. *The Human Act:* 1 human act, 2 its principles, 3 habit, 4 virtue and vice, 5 cardinal virtues, 6 freedom of choice, 7 exercise, specification, 8 components, 9 motion of will. §51. *The Ends of Human Action:* 1 end, 2 end in ethics, 3 kinds, 4 end of man, 5 ultimate end. §52. *Voluntarity and Involuntarity:* 1 voluntarity, 2 explained, 3 involuntarity, force, fear, emotion, 4 nonvoluntarity, ignorance, kinds. §53. *Morality and Responsibility:* 1 morality, 2 kinds, 3 determinants, 4 rule, 5 consequences, double effect, 6 indifferent act, 7 responsibility, imputability, 8 co-operation. §54. *Law and Right Reason:* 1 common good, 2 law, civil law, 3 natural law, 4 eternal law, 5 synderesis, 6 first principles, 7 prudence, 8 conscience. §55. *The Life of Virtue:* 1 virtue, 2 subject, how acquired, 3 temperance, 4 fortitude, 5 the mean and right reason, 6 right appetite. §56. *Justice and Rights:* 1 justice, 2 positive law, epikeia, 3 commutative, legal, distributive justice, 4 right, 5 natural rights, 6 hierarchy of rights.

PART II. SYSTEMATIC PHILOSOPHY:
SPECIAL DISCIPLINES

Chapter 9. Philosophy of the Humanities ............... 179
    §57. *Philosophy of Language:* 1 language, linguistics,
    2 semantics, 3 linguistic analysis, 4 hermeneutics. §58. *Philosophy of Art:* 1 art, 2 poetics, 3 aesthetics, 4 beauty.
    §59. *Philosophy of History:* 1 history, historicity, 2 philosophy of history, metahistory, 3 positions. §60. *Philosophy of Religion:* 1 religion, 2 myth, 3 symbol, 4 philosophy of
    religion. §61. *Philosophy of Education:* 1 philosophy of
    education, 2 theories, 3 liberal arts. §62. *Philosophy of
    Value:* 1 philosophy of value, 2 value, kinds of good.

Chapter 10. Philosophy of Mathematics ................ 191
    §63. *Philosophy of Mathematics:* 1 mathematics, 2 its philosophy, 3 science of quantity, 4 logicism, formalism, intuitionism, 5 pure mathematics, 6 applied mathematics. §64.
    *Number and the Continuum:* 1 number, 2 prior notions,
    3 nature and reality, 4 continuum, 5 extension, contiguity,
    6 indivisibles, 7 continuity of the discrete. §65. *Symbolic
    Logic:* 1 symbolic logic, 2 variables, constant, function,
    3 functors, arguments, kinds of logic, 4 propositional logic,
    5 material implication.

Chapter 11. Philosophy of the Natural Sciences ......... 201
    §66. *Philosophy of Science:* 1 modern science, 2 philosophy
    of science, 3 scientific revolutions, 4 truth, objectivity.
    §67. *Methodological Concepts:* 1 hypothetico-deductive
    method, 2 fact, 3 measurement, 4 law, 5 problem of induction, 6 theory, 7 models, analogies. §68. *Physical Sciences:*
    1 force, mass, energy, 2 laws of motion, 3 laws of thermodynamics, 4 quantum theory, 5 relativity, 6 structure of
    matter, 7 the universe. §69. *Life Sciences:* 1 biology, 2 biological mechanism, 3 biogenesis, 4 evolution, 5 dynamic
    order, designer, 6 genetics. §70. *Technology:* 1 technology,
    2 philosophy of technology, 3 assessment.

Chapter 12. Philosophy of the Behavioral Sciences. . . . . . . 219
§71. *Anthropology:* 1 physical anthropology, 2 human evolution, 3 cultural anthropology, 4 cultural evolution, 5 archeology, ethnology. §72. *Modern Psychology:* 1 science of
psychology, 2 methodology, 3 measurement, 4 psychometrics, 5 experiment, 6 comparative psychology, 7 other
branches. §73. *Systems and Theories of Psychology:* 1 systems
and theories, 2 structuralism, 3 functionalism, 4 behaviorism, 5 Gestalt psychology, 6 psychoanalysis, 7 theories,
8 learning, perception, personality, 9 normality, abnormality.
§74. *Philosophy of the Behavioral Sciences:* notion.

Chapter 13. Social Philosophy . . . . . . . . . . . . . . . . . . . . . . .231
§75. *Social Philosophy and Social Science:* 1 social philosophy, 2 social science, 3 models, methodology, 4 sociology,
economics, social work. §76. *Society:* 1 notion, 2 ontological
basis, 3 unity of order, 4 function, reality, 5 structure,
6 moral person, 7 kinds of society. §77. *Authority:* 1 notion,
its necessity, 2 function, 3 source. §78. *Marriage:* 1 notion,
2 kinds, 3 motive behind, 4 ends, primary and secondary,
5 properties, unity and indissolubility, 6 abuses. §79. *The
Family:* 1 notion, 2 functions, 3 objectives, 4 children.
§80. *Social Justice:* 1 notion, 2 right to work, 3 private property, 4 principle of solidarity, 5 principle of subsidiarity.

Chapter 14. Political Philosophy . . . . . . . . . . . . . . . . . . . .251
§81. *Political Philosophy and Political Science:* 1 political
philosophy, 2 classical, 3 medieval, 4 modern, 5 political
science. §82. *The State:* 1 notion, 2 elements of, 3 society
and, 4 nation and, 5 international law, 6 just war. §83. *Government:* 1 notion, 2 power, 3 checks and balances, 4 separation of powers, 5 forms of government, 6 communism,
socialism. §84. *Philosophy of Law:* 1 notion, jurisprudence,
2 positivism, natural law, 3 basic problem, 4 natural vs. civil.
5 civil law, 6 misunderstandings, 7 goal of civil law.

## PART III. HISTORY OF PHILOSOPHY

Chapter 15. History of Philosophy .................267
§85. *Philosophy and History:* 1 philosophy, 2 history, 3 history of philosophy, 4 philosophy and philosophies. §86. *Philosophical Systems:* 1 systems, 2 being, 3 truth, 4 knowledge, 5 God, 6 ethics. §87. *Historiography of Philosophy:* 1 methodology, 2 divisions, various bases, 3 metahistory of philosophy.

Chapter 16. Ancient Philosophy .................277
§88. *Early Thought:* 1 ancient philosophy, 2 Greek philosophy, 3 Chinese, Indian philosophy, 4 pre-Socratics, nature, 5 Heraclitus, Parmenides, being, 6 elements, atomism. §89. *Classical Greek Period:* 1 Sophists, Socrates, 2 Plato, 3 Aristotle. §90. *Post-Aristotelian Developments:* 1 Cynics, Stoics, Epicureans, 2 Jewish, Roman philosophy, 3 Platonism, Neoplatonism, 4 end of an era.

Chapter 17. Medieval Philosophy .................285
§91. *Patristic Philosophy:* 1 medieval, patristic, scholastic philosophy, 2 Greek apologists, 3 Origenism, Hellenism, 4 Greek Fathers, Cappadocians, 5 Latin Fathers, Augustine, 6 Boethius. §92. *Scholasticism and Its Prelude:* 1 Carolingians, Erigena, 2 dialectics, early scholasticism, 3 School of Chartres, 4 new learning, translations, Arab Aristotelianism. §93. *High Scholasticism:* 1 Grosseteste, Augustinianism, 2 Albert, Aquinas, Thomism, 3 Latin Averroism, 4 correctoria, Scotus, Scotism. §94. *Late Scholasticism:* 1 Ockham, Ockhamism, 2 nominalist logic, science, 3 scholastic systems, 4 humanism, the Reformation.

Chapter 18. Modern Philosophy.................297
§95. *Renaissance Philosophy:* 1 modern philosophy, 2 Renaissance philosophy, Cusa, 3 Platonism, Aristotelianism, 4 Stoicism, skepticism, 5 politics, nature, 6 second scholasticism, 7 the Jesuits, Suarez, Suarezianism. §96. *Mechanical*

*Philosophy and Empiricism:* 1 mechanical philosophers, Bacon, Galileo, Newton, 2 Hobbes, Descartes, 3 empiricists, Locke, Berkeley, Hume. §97. *Rationalism and Other Movements:* 1 rationalists, Spinoza, Malebranche, Leibniz, 2 Cambridge Platonists, common sense, enlightenment, 3 Kant, Wolff. §98. *Philosophical Reconstruction:* 1 romanticism, 2 idealists, Fichte, Schelling, Hegel, 3 Kierkegaard, Feuerbach, Marx, Engels, 4 positivism, Comte, Mill, 5 life and will, Schopenhauer, Darwin, Nietzsche, 6 traditionalism, ontologism, neo-Kantianism.

Chapter 19. Contemporary Philosophy ................309
§99. *Life, Idea, and Spirit:* 1 contemporary philosophy, 2 life philosophies, Bergson, Dilthey, 3 idealism, Bradley, 4 Royce, personalism, 5 Croce, Gentile, actualism, 6 philosophy of spirit, Blondel. §100. *American Philosophy:* 1 Peirce, James, pragmatism, 2 naturalism, Santayana, Dewey, 3 process philosophy, Whitehead, 4 Hartshorne, 5 realism. §101. *Logic and Analysis:* 1 logical positivism, Ayer, 2 analytical philosophy, Moore, Russell, 3 linguistic analysis, Wittgenstein, 4 religious and ethical language, metaethics. §102. *Phenomenology and Existentialism:* 1 Husserl, 2 Scheler, Merleau-Ponty, 3 phenomenology, intentionality, objectivity, reductions, 4 idealist elements, Lebenswelt, 5 existentialism, 6 Heidegger, Sartre, Marcel, Jaspers, 7 Bultmann, Tilich. §103. *Recent French and German Philosophy:* 1 French philosophy, 2 Lévi-Strauss, 3 Ricoeur, 4 German philosophy, 5 Gadamer, 6 Frankfurt School, 7 Catholic existentialists. §104. *Thomism: Existential and Transcendental:* 1 Thomistic revival, 2 Maritain, 3 Gilson, 4 transcendental Thomism, Maréchal, 5 Rahner, Lonergan, 6 preconceptual knowledge, 7 transcendental method, 8 knowing God, 9 implicit intuition, Schillebeeckx.

Index ...........................................333

# THE ELEMENTS OF PHILOSOPHY

# CHAPTER 1.

# INTRODUCTION

## §1. INTRODUCTION TO PHILOSOPHY

1. *Philosophy* (11:294c) means literally "love of wisdom," a type of perfect and even divine knowledge that enables one to judge of all things in terms of their ultimate causes. As understood in the tradition of the Church (11:296c), it is a habit of mind or a body of natural knowledge that results from disciplined inquiry and that enables one to explain in a more or less profound way the sum of human experiences. It differs from common knowledge in that it is acquired and evolved systematically, although it must take its beginnings from ordinary experience. Insofar as it considers everything knowable by reason and is not restricted to one or other species or kind of entity, it is more universal in its concern than are the special sciences; in a certain way it includes even them and their objects in its considerations.

2. Thinkers in the Thomistic tradition accent the certain and causal character of philosophical knowledge. Though not holding that every subject investigated by philosophers permits of absolutely certain judgment, they regard truth [§39] and certitude [§40] as the goal of philosophy and insist on the availability to the human mind of at least some starting points on which philosophical reasoning can be solidly grounded. Philosophy, in their understanding, remains ever open to further extension and development, but it is not subject to change with regard to first principles and other self-evident truths on which this development is based, except in the sense that these come to be more deeply comprehended and understood with the passage of time.

Thus they define philosophy as all certain and evident knowledge, grasped either directly or through causal analysis and demonstration, together with its dialectical extension, that man can attain through human reason alone, and this both in the speculative order and in the practical order, but in the latter only as it enables man to reach his ultimate end.

3. Being concerned with all knowledge, philosophy is not merely one discipline but is an aggregate of several different disciplines; since its unity is merely analogical, it cannot be defined strictly. Its certain and evident character separates it from conjecture and from mere personal opinion, and also from divine faith which, though certain, is not evident to the human mind. Again, it is purely natural knowledge, and this separates it from sacred theology, which makes use of knowledge that can be had only through the acceptance of divine revelation.

4. The various *branches* of philosophy (11:297c) follow from the traditional classification of knowledge into speculative, with its three degrees or levels, and practical, with its realm of art and ethics.

5. *Speculative knowledge* is knowledge for its own sake: it is divided into three parts depending on the way in which the object it considers is related to matter [§13.4], namely: metaphysics, the most abstract; mathematics, of intermediate degree; and natural philosophy, whose objects have sensible matter as part of their definition. *Logic* [§2] is usually not included in such a classification as a separate type of knowledge; rather it is a discipline demanded of the human mind prior to its comprehension of any subject matter. *Natural philosophy* [§15] investigates the world of nature, matter, motion, time and space. *Psychology* [§21] is the part of natural philosophy that focuses on the soul and its relation to body; it investigates problems of life, cognition, and appetition. Mathematical entities have long been of special interest to philosophers, but in the present day mathematics is no longer considered a part of philosophy; rather the philosophical problems it generates are considered in the philosophy of mathematics [§63]. *Metaphysics* [§30] is the science of being, its attributes, its categories, and its principles. Because of its wide general

concerns, it alone is capable of defending knowledge claims in all disciplines, a task which it undertakes in its part known as *epistemology* [§37]. Yet another part of metaphysics is *natural theology* [§41], which uses reason to investigate the existence and attributes of God as a principle of being itself.

6. *Practical knowledge* is knowledge for the sake of operation or conduct. Its main branches are the arts of making [§58.1] and the arts of directing human activity; the latter are considered a basic part of philosophy under the names of *ethics* [§49] and *politics* [§81], and are concerned with the study of morality, social and political life, the nature of law and other institutions that preserve the common good.

7. Apart from these basic disciplines that go to make up philosophy in its traditional sense, there are a considerable number of interesting problems that are considered by philosophers under the title "the philosophy of *x*," where *x* can stand for language, art, religion, and so on. The fact that such titles are accepted in the present day attests to the pervasive influence of philosophical reasoning and the recurrence of problems that invite solution by philosophers in a variety of new disciplines—most of which, of course, originally came into being as an offspring of philosophy. These problem areas are considered in what follows not as basic disciplines but as special disciplines [§§57-84]; their study enables one to recover the wisdom of the past and apply it in new contexts, so that the philosophical relevance of the newer disciplines may be made more manifest.

8. If philosophy is understood as defined above, a special problem arises when one applies the adjective "Christian" to it so as to speak of a *Christian philosophy* (3:640c). The expression has been used by contemporary Thomists such as Etienne Gilson [§104.3] and Jacques Maritain [§104.2] and by others such as Maurice Blondel [§99.6]. The problem is that the term "Christian" when applied to philosophy has itself the connotation of grace and divine revelation and thus suggests that the philosophy it modifies, being under supernatural influences, can no longer be regarded as pure philosophy. Yet there are a variety of ways of understanding the expression "Christian philosophy" that need

not involve such obvious contradiction. One way is to speak of the control exercised by revelation over philosophy as negative and exclusive, i.e., as notifying a philosopher who may have come to a conclusion manifestly contrary to faith of his error. There then remains for the philosopher, as Christian, the task of rethinking his arguments and discovering his error. This solution implicitly assumes that God is the Author both of nature and of revelation, and that the truth of the one can never contradict that of the other. Another solution, obviously more nuanced, is the following (3:644a): A Christian philosophy is one that takes account, from its beginnings, of the fact of Christianity no less than the existence of stars and planets. It aims to form a system in which Christianity is reduced to the object of an abstract dialectic, or, alternatively, it would conduct its inquiry in a way that, without altering its natural character, opens philosophy to wait upon, or even to make appeal to, the order of grace [cf. §§43.2, 47.3].

9. The expression *scholastic philosophy* (12:1146d) does not have the same connotation as Christian philosophy, although it has been derided by its adversaries as a disguised form of theology. Properly speaking, scholastic philosophy refers simply to the philosophy of the Schoolmen, meaning by this the philosophy that was first elaborated in the universities of the Middle Ages. As such it is characterized by its emphasis on system. Scholastic philosophy is a synthesis that attempts to organize all questions philosophy asks and to present the answers in a strictly logical format. This systematization most frequently uses the Aristotelian concept of science or *scientia* [§13] as its internal principle of organization. The scholastic philosopher attempts to explain things in terms of their causes with the aid of definition, division, and argumentation, and preferably with the type of argumentation that leads to strict demonstration. The method he employs, sometimes called "scholastic method" (12:1145a), must be understood in the context of its historical origins to be properly appreciated [§§92-94]. In the minds of many scholastic philosophy connotes an arid verbalism, a closed system of thought perpetuated by rote memorization. Yet the technical vocabulary

of scholastic philosophy is a necessary instrument of its precision. Behind its apparently abstract terminology lies an intense effort to gain insight into the nature of reality as manifest in the facts of experience. (For an explanation of the principal Latin expressions used by scholastics, see 12:1147c).

10. An interesting problem that arises in contemporary scholasticism is that of the relationship between *philosophy and science* (11:317a), or, more precisely, between natural philosophy and recent science, two disciplines that prior to the nineteenth century had been regarded as one. Many scholastics of the present day urge a radical distinction between philosophy and science, some regarding natural philosophy as a specialized branch of metaphysics and science as positive knowledge at a wholly different level. Others see both disciplines as operating on the same level, i.e., that of nature, but claim that natural philosophy attains ontological knowledge whereas modern science attains only empiriological knowledge. Yet others question whether so-called empiriological knowledge really represents a distinct type of knowing; they regard it as merely a dialectical extension of the knowledge gained in natural philosophy. A final position is that modern science is a continuation of natural philosophy into ever more specialized areas of concern, and that its methods are for the most part, although not exclusively, dialectical; thus this view allows for the possibility of demonstration, and so for a cumulative growth of certain knowledge, even in the realm of modern science. It is this last position, as more open to philosophical innovation from within science, that will be implicitly adopted in the subsequent exposition.

11. The problem of *philosophical pluralism* (11:448d), namely, "why are there many philosophies and not one?", poses a scandal for many beginners in philosophy. Yet a characteristic of philosophy as it is known in history is the multiplicity and diversity of philosophical systems. This is not merely a question of historical development, which obtains in all fields of human learning, nor is it a question either of the proliferation of divisions of philosophy as in the proliferation of the positive sciences, or of division within the sciences. Rather the historical situation is

that philosophy exists not simply as philosophy, but as individual philosophies that are wholes or systems; these systems are in varying degrees different from and opposed to each other, and some tend to endure and to recur in the course of history [§86]. It should be noted, moreover, that the problem of philosophical pluralism is broader than the question of philosophy in the Catholic Church. Catholicism adds another dimension and context to the problem because of the unity of faith and the completion of the deposit of faith at a definite time in the past. But the question arises also from the pluralism of Greek and modern philosophies. It is a question of ultimate truth and whether truth is one or many: and if one, in what way; and if many, in what way. There have been many responses to these questions. They can be summarized into the following five types:

a. First, there are the various types of denial of a unified ultimate truth. The very phenomenon of the diversity and disagreement of philosophies was one of the arguments used by the Greek skeptics and by the skeptical tradition for rejecting absolute knowledge and speculative truth.

b. At the opposite pole is the response asserting the absolute and univocal unity of ultimate truth and identifying this truth with a particular historical system or tradition in such a way that all other philosophies are measured by this system and are judged false or inadequate insofar as they differ from it.

c. Next there is an intermediate response, the ideal expressed in the term *philosophia perennis*. According to this view philosophy is not a collection of different systems, but rather a continuous and gradual development by many philosophies and philosophers of an increasingly more adequate explanation of reality. Philosophy itself is continuous with non-philosophical thought; there is continuity between pre-Christian and Christian philosophy, between medieval thought and that of the present day.

d. Next there is the response that considers all particular philosophies even in their contradictions as parts of a whole or of an infinite unity. In one form of this position, the infinite can be expressed only in finite modes that are contradictory or opposite. In another, reality is dialectically structured so that opposition forms a stage in the process of the whole.

e. Finally there is the response judging that, though the many philosophies are apparently diverse and opposed, they are simply different expressions from different viewpoints and by different methods of one ultimate truth. They can either be translated into each other if one studies the semantics involved or they simply point at the ineffable truth across the dialogue, as is stated in Plato's seventh letter.

12. In what follows, to take adequate account of this peculiar character of philosophy, the presentation is divided into three parts. The first two are called SYSTEMATIC PHILOSOPHY and consist essentially of an attempt, in line with the ideal expressed in the third response above [§1.11c], to give a consistent exposition of the main conclusions of philosophy that provide the most adequate explanation of reality now available. The third is called HISTORY OF PHILOSOPHY and aims to survey the vast diversity of philosophical systems in their chronological development so as to fill out, and complement, the synthetic account given in the first part.

13. Pre-theology students should recall here that Vatican II's Decree on Priestly Formation, *Optatam totius,* specifies that philosophy be taught to seminarians in such a way as to convey "a solid and coherent understanding of man, of the world, and of God," and that its teaching should: (1) be based "on a philosophical heritage that is perennially valid"; (2) include "contemporary philosophical investigations," especially those influential in the student's own country, and be abreast of "recent scientific progress"; and (3) feature a critical study of "the history of philosophy." The first requirement is summarized in what follows under the BASIC DISCIPLINES sections of SYSTEMATIC PHILOSOPHY; the second, partly under the later sections of the HISTORY OF PHILOSOPHY and partly under the SPECIAL DISCIPLINES sections of SYSTEMATIC PHILOSOPHY; and the third, under HISTORY OF PHILOSOPHY generally.

# PART ONE

# SYSTEMATIC PHILOSOPHY

## BASIC DISCIPLINES

*The materials presented in this part are arranged in pedagogical order, in the sense that simpler topics are presented first and those of greater complexity later; also concepts that are requisite for their understanding are introduced gradually and then developed as needed. Thus it is best to study the material in the order given from beginning to end. Should one wish to cover all of philosophy in a two-year sequence, it is suggested that Chapters 1 through 4 be studied in the first year, together with related selections from Parts II and III, and then in the second year Chapters 5 through 8, together with the remaining material in the other parts.*

*The titles adopted for chapter headings are the traditional divisions of philosophy. Modern authors frequently use other names, e.g., for psychology, philosophy of man, philosophical anthropology or philosophy of mind; for metaphysics, philosophy of being; for epistemology, philosophy of knowledge; and for natural theology, philosophy of God. Such terminological diversity usually does not affect the scope of the material covered.*

# CHAPTER 2.

# LOGIC

## §2. ARISTOTELIAN LOGIC

1. _Logic_ (8:954d) can be defined as the _art_ of sound discourse. It is an intellectual habit or virtue that strengthens the mind of man for its characteristically human operation. Man's intellectual life is in constant development; it proceeds from knowledge already won, through this, to knowledge that follows from it. Insofar as man is required to engage in discourse his intellect is called reason, and from this he is defined as rational. There is a method to rational procedure or discourse, and this method is logic. Accordingly logic can be described as an instrument proper to man precisely insofar as he has reason or is rational [§29.2].

2. Logic may also be viewed as a _science,_ and when so viewed its subject matter (8:955c) is quite distinctive, being spoken of as the second intention. Speaking very generally, discourse may be described as a mental manipulation of objects. This mental manipulation of objects is sound only so long as it is achieved according to the demands of the relations that accrue to objects as known and that order them one to another. These relations, from which the rules of discourse are taken, are called second intentions [§§6, 8.1, 9.1-2]. Logic is equivalently, then, the science of second intentions (8:955d-956a).

3. There are three orders of rational operation (8:956c), traditionally spoken of as the _three acts_ of the mind: (1) simple apprehension [§3], i.e., grasping an object without affirming or denying anything about it; (2) judgment [§4], i.e., affirming or denying something of something else; and (3) reasoning [§5],

i.e., proceeding to new knowledge from previous knowledge. These suggest a natural threefold *division* of logic into (1) the logic of the term or concept, in which second intentions accruing to objects at the level of simple apprehension (e.g., species or definition) are studied so as to ascertain the rules of thought for this level; (2) the logic of the proposition, where second intentions accruing to objects on the level of judgment (e.g., subject and predicate) are studied; and (3) the logic of argument, where second intentions accruing to objects on the level of reasoning (e.g., syllogism and middle term) are studied.

4. Logic is divided according to another principle of division into *formal* logic and *material* logic. The first studies discourse to see whether it is valid or not, whereas the second studies discourse assumed to be valid to see what requirements it must fulfill to achieve a determinate degree of scientific force (8:956d-957a). In what follows the three acts of the mind will first be examined essentially from the viewpoint of formal logic, then from the more demanding viewpoint of material logic (see also §65).

# FORMAL LOGIC

## §3. SIMPLE APPREHENSION

1. *Simple apprehension* (1:706c) is the first act of the intellect whereby it simply grasps what a thing is, i.e., its essence or quiddity, without affirming or denying anything of it. In apprehending a quiddity (12:25a) the intellect forms within itself the formal concept or mental word, whose external sign is the oral or written term.

2. The *concept* (4:106c) is both intellectual knowledge, "that which" (*id quod*) is understood, and the means "by which" (*id quo*) the thing known is understood [§§23.4, 25]. These two features of the concept are spoken of as the objective concept and the formal concept respectively (4:107a-b). In objective con-

cepts two different aspects can be considered, their extension and their comprehension (or intension). The two are related by the general rule: as the extension of concepts increases their comprehension decreases, and vice versa (4:107d).

3. As the concept is the internal representation of a thing's essence or quiddity, so the *term* (13:1018b) or word is the external sign of the concept. The term is the ultimate significant element into which a sentence or a proposition may be resolved, or it is the elementary part of a proposition. There are three types of term: univocal, equivocal, and analogical. A univocal term is one that signifies the things represented by one and the same concept, e.g., the word "man" signifies all men as identified in one and the same concept of human nature. An equivocal term is one that signifies things represented by several essentially different and unrelated concepts, e.g., the word "bark" as signifying a canine sound and a tree's covering. An analogical term is one that signifies things represented by a concept that has a unity of proportion, e.g., "healthy" as referring to an animal and to a food, to the first as possessing health, to the second as causing health in the animal possessing it [§31.5-6].

4. The notion of *sign* (13:209a) is helpful for clarifying the meanings of both term and concept. A sign is anything that represents to a knowing power something other than itself. There are three basic modes of division of sign: natural or artificial, instrumental or formal, and imaging or non-imaging. A natural sign receives its significative force from nature itself, as smoke is a sign of fire; an artificial sign, on the other hand, receives its significative force by convention from those using the sign, as a white color signifies joy for some people. An instrumental sign must be known apart from and before the thing signified, as the connection between white and joy; a formal sign, on the other hand, is known together with the thing signified, somewhat as a bird's danger cry, which conveys its meaning at once even though never heard before [§24.2]. An imaging sign is one that pictures the thing signified, as in picture writing; a non-imaging sign is one that does not picture the thing signified, as in writing employing an alphabet. With these distinctions understood, one

can say that the concept is the natural, formal, and imaging sign of the essence apprehended in extramental reality, whereas the term is the artificial, instrumental, and non-imaging sign of the concept. [See also §57.1 and §60.31].

5. Simple apprehension seeks a clear and distinct knowledge of objective concepts by an explicit grasp of their comprehensive notes and extensive parts. The act whereby the intellect explicitly expresses the comprehension of a concept is the act of *defining that concept*. The act whereby the intellect explicitly expresses the distribution of a concept into its subjective parts or components is the act of logically *dividing* that concept. Hence both definition and division pertain directly to the first act of the mind.

6. *Definition* (4:718b) is a mental process of clarifying the meaning of a term by analyzing and relating the elements involved in it; or, alternatively, it is the product or result of a mental process, an expression explaining the use of the term or its meaning. As the product of a mental process, definition is distinguished from the term or thing defined (the *definitum* or *definiendum*). Definition need not be a sentence or a proposition; the mere juxtaposition of *definitum* and definition by a colon suffices, e.g., "man: social being." Thus definitions are not true or false, but good or bad, adequate or inadequate.

7. There are two major groups of definitions, (nominal (explaining the use of a term) and real (explaining the meaning of the concept it signifies). Instances of nominal definitions are those that employ synonym, etymology, history of the term's use, and imposed or stipulated usage. Among the many varieties of real definitions are those made in terms of efficient causes, end or purpose, and intrinsic principles (physical definition); properties or accidents (descriptive definition); and genus and difference (metaphysical definition). The following are the rules of definition: a good definition should be (1) coextensive with the *definitum*, (2) non-circular, (3) in univocal terms, (4) in positive, affirmative terms, and (5) expressed through a genus and a difference—best when the genus is proximate and the difference specific (4:718c-719b).

8. *Division* (4:926c) is a mental process of clarifying the

meaning of a term or concept by showing how it is distributed into its various parts. The objective concept may be taken as a whole in several physical or natural senses of whole (14:901a), or in the more properly logical sense of universal [§7]. These give rise to various kinds or species of division, namely, nominal, integral, physical, essential, logical, and dynamic or potestative (4:927b-c). The rules of division are as follows: a good division (1) should be into inferiors, i.e., parts, (2) the parts reunited should equal the whole, and (3) there should be at least formal opposition (some insist on contradictory opposition) between the parts (4:927c-d).

## §4. JUDGMENT

1. _Judgment_ (8:22d) is the second operation of the intellect by which something is affirmed or denied of something else. It is referred to as composing or dividing, or as combining or separating, since by it the essences apprehended in the first operation are associated or dissociated. Its necessity arises from the limitation inherent in simple apprehension, which is abstractive and attains only a partial aspect of a thing at a time. To know the thing as it is in reality, a single whole, one and concretely existing, a mental operation is required that reintegrates the intelligible aspects of the thing and signifies it as existing. This requires a comparison, the establishment of a relation, which is the unity of its terms. This comparison is judgment, combination and separation. As an operation it is always a combination or composition, though from the standpoint of the apprehended essences it is either combination or separation according as they are perceived to belong together or not. By judging and forming a proposition the intellect restores natures to subjects and accidents to substances, thus re-establishing the condition in which things exist.

2. The two elements joined in judgment are referred to as the _subject_ and the _predicate_. The first, representing the thing to be understood, is regarded as determinable, whereas the second, signifying what one understands about the thing, is regarded as

determining. When the apprehended aspects of the thing are connected in their very notions or essence, the judgment is *per se* or essential; when the connection is only factual or existential, the judgment is *per accidens* or accidental. The latter must be perceived through the senses, whereas the former is directly intelligible.

3. The second operation of the mind is said to be concerned with the *existence of the thing*, whereas the first operation is concerned with its essence. This does not mean that apprehension has no reference to existence, or that every judgment is directly a judgment of existence. But the verb "to be" that effects the composition (the *copula*) retains the meaning of existence even when the judgment is attributive. So "This paper is white" means "This paper exists in a white way."

4. Because judgment signifies existence, it always involves *truth* or *falsity*. For "true" means that what is *is*, and that what is not *is not*; and "false" means just the reverse. The judgment affirms that the thing *is* precisely as the intellect has conceived it, and this known conformity is what is required for formal truth [§39].

5. The *proposition* (11:872c) stands in the same relation to judgment as the concept to simple apprehension. A proposition is the sense of the sentence that expresses it, and both are true or false because the judgment they signify is true or false. Propositions are either assertoric, declaring that a given state of affairs obtains, or modal, qualifying such declarations as necessary, contingent, possible, or impossible. Assertoric propositions are of two kinds, categorical and compound. The subject and predicate of a *categorical proposition* constitute its matter; its form is the copula affirming or denying the predicate of the subject. On the basis of its form a categorical proposition is either affirmative or negative; on the basis of its matter it is either particular or universal. The four main types are thus universal affirmative (A), particular affirmative (I), universal negative (E), and particular affirmative (O).

6. Modification of a proposition's matter or form produces a new proposition. *Conversion* affects the matter: it is the inter-

change of subject and predicate, the copula remaining unaffected. *Obversion* has to do with the proposition's form: it is the change of quality from affirmative to negative or vice versa, with the compensating substitution for the predicate of its contradictory term. The product of obversion is a proposition whose subject is the predicate of the original. Two other processes, *contraposition* and *inversion*, consist of alternating obversions and conversions. The contrapositive is a proposition whose subject is the contradictory of the original predicate, whereas the inverse has for its subject the contradictory of the original subject. Various rules have been worked out by logicians to ascertain what pairs of propositions imply each other or are equivalent: the usual condition is that the distribution and existential import of the terms involved be the same (11:873b-d).

7. A *compound proposition* has for its matter two propositions; its form is a conjunction affirming or denying a given relation between these two. There are four basic relations: implication, subimplication, contrariety, and subcontrariety. Depending on how these relations are affirmed or denied there arise four species of compound propositions, namely, the conditional, the disjunctive, the alternative, and the conjunctive. Pairs of these can be shown to be equivalent through rules similar to those for the equivalence of categorical propositions (11:874a-b). [See also §65.4-5.]

8. The most important relationships between pairs of propositions having the same subjects and predicates but varying in quantity or quality are given in the *square of opposition* (10: 706a). Depending on the position one takes with regard to the existential import of categorical propositions he can use the square to illustrate the relations of contradiction, subalternation, superalternation, contrariety, and subcontrariety (10:706b-d).

## §5. REASONING

1. *Reasoning* (12:119b) is the third operation of the intellect by which it passes from what it already knows to what it does not

yet know. Since knowledge is expressed in propositions, reasoning may be characterized also as the process by which the mind passes from two or several propositions, called the premises or antecedent, to another proposition, called the conclusion or consequent. It should be noted that passing directly from one proposition to another proposition by the methods of conversion just discussed [§4.6] is not considered reasoning because the conclusion has the same content as the premise, differing from it only in arrangement; thus no new knowledge results.

2. The consequence (*consequentia*) is the logical link that the reasoning establishes between the antecedent and the consequent; it is the manifestation of an inference. Reasoning, as an act, is really a movement of the mind, a *discursus* wherein the mind, perceiving two propositions as true and as standing in some type of mutual relationship, perceives in this very connection the truth of a third proposition, which it itself forms and to which it gives its assent. Thus the mind, put in motion by the antecedent, finds its rest in the consequent. The antecedent may therefore be regarded as a cause of the consequent. The essential law that governs this process is the following: in a correct reasoning, it is impossible that the antecedent be true and the consequent false.

3. An *argumentation* (1:788b) is an expression that signifies the inference from one truth to another. Just as a term is the sign of a concept, and a sentence the sign of a judgment, so argumentation is the sign of the act of the intellect known as reasoning. Every argumentation consists of the three elements found in reasoning: the antecedent, the conclusion, and the inference. The first two elements are stated explicitly in the argumentation, while the third is indicated implicitly by a "therefore," "so," or "hence." Of the three, inference is the most important element because it gives unity and meaning to the other two, fashioning them into a logical unit. Apart from the essential law given above there are two additional rules of argumentation: from a false antecedent a true conclusion sometimes follows; and the conclusion always follows the weaker part (i.e., if the antecedent is negative or particular, the conclusion will correspondingly be negative or particular).

4. An argumentation is either good or valid, or it is only apparently good, in which case it is known as a fallacy. Good or valid argumentations are of two types, *inductive* and *deductive*. The inductive process is one whose antecedent is less general than the conclusion; the deductive process is one whose antecedent is more general than its conclusion.

5. A *syllogism* (13:856b) is an artificial, logical arrangement  of a deductive argumentation. It is said to be artificial, not that the inference it signifies is artificial (indeed this results from the natural act of the mind called reasoning), but because the forced disposition of the antecedent and the conclusion according to logical laws is an artifact, i.e., something constructed by the mind to attain truth and eliminate error. The two principal types of syllogisms are the categorical and the hypothetical; they differ in their formal structures and in the types of inference they allow.

6. The *categorical syllogism* is an argumentation in which two terms are compared with a third term in the antecedent, and the conclusion states that the two terms agree or do not agree with each other. The subject term of the conclusion is called the minor term and the premise that contains this term is called the minor premise. The predicate term of the conclusion is called the major term and the premise that contains it is called the major premise. The term repeated in both premises but not found in the conclusion is known as the middle term.

7. The categorical syllogism is validated by two basic *principles* of logic, the so-called *dictum de omni* and *dictum de nulla*.  The first states that whatever is distributively and universally predicated of some subject must be affirmed of all included under that subject; the second states that whatever is universally and distributively denied of a subject must be denied of all included under that subject.

8. From the nature of the categorical syllogism certain *laws* follow that govern its use. These may be summarized as follows: (1) There can be only three terms in a syllogism, one of which (the middle) cannot appear in the conclusion. From this law it follows that only four figures of the categorical syllogism are possible (see 13:856d). (2) A term in the conclusion cannot have a

wider extension than in the premises. (3) The middle term must be used universally at least once. (4) If one premise is negative or particular, the conclusion must be negative or particular. (5) When both premises are negative or particular, no conclusion is possible. When these rules are applied to the various figures of the categorical syllogism it is found that only a limited number of forms, or moods, are valid within each figure. The valid moods can be recognized by means of mnemonics (e.g., Barbara, Cesare, Darapti), the first three vowels of which indicate whether the major premise, the minor premise, and conclusion are, in order, A, E, I, or O propositions, and some of the consonants indicate how a syllogism in the second, third, or fourth figure can be converted to the first figure by suitably modifying the propositions it contains (see 13:856d-857a).

9. The *polysyllogism* is a series of categorical syllogisms so arranged that the conclusion of the previous syllogism becomes a premise of the next. The *enthymeme* is a categorical syllogism with one premise suppressed. The *singular syllogism* is one in which the subject is a singular term; if the middle term is singular it is called the *expository syllogism*. The *sorites* is a categorical syllogism resulting from a concatenation of middle terms. The *modal syllogism* is one made up of modal propositions.

10. The *hypothetical syllogism* is an argumentation that has a compound proposition as a major premise. The basic forms of this syllogism derive from the forms of the hypothetical proposition, namely, conditional, disjunctive, and alternative [§65.4]. Most important is the conditional syllogism, which has two valid figures: *ponens,* which posits the condition in the minor premise and posits the conditioned in the conclusion; and *tollens,* which denies the conditioned in the minor premise and denies the condition in the conclusion [§67.1].

11. *Induction* (7:481b) is generally regarded as the opposite of deduction (4:715a); more properly it is the counterpart of demonstration, since its use leads to the acceptance of principles from which conclusions can be demonstrated [§11]. It may be defined as the method or activity by which one proceeds from observation to generalization, and it is based on the resemblance

or similarity among particular objects. The main justif
induction would seem to be the existence and recognition of
causal relations (see §67.5).

12. A *fallacy* (5:818b) is a statement or argument that leads
one to a false conclusion because of a misconception of the meaning of the words used or a flaw in the reasoning involved. Related
terms with different shades of meaning are the following: (1) a
sophism, which is a false argument offered with deliberate intent
to deceive; (2) a paralogism, which is an unintentional violation
of the rules of logic; and (3) a paradox, which is a statement
that sounds absurd or contradictory, but yet may be true in fact.
There are various ways of classifying fallacies. A common one
is in terms of fallacies of induction (insufficient observation,
unwarranted generalization, and false analogy), and fallacies of
deduction (formal error in the proposition or in the syllogism—
illicit premises, undistributed middle, extended conclusion; material error in diction or extra diction). Fallacies in diction include equivocation, amphibology, composition, division, metaphor, and accent. Fallacies extra diction include accident, false
absolute, pretended cause, evading the issue, begging the question, and the complex question. For examples see 5:818d-819b.


# MATERIAL LOGIC

## §6. MATERIAL LOGIC

Much of what has been said thus far pertains to the formal
aspects, to requirements for assuring validity, of the various operations of man's intellect. There now remains the task of reviewing
each of the three acts of the mind from the viewpoint of their
content, the matter with which they are concerned, to discuss
additional second intentions that accrue when one is concerned
with the truth and certitude of the results attained through the
mind's operations. These also can be classified according to the
three acts: at the level of simple apprehension there are universals—their nature and reality, how they are formed in the intel-

lect, the various types they assume as modes of predication (i.e., as predicables) and of being (i.e., as categories), and the kinds of distinction among them; at the level of judgment there are first principles, to which the mind gives immediate assent and which ground all of its subsequent reasoning processes; and at the level of reasoning there is demonstration and the necessary knowledge it generates, called science, which likewise can be classified into various types. The coverage of these matters will permit a reflection on the nature of logic itself so as to make more precise the kinds of universals it considers and the sense in which it is a science related to other sciences, entering more or less intimately into their various thought processes.

## §7. UNIVERSALS

1. The term *universal* (14:452c), derived from the Latin *universalis* (*unum versus alia*, one against many) signifies a unity with reference to some plurality. Unlike the singular, which cannot be communicated, the universal is by definition something that is communicated or communicable to many.

2. In the history of thought the term is used in three distinct senses: (1) In the context of being (*in essendo*), an essence is said to be universal when it is possessed or can be possessed by many individuals. (2) In the context of causality (*in causando*), a cause is said to be universal when it is capable of producing specifically different effects. (3) In the context of thought (*in significando*), a concept, an idea, or a term is said to be universal when it signifies a certain plurality. This plurality is signified in two ways: (a) by representing many (*in repraesentando*), e.g., many individual men are represented by a single term or concept; and (b) by being predicable of many (*in praedicando*), e.g., the specific term man can be said univocally of many individual men.

3. The controversy over universals is a metaphysical discussion concerning the objective, ontological status of essences that are perceived universally by the intellect and that are seen to exist in many individuals. For Plato and the absolute realist tradition

(12:110b) universal essences have, as such, some kind of reality independent of the mind. For Aristotle and the tradition of moderate *realism* (12:111b) essences exist as individuals in reality, but these individuals possess a real basis in reality for the intellectual perception of universality. For *nominalism* (10:483a) only words are universal, since one word can be applied to distinct individuals that appear to be similar, but have no ontological similarity in reality. For *conceptualism* (4:108d) universal terms signify universal concepts that are mentally constructed and correspond to nothing in reality.

4. In a broad sense universals are taken to mean any intellectual concept obtained by *abstraction* (1:56d). Abstraction may be defined as a mental separation of things not, or at least not necessarily, separated in the real. The most radical separation is the abstraction of the intelligible object from the data of sense experience. Both the intelligible and the sensible are given together in human knowledge, but the intelligible is cognized by way of insight in and through the sensible. The sensible is the phenomenal in things—their colors and shapes, their sounds, odors, flavors, their heat and heaviness, whereas the intelligible is the meaningful in them—the stable, definable object of an intellectual insight. The sensible as a datum of experience is exclusively singular, tied to an individual thing in this place at this time. The intelligible is, at least as the object of the direct act of intellection, universal, i.e., it can be said of many, indifferent to individual differences, indifferent to shifts in place and time.

5. To understand how the intelligible is cognized through the sensible it should be noted that the objects of man's direct experience are actually sensible and only potentially intelligible. The thing understood which is potentially intelligible is originally present in human knowledge through its sensory representation, which is called the *phantasm* [§24.8]. The intelligible aspect contained in the phantasm is illumined by the agent intellect; this illumination process actualizes the intelligible so that it can be actually cognized by the possible intellect [§25.2]. The agent intellect as principal cause uses the phantasm of the thing as instrumental cause, and together they actualize the possible

intellect so that it knows the object as intelligible. The intelligible remains an object irreducibly other than the sensible. Intellection is never reduced to sensation. But the intelligible is known only in and through sense experience by way of an intuitive penetration that is most strictly an abstractive act.

6. The object cognized in the abstractive intuition just described differs from the data of sense experience in that the latter are singular whereas the object intellectually cognized is universal. The reason is that the intelligibility of the physical thing is shrouded by its matter (so that it is only potentially intelligible), and this matter is also its principle of individuation [§19.6]. To get to the intelligible man must (and does, through the light that is the agent intellect) slough off matter as a principle of non-intelligibility. In doing so, of course, he also sloughs off the principle of individuation and cognizes an object that is universal. The intellect is essentially ordered to the *intelligible*, but the price of knowing the intelligible is knowing it as a universal.


## §8. PREDICABLES

1. In the broad sense just described all concepts obtained by abstraction are universals. Most properly, however, the word universals has been reserved in philosophical discourse for the five ways in which one term can be predicated univocally of another. These logical universals, or *predicables* (14:452c), are second intentions that can be discussed as such, viz, genus, difference, species, property, and accident, or as applied to a particular nature or essence known in first intentionality, e.g., man as species, animal as genus.

2. The *five* predicables, like the ten supreme categories of being, are most useful for classifying and defining natural objects. In the most complete type of definition several concepts, generic and differential, are ordered in such a way as to express distinctly the determinate kind of being of an object, thus setting it off sharply from other objects. The thing to be defined, the whatness or quiddity, is thus manifested through the use of these concepts,

of which there are only five general types corresponding to the possible relations they can have to the object being defined. These relations are attained in the following way: When something is said of an object it can either (1) belong to the nature or essence of the object and express its quiddity, or (2) belong to the object in some other way beyond its essence, i.e., as accidental to it. In the former case, it will manifest either the whole nature or essence of the object, or part of that nature. The predicable designating the whole nature is called species. That part of the essence that the object has in common with other classes of things resembling it is called genus, or including class. The part that distinguishes the object from all other classes is called the difference. In the latter case the predicate may indicate something outside the essence but necessarily following on it, the property; or may indicate something contingently associated with the object, the predicable accident.

3. On this basis the definitions of the predicables are as follows. *Genus* (6:339c) is the universal said of many differing in species, in answer to the question "What is it?" ("animal," of man and brute). *Species* (13:554d) is the universal said in answer to "What is it?" of many that differ only in number ("man," of Plato and Socrates). *Difference* is predicated as the qualitative part of the essence (*in quale quid*) of those differing in number and also in species or kind ("rational," of man; "sensitive," of animal). *Property* (11:847:b) or *proprium* is a universal said of a species as belonging only, necessarily, and always to that species and its individuals ("able to learn," of man). *Accident* is a universal said of a species as belonging contingently to that species and its individuals ("white," of man).

4. The *order* in which the predicables are given reflects a proportionate share in the notion of universality. This is found more formally in essential predicates than in those that are outside the essence of the subject. And of the essential predicates, the generic are more universal than the specific, so that genus and species are given first as substantial predicates, then difference as a qualitative predicate, followed by property and accident as yet more distant from the essence of the subjects.

## §9. CATEGORIES

1. First intentions represent perfections characteristic of things as they exist outside the mind. There are ten basic modes of such real finite being, and these are called the *categories* (from the Greek *katēgoriai,* meaning predicates). The categories of being (3:242a-243c) form ten supreme genera that serve as the starting point for an orderly classification of all essential predicates attributed to an individual. Such a procedure is exemplified in the *Porphyrian Tree* (11:593ab), which is a diagrammatic representation of the relationship of genus, species, and individual in the category of substance.

2. As *modes* of real being the categories are not merely logical entities; rather they are first intentions in the sense that what they categorize is real being. On the other hand, when something is so categorized it takes on a logical relation, and in so doing has the second intentional character of a *universal.* There is nothing merely logical about being a substance, but to say of substance that it is a supreme genus is to relate the content of one concept to the meanings of a number of predicates subordinate to it and, like it, expressive of the natures of things like Socrates and Plato. To say of substance that it is a category, then, is like saying of horse that it is a species; in both cases one is asserting of something real a kind of predicability that is consequent upon man's abstractive manner of knowing real things, and so conferring on it the characteristics of a second intention. Viewed in this way both the predicables and the categories may be seen as universals: the five predicables are universals formally considered, whereas the ten categories are universals materially considered, the various natures to which different formal relations of universality are affixed when such natures are ordered from the supreme modes of being all the way to the individual.

3. Aristotle enumerated the *ten categories* as follows: substance, quantity, quality, relation, place, time, situation, vestition, action, and passion. Of these the first category is unique in that it exists in itself; the remaining nine categories share in common that they are predicamental accidents, or exist in another [§34].

Of the accidents only quantity and quality are absolute and intrinsic; the rest are relative and extrinsic (1:76a-c). Relation designates how the substance to which it belongs is related to another subject; action and passion are correlative accidents that arise from the exercise of efficient causality. The remaining four accidents are modes [§34:6] or extrinsic denominations that are based in various ways on the quantity of the substance in which they are found. To be more specific:

4. *Substance* [§34.1] is what is basic and independent in existence, standing under (*substans*) and sustaining accidents in their being, and a source of activity. It is in the nature of substance to be in every part of a thing as whole and entire. An individually existing substance with all its attributes and accidental modifications is called first substance; when precision is made from individual existence and substance is taken as a category and universal it is called second substance. A complete substance is one that can exist *per se*. Incomplete substances, such as primary matter [§16.3] and substantial form [§16.4], are incapable of actual existence by themselves; each requires the other for the actual existence of their composite. (For an exception, see §29.3).

5. *Quantity* (12:5d) is that by which a thing is said to be large or small, or to have part outside of part, or to be divisible into parts; it answers the question "How much?" (*quantum*). There are two kinds of quantity, the discrete [§64.1] and the continuous [§64.4]. Unlike quality, quantity has no contrary and does not permit of more and less; however, quantities can be said to be equal and unequal.

6. *Quality* (12:2b) is what makes an already essentially determined substance to be of a certain kind (*quale*). There are four main divisions: (1) habits [§50.3] and dispositions; the former are firmly established conditions of some nature, the latter conditions that are easily changed; (2) power [§21.7] and incapacity, which indicate a nature's ability to operate well or not; (3) sensible qualities, which modify the substance insofar as it is capable of affecting the senses [§24.5] and (4) figure and shape, which are modifications of the substance's quantity. Some

qualities have contraries, and some admit of degrees. Insofar as qualities are rooted in quantity they are indirectly quantified through the quantity of the subject in which they exist, and so they are indirectly measurable also [§67.3].

7. *Relation* (12:216a) is that by means of which the substance to which it belongs is related to another subject; its entire being is one of reference or order (8:720d) to another (*ad aliud*). Relation as a category is referred to as predicamental relation, and as such is distinguished from logical relation, or relation of reason, which exists only in the mind, and from transcendental relation, which is the very nature of some essence or principle as this relates to a complementary principle. Predicamental relation is distinguished from the foundation that serves as the cause of the relation; thus tallness is the foundation for the real relation of similarity between tall people.

8. *Action and Passion* (1:94b) are correlative accidents related to the operation of an agent [§35.8]. Action designates the activity of the agent, but it is extrinsically denominated by reference to the patient upon which the agent operates. Passion, on the other hand, is the accidental modification that the patient undergoes by receiving in itself the efficiency of the agent. Action and passion as categories are really distinct, although both are only rationally distinct from the change initiated by the agent [§18.6].

9. *Time* (14:155d), or more properly the accident "when" (*quando*), confers on corporeal substances that exist in the changing world of time a type of accidental existence by reason of their temporal situation. "When" is therefore a category of real being; it has extrinsic denomination from time [§19.4] as its measure.

10. *Location* (8:948d) in place [§19.2] provides the basis for another category, the accident "where" (*ubi*). This inheres in a subject through its quantity, because of the circumscriptive containment of the subject arising from the surrounding quantities of other bodies. *Situation* (13:268b) or *situs* is an accident presupposing the category "where," which it further determines by specifying the order of parts of the body in place. Posture or posi-

tion would thus be synonyms for situation. *Vestition* or *habitus,* also called possession or condition (1:76d), is the accident proper to a body by reason of something extrinsic and adjacent to it that does not measure it, as does place. An example would be "clothed," whereby a body is denominated by something extrinsic to it, viz, clothing.

## §10. KINDS OF DISTINCTION

1. The predicables and the categories furnish valuable tools of definition. They also give rise to problems of distinction, however, because not all of the predicates that can be assigned to a given subject are really distinct one from the other—some distinctions originate as a result of the mind's operation alone. To clarify the relationships between various predicates or universals a rather extensive teaching on the kinds of distinction (4:908d) has developed; this will now be summarized for the additional insight it provides as to the nature of universals and the relationships that obtain between them.

2. A distinction may be either *formal* or *material,* i.e., numerical; the former indicates a difference of species or form, a difference properly so called, and the latter, a difference in number, i.e., a diversity.

3. Objects distinct according to a *real distinction* are nonidentical as things in their own right, prior to and independent of any objectifying insight by the human reason. Thus two individuals of the same species, while not at all formally distinct, are distinct from each other by a real, absolute, material or numerical distinction. They are diverse as beings, though altogether alike in essential form. If the two individuals differ also in species, then they are distinct by a real, absolute distinction that is both material and formal; they are diverse and different. If one abstracts from the individuals as such and considers their essences either as natures in themselves or as so-called "metaphysical universals," then these essences are distinct from each other by a real, absolute, formal distinction.

4. The real distinction may be either *absolute*, as in the three ways just enumerated, or *modal*. A modal distinction holds either (1) between a thing and its mode [§34.6] of being or acting, e.g., between Socrates and his being seated, or (2) between two modes of the same thing, e.g., between Socrates' being seated and his being in prison. It is generally held that the distinction between a continuum and its actual indivisibles [§64.6] is a modal distinction; analogously, the distinction drawn in metaphysics between an essence and its act of subsistence is also modal [§34.4].

5. The *separation* of two objects is a sufficient but not a necessary sign that a real distinction obtains between them. An object may be a principle rather than a thing. Real principles such as primary matter and substantial form are really distinct from each other [§16.7]; at the same time, being incomplete substances, neither can exist apart from the other.

6. The rational distinction, or *distinction of reason,* is of two sorts: the less (or minor) of the two is titled the distinction of reason reasoning (*rationis ratiocinantis*), because it originates exclusively in the mind that understands or reasons; hence it is called also the distinction of reason without a foundation in reality (*sine fundamento in re*). The greater (or major) is titled the distinction of reason reasoned about (*rationis ratiocinatae*), because it has a double foundation, viz, in the reasoning mind and in the thing affording rational analysis (*cum fundamento in re*).

7. The *foundation* of the distinction of reason reasoning is extrinsic to the thing being distinguished. For example, there is a distinction of reason reasoning between the object that is subject and the object that is predicate in either of the following two propositions, "Man is man," and "Man is a rational animal." In the first case the intellect sees the object "man" as subject to be extrinsically affected by the rational condition of being subject, and sees the same object as predicate to be extrinsically affected by the rational condition of being a predicate. The same situation holds in the second case, except that there the predicate is the definition of the subject; in neither case, however, is there any

intrinsic difference in intelligibility between the subject and the predicate.

8. In the distinction of reason reasoned about, which is also called the virtual distinction, there is a difference of objective contents taken intrinsically as such. Its mental foundation is the mind's passage from potency to act through a series of concepts such that not all the features revealed in one objective concept are revealed in the other. For example, in the Porphyrian Tree, for Socrates the predicates "body," "living," "animal," and "man" are all distinct from each other and from Socrates—whom they, in fact, are—by a distinction of reason reasoned about. Because they all indeed are Socrates in point of fact, there is no real distinction between them. On the other hand they each designate different metaphysical grades of the same being and thus they each have different objective contents or different intrinsic intelligibilies. (For the Scotistic formal distinction, see 4:910d-911d.)

## §11. FIRST PRINCIPLES

1. The foregoing exposition of universals, predicables, categories, and kinds of distinction all relate to the first act of the mind; the apprehension of first principles, on the other hand, relates to the second act of the mind when seen from the viewpoint of material logic.

2. *First principles* (5:937) are truths on which scientific reasoning is based and to which the intellect gives direct assent; they are called "first" because they are immediately known as indemonstrable truths and because demonstrations are built upon them as premises. They are also known as *immediate propositions* in the sense that, in them, the predicate is so connected with the subject that the relationship affirmed between them admits of no middle term. There are two types of first principles, viz, proper principles and common principles; these may be equivalently distinguished as definitions and axioms.

3. While a definition as such is not yet a proposition, any

proposition that directly applies a definition to the thing defined is an immediate proposition. *Proper principles* are always immediate, with the immediacy, so to speak, of definitions. Their designation as "proper principles" arises from the fact that their definitions derive from the proper subject matter of a particular science.

4. From this it can be gathered that *common principles* or axioms go beyond the limits of a particular science, that the truth they convey has a common value for all science. They are also common in the sense that they express thoughts or opinions that all accept and share. Their terms are so simple and current, their evidence so compelling, that no one can be mistaken about them. An example is the principle of contradiction: the same predicate cannot be affirmed, and at the same time denied, of the same subject. Other examples are the *dictum de omni* and *dictum de nullo* already referred to [§5.7].

5. All things being equal, common principles enjoy a certain superiority over proper principles; this does not mean, however, that proper principles must be demonstrated from common principles. The terms of the former also are joined without need of a third term and their evidence comes from proper considerations. Yet common principles are said to be more certain than proper principles because of their greater simplicity. Again, common principles would not be the most common if they were not included in the proper, and the proper are not such because they are totally different from the common, but rather because they imply an addition to the common.

6. Except for one who studies a science, knowledge of principles proper to that science is not indispensable. Nor is there need to know such principles before taking up the science, for it is understood that the instructor begins by laying down these principles. Whatever the discipline in which one engages, however, the possession of axioms or common principles is a prerequisite. Proper principles are already a part, initial though it be, of a science or particular treatise, whereas axioms are completely prior to any science. Thus Boethius has formulated the classical distinction between immediate propositions that are such for

specialists alone (*quoad sapientes tantum*) and immediate propositions that are such for all (*quoad omnes*). These are further
divided into immediate propositions that are readily seen by us
(*quoad nos*), and those not recognized as such (*quoad se tantum*)
that require *a posteriori* demonstration, such as the proposition
"God exists." Thus not all immediate propositions are principles,
for the criterion of a principle is that it be better known to us,
and even to all in the case of first principles.

## §12. DEMONSTRATION

1. When reasoning, the third act of the mind, is considered
from the viewpoint of material logic, it is seen as generating
various types of argumentation with distinctive probative force
depending on their matter or content. Argumentation is apo-
dictic when the matter involved is necessary, i.e., the various
terms of the antecedent cannot be related otherwise than they
are; when this obtains within the deductive process the result
is a *demonstration*. When the matter is only contingent or probable the argumentation is said to be dialectical; this is discussed
in the branch of logic known as *dialectics* (4:843a). When the
matter is such that it involves the emotions, but in a hidden way,
the argumentation is rhetorical; its study pertains to *rhetoric*
(12:458a). Finally, when open appeal is made to the emotions,
the argumentation may be called poetic; this is the subject of
Aristotle's *Poetics* [§58.2]. Thus argumentation can express a
reasoning process in a variety of ways, from the strictest scientific
reasoning (the focus of interest in what follows) to the subtle
intimations of poetry; it embraces inductive and deductive processes, and often combines both.

2. A *demonstration* (4:757c) is a syllogism that is productive
of scientific knowledge, i.e., knowledge that is true and certain
because based on the cause [§35] that makes the conclusion be
as it is. Effectively a demonstration is had whenever a statement
is given together with the reason (or cause, or explanation) for
its truth, that is, whenever the question "why" is answered.

Because there are different senses of "why" there are different kinds of demonstration. Since the reason "why" is expressed by the middle term [§5.6] of the demonstrative syllogism, it can be equivalently said that the types of demonstration correspond to the condition of the middle term that links the subject and predicate of a scientific conclusion.

3. The two main *kinds* of demonstration are: (1) that which yields knowledge of the fact (*quia*) and (2) that which yields knowledge of the reasoned fact (*propter quid*). Only demonstration of the reasoned fact is demonstration in the strict sense; knowledge of fact is called demonstration analogously by reason of its similarity with, and ordination to, demonstration *propter quid*.

4. Demonstration *propter quid* assigns the proper ontological cause of an attribute's inherence in a subject. Thus the human soul is immortal because it is incorruptible [§29.4]. In the most perfect type of *propter quid* demonstration all the terms are convertible, or commensurately universal. However, as long as the middle term and the attribute are convertible there is *propter quid* demonstration, even though the subject of the given demonstration is only a subjective part of the proper subject of the attribute; e.g., every isoceles has three angles equal to two right angles because it is a triangle. What is essential to this sort of demonstration is that the cause of the attribute be proper.

5. Demonstration *quia* is had whenever the middle term is not the proper cause of the attribute. This demonstration can be *a priori* or causal when a remote cause is assigned; e.g., a wall does not breathe because it is not living (the proper cause is that it has no lungs). Demonstration is *a posteriori* when the middle term is not a cause at all, but an effect of the attribute. If the effect is not adequate or convertible with the cause, the demonstration yields knowledge of the existence of the cause and some of its conditions, e.g., God as known from his creation [§43]. If, however, the cause and effect are of commensurate universality, e.g., the intellect as the cause of abstract reasoning [§25], then the demonstration makes known the proper cause,

and hence the terms may without circularity be recast as a *propter quid* demonstration.

## §13. SCIENCE

1. *Science* (12:1190b) is the result of demonstration; it is mediate intellectual knowledge, as opposed to the immediate knowledge of universals and first principles, because it is acquired through the prior knowledge of principles or causes. As a type of knowledge it can be further considered as the act itself by which such knowledge is acquired or the habit of mind resulting from one or more such acts. And apart from the act and the habit, the body of knowledge that is known by one possessing the habit—the body of truths and conclusions attained—also is said to constitute the science.

2. The *classification of the sciences* (12:1220d) follows the general division of knowledge into speculative and practical (13:557c): speculative science is concerned primarily with knowing and not with doing, whereas practical science is concerned with knowing as ordered to doing.

3. The object of any *speculative science* must fulfill two conditions: it must be something that has prior principles and it must have parts or attributes that belong to it essentially (*per se*). The distinction of the sciences, however, does not arise precisely from a diversity of things or objects considered, but rather from a diversity of principles or of formalities that can be found in the object. Thus, for the unity of a science it is necessary to have one subject genus that is viewed under one formal light or way of considering, whereas for the distinction of sciences it suffices to have a diversity of principles.

4. All human sciences have their origin in sense knowledge, and all therefore commence with the same material objects. The *differentiation* of the sciences comes about from the different ways of demonstrating properties of these objects, and this in turn is traceable to the different middle terms or definitions that are

employed. Again, such middle terms are grasped intellectually by a type of *abstraction* (1:58c) characteristic of the science [§7.4]. So, to the extent that objects are differently freed from the restrictions of matter as a principle of non-intelligibility they are differently scientific. (1) Freedom from individual sensible matter yields an object that is scientifically relevant on the level of natural philosophy [§15]; this is said to constitute the first order or degree of abstraction, i.e., physical abstraction. It is also referred to as abstraction of a whole (*abstractio totius*) because it is the abstraction of the whole essence of the natural thing from the matter that individuates it; it yields an object sufficiently free from matter to be intelligible, but an object defined nevertheless in terms of common sensible matter. (2) Freedom from all sensible matter yields an object that is scientifically relevant on the level of mathematics [§63.3]; this is said to constitute the second order of abstraction, i.e., mathematical abstraction. It is also referred to as abstraction of a form (*abstractio formae*) because it yields the form of quantity that is abstracted from all matter save common intelligible (or imaginable) matter. (3) Freedom from all matter yields the object of metaphysical inquiry [§30.2]; this is said to constitute the third order of abstraction, i.e., metaphysical abstraction. It is also referred to as separation (*separatio*) because it yields an object separated from all matter and so seen to be independent of matter both in meaning and existence.

5. Should the principles of one science be applicable to the object of another science, moreover, it is possible to generate a hybrid science, usually referred to as an intermediate science (*scientia media*) or mixed science (*scientia mixta*). Thus mathematical physics can be seen as *scientia media* intermediate between mathematics and physical science, insofar as it considers the same object as does physical science but under the light of mathematical principles [§17.7]. This possibility gives rise to what is known as the *subalternation* of speculative sciences, when, for example, mathematical physics is subalternated to mathematics and natural science is subalternated to mathematical physics.

6. *Practical science* is distinct from speculative science, al-

though as sciences they both seek knowledge through causes. What distinguishes them is that speculative science seeks causal knowledge of what man can only know, viz, universals, whereas practical science seeks causal knowledge of what man can do or make, viz, singular operables such as the human act. To the extent that a practical science engages in causal analysis, it can speculate and use analytical procedures similar to those of the speculative sciences. But whereas a speculative science seeks demonstrative knowledge of its object, a practical science seeks actually to produce or construct its object, and needs scientific knowledge in order to do so. It should be noted, however, that a practical science (e.g., ethics) does not attain its singular operable (e.g., the human act) directly, but must be complemented by an art or habit (e.g., prudence) that has for its proper concern the individual act in all its concrete circumstances.

## §14. NATURE OF LOGIC

1. Logic, as has been noted earlier [§2], is both an art and a science. It is an *art* [§58.1] because it involves a constructive effort: man advances through discourse in knowledge only insofar as he constructs sound definitions, divisions, and arguments within his mind. Insofar as art by definition is an intellectual habit that readies the mind for the direction of a constructive activity, then logic, which is a habit readying the mind for discourse, which is constructive, is an art.

2. However, if logic is to be the art it must be to realize its purpose, it must at the same time be a *science,* and a demonstrative science at that. Clearly the logician must know the rules of discourse, but if his knowledge is to be reflectively assured, i.e., if he is to know these rules scientifically, he must know also the necessity that imposes them upon his discourse. He can know this only if, by an inductive intuition, he sees into the self-evident character of the basic canons of logical procedure, and if, by a resolution back to these, he can defend the other (more particular) rules of logic. This means that for logic to be adequately

an instrument for discourse it must be itself a demonstrative science, while it is, of course, at the same time a *liberal art* [§61.3].

3. Since it is of value only for its use, logic is sometimes called a practical science. However, it seems more accurate to say it is speculative, for it is of value for the sake of knowing—its use is for the sake of knowledge elsewhere, beyond itself in the other disciplines. Logic can be said to be a tool of the other sciences, but it is better to say it is a tool or *instrument* of the intellect as the intellect looks to the other sciences. For logic is at best a common method, and each science, in virtue of the demands of its own specifying subject matter, calls for a particular contraction of logic. This particular contraction of logic for any given science is known as the methodology of that science. (For the distinction between *logica docens* and *logica utens,* see 8:957b; for extensive treatments of *methodology* in philosophy and various disciplines, see 9:744b-757d and also §§63.3, 67, 72.2, 75.3.)

# CHAPTER 3.

# NATURAL PHILOSOPHY

## §15. PHILOSOPHY OF NATURE

1. _Natural philosophy_ (11:319c), variously referred to as the philosophy of nature and cosmology (4:364b), is the science of nature, i.e., the discipline that treats of the world of nature or the physical universe in its most general aspects. It operates at the first level of abstraction, and so considers its objects as they contain common sensible matter [§13.4]. Its abstractive process starts from the individuals that impress themselves upon man's senses and terminates in universals whose definitions contain a reference to sensible matter. Because the universal leaves aside individual sensible matter it is said to involve only common sensible matter, e.g., the flesh and blood found commonly in men and not that of a particular individual.

2. The _subject of_ natural philosophy may be defined in a general way as mobile being (_ens mobile_), where "mobile" means capable of being changed in any way. It is by their mobile character that things in the physical world first come to be understood. Water, copper, maple trees, cows, even men, are initially known by their behavior, their reactions, their growth and other such activities and characteristics. Since changeability is thus a pervasive attribute of physical reality, it is appropriate to start with it when investigating the requirements of a science that would have nature for its object.

3. To be a science in the sense already described [§13], natural philosophy must first investigate the _principles_ of mobile being and then use these principles to delineate the proper ob-

jects of its consideration. After this it must investigate the various attributes or *properties* of these objects and show how they can be demonstrated from proper principles or causes. Moreover, for economy of effort, the most general features of mobile being should be examined first and then the characteristics of various types, so as to avoid repeating elements that are common. The treatment of mobile being in general (*ens mobile in communi*) forms the basic content of natural philosophy; particular types of mobile being are studied in the various physical, biological, and behavioral sciences (11:320b-d).

## §16. MATTER AND FORM

1. An analysis of *change* (3:448d) or of the process of *becoming* (2:214b) reveals that every change involves three factors or principles in terms of which it can be explained: it involves two contraries, or opposites within the same category, that succeed one another, and it involves a subject in which the contraries successively come to exist (9:484c-485b). The positive principle present in the subject at the end of any change is called *form*; it is the final term or *terminus ad quem* of the change. Its contrary term, or *terminus a quo*, is referred to as *privation*; sometimes it is a positive opposite of the form that terminates the change, sometimes not. The subject that persists throughout the change is generally identified as *matter.* Thus all natural change involves matter, form, and privation as its most general principles. In a further refinement of this analysis, matter and form, entering as they do into the intrinsic constitution of the product of change, are called essential or *per se* principles; privation, not entering into that constitution, is spoken of as an incidental or *per accidens* principle.

2. Deeper reflection shows that there are two basic types of change, accidental and substantial, depending on whether the *terminus ad quem* is an accident or a substance. In the first case, as in the reddening of the human skin or the growth of a puppy into a dog, a thing changes only in a qualified way; in the second

case, as in the burning of wood or the death of a dog, a thing
changes in an unqualified way, i.e., wholly into another thing.
The latter type of change is referred to as *substantial change*
(13:771b). This has two subdivisions, *generation* and *corruption*
(6:323b): the former is a change from non-being to being (from
non-dog to dog), the latter a change from being to non-being
(from dog to non-dog).

3. *Matter* (9:473d), as the subject of change and as capable
of taking on new forms, is itself a *potency* [§33.2] or capacity.
The subject of substantial change is called *primary matter*, while
the subject of accidental change is known as *secondary matter*.
Secondary matter, such as the dog undergoing the accidental
change known as growth, is potential with respect to its new size;
yet it possesses an actuality of its own insofar as it is a dog. By
analogy [§31.5] to the subject in such accidental changes one can
know that there is a subject also in substantial change. Experience
manifests that something abides in such changes as the burning
of wood, the death of a dog, the coming to be of a new organism.
In the order of nature nothing comes from nothing (*ex nihilo
nihil fit*): the new substance emerges from a material or a matrix
that survives the change—charcoal from wood, cadaver from dog,
organism from seed. If the emergent entity is to have more than
an accidental unity, moreover, the perduring substratum must
lack substantial determination; it is therefore not matter in the
ordinary sense, but rather a protomatter devoid of specific characteristics. This first subject in any physical substance is called
primary matter, and its reality is that of potency devoid of all
actuality [§42.2]. Aristotle defines it as "the primary substratum
of each thing, from which it comes to be without qualification,
and which persists in the result." The "primary" of this definition
and the "to be without qualification" mark the *definitum* off
from secondary matter, and "substratum" distinguishes it from
form; the last two clauses further distinguish it from privation.

4. *Form* (5:1013c) is, in general, the complement or the
actuation of matter. The form that terminates an accidental
change is called *accidental form*—examples would be the color,
size, or shape of a thing, or its place; in the substantial order,

the form is called *substantial form*. Accidental form makes its matter to be qualified in this way or that; substantial form makes its matter simply to be, it confers being in an unqualified way. Whereas matter is that out of which a thing is made, like marble in the case of a statue, form is what makes a thing to be what it is, the shape in the case of the statue. Arguing analogously, primary matter is the potential substantial principle from which a physical thing is made, whereas substantial form is the actuating principle that makes it be a dog, a tomato plant, water, or charcoal.

5. *Privation* (11:807d), unlike matter and form, is not divided into substantial and accidental kinds, for non-being cannot be divided into species. Privation is contrasted with form but associated with matter, primary or secondary, for matter in either case is never without privation. When it has one form it lacks all others, and when it acquires a new form it lacks the one it previously had. Thus privation connotes some kind of lack or loss; it is usually defined as the absence of form in a suitable subject.

6. Since form terminates or ends a change it is said to be the end, or *final cause*, of the change; thus form completes and satisfies the inclination of matter toward its actuation. As will be seen in the next section, nature is an intrinsic principle or source of motion and rest, and both matter and form are able to satisfy this definition of nature, albeit in different ways [§17]. Matter is the source from which physical things come to be, and as such is an intrinsic principle of change. Form, as terminating matter to give physical things their essential and original character, is also such an intrinsic principle.

7. On this accounting primary matter, substantial form, and the previous privation of such form are the three first principles of mobile being. A *principle* is usually defined as that from which something proceeds in any way whatever; it differs from a *cause* in that the latter is that from which something proceeds with a dependence in being [§35.1]. Matter and form, in addition to being principles, are also causes: matter satisfies the definition of material cause [§35.7] and form the definitions of formal cause [§35.6] and final cause [§35.10]. Privation, on the other hand,

not being a positive reality, can exert no positive influence in the production of a thing and is therefore not a cause. The material and formal causes, though both intrinsic to the effect, are really distinct from it and from each other, since the effect is neither matter nor form but the result of both [see §§33.2-6, 35.6]. There is thus a sufficient difference between matter and the result, on the one hand, and between form and the result, on the other, to preserve the real distinction required for a true cause-effect relationship.

## §17. NATURE

1. *Nature* (10:276a) is commonly said to be the subject matter of natural philosophy, and as such it requires definition and distinction from other concepts. Its definition is best sought by comparing things that exist by nature (viz, animals and their parts, plants and minerals) with those that exist by other causes, in particular by *art* [§58.1]. The former are seen to have within them a tendency to change or to motion. The artifact as such has no similar tendency; it has an inclination to change only insofar as it is made of a natural substance. In this context nature is defined as "the principle or cause of motion and of rest in that in which it is primarily, by reason of itself and not accidentally." Here "motion" refers to any kind of corporeal change, accidental or substantial, and "rest" implies the attainment of the end to which the change was directed; "primarily" excludes secondary principles and forms that make things artifacts; and "by reason of itself and not accidentally" is added to exclude chance events and such cases as the doctor who cures himself, where the art of medicine would be intrinsic but merely accidental to the one being cured.

2. Thus defined, nature can be identified with *matter* as the substratum of change, i.e., as the passive, potential principle of being moved [§16.3]. It should be noted, however, that the matter from which becoming proceeds, taken in its concrete existence, is always determined matter. The substantial form currently possessed, determining the matter in a particular way,

always limits and defines matter's immediate potentialities. Moreover, since the form already possessed by the matter can be the source of certain activities as well, the matter on which a natural agent operates need not be entirely passive; its activity, in fact, may run contrary to the aim of an *agent* [§35.8] that acts upon it.

3. Since substantial form is the principle of essential determination, the source of activity, and the end of generation, it should be obvious that *form* deserves to be called nature even more than matter [§16.6]. As the active principle of movement, therefore, nature is substantial form. Its activity as form is twofold: first and most obviously, it is the intrinsic source of the vital activities of the living body, and as such is known as *soul* [§22]; second, it is the intrinsic source of the spontaneous activities of any given body, e.g., a chemical element. Inanimate bodies, not having differentiated organs, do not move themselves; rather their activities are directed to other bodies that in turn may affect them. Their forms, in this case, satisfy the requirement of interiority in the definition of nature insofar as they are parts within a system of interrelated active and passive powers and capabilities.

4. In the world of nature there are powers that are not strictly natural, e.g., the power of a natural body to take on an artificial form. A natural power differs from these in that it has a positive inclination to an act that perfects or fulfills the being so inclined, or else contributes to the good of the species or of the whole of nature. Passive principles in nature, moreover, are normally related to natural agents, through the activity of which they are brought to their proper actualizations for the most part. Thus the acts to which agents naturally direct matter by their activity are determinate acts. It is in this sense that nature is said to act for an *end* [§35.10]. Consequently it is the act or form, considered as the end to which a natural being tends either actively or passively, that determines whether a process is or is not in accordance with nature. On this account the form as end is itself properly called nature: it is a principle of becoming, of natural movements that are for the sake of the form from which they spring. So the natural form seeks its own preservation and de-

velopment within the individual; it tends by generation to its own continuance, as a specific form, in other individuals; and ultimately, by realizing its specific ends, it contributes to the order and preservation of the universe, i.e., to the good of the whole of which it is a part (see 14:457b).

5. *Chance* (3:444a) is different from nature and indeed quite its opposite. It is defined as an incidental or *per accidens* cause in things that are for an end and that happen seldom, rather than for the most part. Moreover, as happening seldom, the effect in chance is something neither intended nor expected by the agent. Another definition of chance is that it is an interference between, or an intersection of, two lines of natural causality not determined, by the nature of either, to interfere with one another. Such happens when, say, a cosmic ray strikes a gene and results in the production of abnormal offspring. As the example suggests, chance events occur in nature and keep it from being completely determined in its operation. A related concept is *fortune* (5:1035b) or luck, which is said properly of events wherein an agent who acts with intelligence and will attains an unintended end. The classic example is the person who is digging a grave and finds a buried treasure. Unlike chance, fortune is called good or bad (misfortune) depending on the event that happens to the agent.

6. *Violence* (14:690a), i.e., compulsion or force [§52.3], is even more opposed to nature than is chance. The violent arises not from an intrinsic principle, as does the natural, but from an extrinsic principle, and in such a way that the thing suffering the violence contributes nothing to the result. The action of the extrinsic principle either prevents the thing acted upon from following its own inclinations or forces it to act contrary to them. These inclinations are intrinsic sources of activity, e.g., the will for rational life, the appetites for sentient life, and the tendency of form or nature for vegetative life and for non-vital activities and reactivities. Just as such inclinations give rise to natural movements, so force or compulsion gives rise to violent movements. It is to be noted, however, that when one is dealing with the inanimate, where the ends intended by nature are not always

clearly discernible, the distinction between natural and violent movements becomes much less sharp than in the sphere of human activity and even of living things in general.

7. Art, chance, and violence differ from nature and so aid in its definition, but a perhaps more significant opposite of the natural or the physical in our day is the _mathematical_ (11:321b). This opposition becomes important when differentiating natural science from mathematical knowledge as this is applied to nature [§63.6]. In mathematical physics, for example, the object of consideration is not the natural as such but rather the sensible or physical as compounded with the quantified or mathematical. It is for this reason that mathematical physics is called a mixed science [§13.5]. The middle terms or explanatory factors it employs are physico-mathematical, but the formality under which it demonstrates is mathematical and its conclusions are only terminatively physical. The mathematical physicist must measure motion or time in order to treat it; the philosopher of nature has the problem of defining motion or time regardless of how it is measured. Again, the results attained by the mathematical physicist require interpretation if one is to give a physical reason or explanation for the facts he knows in only their mathematical reasons. Such interpretation, it can be argued, is itself external to mathematical physics; it is properly the function of the science of nature, where the physical causes of natural things are sought. The mathematical physicist may himself take on this function, but it is noteworthy that difficult problems of interpretation are increasingly becoming the domain of the philosopher of science [§66].

8. As opposed to such mixed disciplines, natural science uses middle terms that are physical and that can serve to provide explanations in terms of any one of the four causes (final, efficient, formal, and material), rather than through mathematical reasons alone (4:759b). The middle terms it employs are defined with sensible matter and in abstraction from individual things, which are themselves contingent and subject to chance. The necessary bond linking the terms in the conclusions of its demonstrations is on this account called conditional or suppositional. The reason

for such necessity rests in natures and essential relations, but the existence of these natures is itself contingent and the perfect realization and operation of the natures may be hindered. However, on the supposition (*ex suppositione*) that the conclusion is to be verified or that a particular end is to be attained by a natural process, the antecedent causes assigned in the premises will be necessarily involved. It is noteworthy that *a posteriori* demonstrations play a prominent role in the science of nature, since sensible effects are usually better known to man than their natural causes.

9. These then are the most general and preliminary considerations relating to the *principles* and *causes* investigated in the philosophy of nature. There remains now the task of investigating and demonstrating, in terms of such principles and causes, the *properties* that characterize mobile being in its most universal aspects, viz, motion, place, time, and the relations that exist between movers and things moved.

## §18. MOTION

1. *Motion* (10:24c) can be taken in a wide and in a strict sense: in the wide sense it stands for any change (*mutatio*) from one state to another; in the strict sense, for continuous and successive change, usually spoken of as movement (*motus*). The latter is found in several different categories of being, and thus the elements of its definition must transcend the categories; the only available prior concepts for defining motion are those basic to being itself, viz, *potency and act* [§33.2]. Motion is situated midway between potentiality and full actuality. When a body is only in potency it is not yet in motion; when it has been fully actualized, the motion has ceased. Therefore, motion consists of incomplete act. But since incomplete act can be the termination of a motion or the starting point of a new motion, it is necessary to indicate motion as the act of being in potency precisely as still in potency to more of the same act. This line of reasoning led Aristotle to define motion as "the actualization of what exists in

potency insofar as it is in potency." This is usually spoken of as the (formal) definition of motion; the (material) definition is that motion is properly "the act of mobile being precisely as mobile." By manifesting the connection between these two definitions one obtains the first demonstration in natural philosophy, which concludes that motion is the pervasive property of all mobile being and so properly exists in the thing moved, not in the mover as such [§20.2-3].

2. Motions are distinguished or *classified* by their goal or *terminus ad quem*. Motion does not belong directly in the categories of being [§9], since it is not being but rather becoming. However, it can be reduced to the category of being in which it terminates, and on this basis there are only three types of motion, since only three categories can directly terminate motion, viz, location, quality, and quantity.

3. The first, most obvious, and easiest motion to observe is change of place, or *local motion,* and the terms used to describe it are applied to other motions as well. Local motion clearly goes from term to term, from point of departure to one of arrival. These two terms are opposed and incompatible, but admit intermediary states: thus, they are called contraries. The motion between them is continuous, or unbroken and successive, that is, traversing the intervening positions. It is divisible by reason of the extension crossed. Since an instant is not divisible, motion cannot be instantaneous, but takes time. Likewise, motion strictly speaking belongs only to bodies, since only they have the divisibility essential to motion. Local motion of some sort is involved in all other motions, and other motions are called such by analogy with local motion.

4. Qualitative motion is called *alteration.* It is realized only in the third species of quality, namely, sensible qualities (12:2b). Only these fit the definition of motion as continuing and successive actualization of potency. Substantial changes are preceded by alterations that dispose matter toward becoming a new being, but the actual generation of a new substance and destruction of the old are instantaneous. Thus generation and corruption are not classified as *motus* in the strict sense, although they are

changes in the wide sense of *mutatio*.

5. Motion in the category of quantity is called *augmentation* or growth and *diminution* or decrease. Augmentation does not consist of mere addition of distinct quantities to form an aggregation; such would reduce to local motion and would be augmentative, but not the motion of augmentation. The latter must take place within the unity of a single substance, and this happens only in living beings. By nutrition these assimilate food into their substance and consequently achieve growth. This is true motion: the growing body expands spatially, it passes through successive stages, and it goes from contrary to contrary. The opposite of augmentation, where this occurs in nature, is diminution or decrease.

6. *Action and passion* [§9.8] do not constitute separate types of motion, for they are really identified with motion. Action is motion considered as being *from* the agent, whereas passion is the same motion considered as *in* the patient. None of the other categories found different types of motion for, though changes occur in them, they do so not directly but through one of the three types of motion already discussed (see 10:25d).

7. Apart from its qualitative parts or types, motion has also *quantitative parts* by reason of the distance between contraries that it traverses. This is best seen in local motion, where the magnitude traversed, known as *extension* [§64.5], itself manifests all the properties of a *continuum* [§64.4]. Although motion is continuous, it is not the same as a static continuum such as a line, where all the parts co-exist and are known immediately; rather it is a "flowing continuum" whose parts, successive in existence, are known only through the re-presentations of memory. Because a flowing continuum is a becoming, its parts do not constitute a being in the strict sense; indeed motion exists only by reason of its *indivisible* [§64.6], i.e., the moment of passage already achieved, and not by reason of its parts, which, as past and future, have already passed out of, or have not yet come into, existence.

8. By reason of its quantitative aspect motion also involves an element of *infinity* [§45.3], as can be seen by comparing it

with the line segment one might hypothetically traverse in local movement. The extension of the line segment is related to its terminating points in somewhat the same way as matter is related to form; it itself is a composite, so to speak, of matter and form. The line segment is also finite by reason of its initial and final terminating points; it becomes infinite only when conceived without one or other of them. This can occur by way of increase, since no matter what its actual length the line can always be imagined as without a termination and thus as extending further. It can occur also by way of decrease, by subtracting parts from the segment in a fixed ratio, say by halves, so that no matter how small the remaining part becomes it can become smaller still, because the remainder is similarly divisible. Now motion is infinite in much the same way as such a line segment. Infinity is attributed to the line when its extension is viewed as lacking terminating points, and so is linked with a state of potentiality and imperfection. Similarly motion is infinite under the aspect of successively traversing a distance that is infinitely divisible or augmentable, and so is characteristic of matter that, as potential and imperfect, is in the process of achieving form without having yet come to the intended termination.

## §19. PLACE AND TIME

1. The infinity thus associated with motion is not an actual infinity; rather it is spoken of as a potential infinity, and as such does not preclude measurement or containment. The measures of most interest for the natural philosopher turn out to be two: place, which can be viewed as a measure of mobile being, and time, which is the measure of the motion the mobile undergoes.

2. Place (11:49d) is defined by Aristotle as "the innermost motionless boundary of what contains." This definition construes place as a container, distinct and separable from the thing contained, but otherwise equal to it and corresponding to it part by part. Every body surrounded by others is in place, and this is what makes local motion, or change of place, a possibility; the

universe as a whole, not being in place, cannot move locally. The definition also leads to two significant distinctions, one between common and proper place and the other between natural and non-natural place. *Common place* is seen as the nearest container or surrounding environment that is immobile, i.e., at rest relatively at least to the body in question. *Proper place* is taken in strict accord with the definition—it is equal to the body in place, but its immobility can be purely formal, as part of the whole system contained within an immobile common place. *Natural place* is the suitable physical environment of a body, i.e., an environment that is adapted to its proper activity and reactivity in accord with its motive powers and other characteristics, and toward which it has a natural tendency to move. *Non-natural place* is any other physical environment. Two bodies cannot occupy the same proper place in virtue of their *impenetrability* (7:396a); nor can one body be in two proper places at once, as in *bilocation* (2:559a), for this would entail a denial of the definition for one or other of the places assigned to it.

    3. *Space* (13:489d) is a concept related to place; in its physical sense it refers to the fundamental dimensional quantity against which one can describe and even measure the motions of bodies. Whether a purely empty three-dimensional space, i.e., a *void* (14:741b), has real physical existence in nature has been much debated in the course of history. Speculative arguments aside, the only evidence for the existence of a void reduces to that for an *ether* (5:568b) or a physical *vacuum* (14:510b), neither of which is known to have all the negated properties of a completely empty space.

    4. *Time* (14:155d), like motion and place, received its first definition as a natural concept from Aristotle, who identified it as "the number of motion according to before and after." This definition develops from three inductive determinations that successively establish (1) time as something of motion, (2) time as continuous, and (3) time as number. (1) Time is not the same thing as motion, for many different motions can take place in the same time, and motions can be fast or slow whereas time remains uniform in its flow. On the other hand, time inevitably accom-

panies motion, for where there is no awareness of motion or change there is no passage of time. (2) Time is continuous because it is associated with motion that traverses a continuous magnitude. A continuum is formally one but materially made up of parts: these parts, joined to each other by indivisibles, constitute an order of local before and after. A motion that traverses such a spatial continuum has also an order of before and after, as does time's passage, e.g., when punctuated by the sun's rising and setting, the moon's phases, the ebb and flow of the tides, the position of hands on a dial. (3) Time is a numbering of the successive 'nows' that serve to mark its passage. To grasp its being one must visualize a before and after under the common aspect of their being a *now* (10:547d) and count them as two nows, i.e., as a now-before and a now-after. These nows, the correlates of the here-before and there-after in motion, are the numbered terminals of the continuum that itself is time. The numbering referred to here is not that of an absolute or mathematical number [§64.1] divorced from passage. Time is rather numbered number, the number of and in motion that is indissociable from its flux.

5. It follows from this analysis that time has the same mode of existence as motion; as a flowing continuum, it exists by reason of its indivisible, the *present* (11:757d), the punctiform now that separates but links past and future. Time is the measure of motion, and so everything in nature is in time inasmuch as it is connected with motion. Every natural substance, precisely as a mobile being, enjoys an existential duration from generation to corruption that is contained within time. Substantial change [§16.2], however, marking the outer bounds of such duration, is measured by the *instant* (7:546d), the limiting now in which it, being instantaneous, alone can take place.

6. A special topic that, like time and place, is associated with the quantitative aspects of mobile being is *individuation* (7:475d). This is discussed in the context of determining a principle within mobile being that accounts for its being this individual and no other. A common determination is the following: (1) form, the basis of substantial specification, cannot be such a principle be-

cause it is universal and thus able to be received in many different subjects; (2) accidents cannot account for individuality, for the individual belongs to the category of substance; (3) matter is the only remaining candidate, and yet primary matter is by nature common and so can be determined by many forms; (4) therefore matter as related to quantity, or matter as signed with quantity (thus called "signed matter" or "signate matter") is what differentiates one mobile being from another. This signing of matter may be understood as an intrinsic ordination of matter to quantity as a dividing and separating form—so allowing, e.g., for monozygotic twins to be identical save only in their numerical or quantitative separation. For other explanations of individuation, see 7:477b-478b; for the associated dispositions of matter in relation to form, see 4:908a-b.

## §20. THE FIRST UNMOVED MOVER

1. Since experience shows that some things in the world are in motion whereas others are at rest, the question arises whether each and every thing is so constituted as to be capable of motion and rest, and can be either a mover or something moved, or whether besides things of this sort something exists that is a mover but is itself unmoved by any other. This is the problem of the *first unmoved mover* (10:28), viz, whether a primal source or first cause of motion can be truly said to exist.

2. That this question can be answered in the affirmative follows from what has already been said concerning motion. Motion is incomplete act, the actual determination of a natural body precisely as this is capable of further actuation. Thus conceived,  motion requires a mobile or potential subject that remains the self-same throughout the change but becomes different from the way it was before the change. When a body passes from rest to motion, motion itself begins to be in this mobile subject. Whatever begins to be does not spring from mere nothing, nor does it produce itself, but depends for its being on some active principle, called the *efficient cause* [§35.8]. The efficient cause is the

mover, or active source of motion, whereas motion is an effect produced in the moved or mobile subject. Each kind of motion requires a mobile subject capable of being moved with that motion, as well as a mover able to produce the motion.

3. For motion to occur, however, several *conditions* must be fulfilled, viz: (1) there must be a distinction between mover and moved; (2) the mover and the moved must be in contact; and (3) the mover and the moved must actuate simultaneously, i.e., they must be together in time. (1) The distinction between mover and moved is expressed in the dictum: whatever is moved is moved by something else (*quidquid movetur ab alio movetur*). If something is in motion and does not have the efficient cause of its motion within itself, then it is moved by something other than itself. But if it does have the cause of motion within itself, then it moves itself by means of its parts, and these are related as mover and moved. In all cases, whatever is in motion is divisible and has parts, and (the whole depends upon the parts both for its existence and for its motion,) whether it is moved by something else or moves itself. (2) The mover is the principle and cause from which the motion proceeds and begins to exist in the moved; without contact the mover would have nothing on which to act. (What appears to be *action at a distance* is found on closer examination to involve at least intermediaries in contact; see 1:96b). Since mover and moved are together and, as it were, one by contact, they share one and the same motion but in different ways: the mover as agent and the moved as patient. (3) At the same time as the mover causes motion, the moved is in motion. Motion itself is one and the same act of both mover and moved, although again in different ways: it is actively from the mover, and as such is known as action; it is passively in the moved, and as such is known as passion. But action and passion are not really distinct from motion, and so occur simultaneously with it [§9.8, 18.6].

4. With these conditions understood one may reason to the *existence* of the first cause of motion as follows. Where there is motion, there must be a mover and a moved, distinct and yet

together in place and time. There may also be an intermediate
mover or instrument of motion. Motion is in the thing moved;
the intermediate mover moves something and is moved by something; there must also be a first cause of motion that is unmoved
by anything else, because the effect (motion as factually perceived) cannot be without such a cause. If anything is a mover
and yet incapable of causing motion by itself, but only as moved
by something else, and this in turn by something else, then such
a series of moved movers cannot be infinite. It must be limited,
in the sense that an unmoved mover must be the first cause of
motion. Besides all the movers moved by something else, however
many they may be, or of whatever kind, there must be a first
cause of motion that imparts motion by itself and is an unmoved
mover, independent of every other.

5. The natural philosopher has limited interest in the *nature*
of this first cause of motion: apart from the obvious understanding it affords him of motion itself, he is concerned only to know
whether or not it is a natural body and so pertains to his discipline.
Now a body or extended whole is not an independent being: it
depends upon its parts for its being and for its being moved, since
motion requires a subject that is extended and divisible into
parts. But the first cause of motion is completely independent
in its action, and hence also in its being. Therefore, the first cause
of motion is not a body, nor does it have parts on which its being
and acting depend. It is not composed of matter and form, nor
of potency and act. It is not capable of being moved or having
motion, either by itself or by something else, but is the unmoved
mover of other things. Because it is unmoved, it is not a temporal
being but eternal. And because it is unmoved and incorporeal,
it does not cause motion mechanically, as one body moves another
from without, but with a higher order of action analogous to the
way in which mind or intelligence moves a body [§§43-46].

6. Knowledge of this first unmoved mover therefore marks a
terminal point in the investigations of natural philosophy. When
one knows, through the study of nature, that there exists a kind
of being that is not mobile or corporeal, he realizes that there

can be a science superior to his own that studies being not merely as mobile, but precisely as being. Such constitutes the subject matter of the science "beyond physics," and called on this account *metaphysics* [§30].

# CHAPTER 4.

# PSYCHOLOGY

## §21. PHILOSOPHICAL PSYCHOLOGY

*Psychology* (11:963c) means literally the study of the soul (*psychē*). In its earlier development it was concerned with all living organisms, i.e., with natural bodies that are able to move themselves, and so could readily be seen as a part of the general study of nature; in more recent times it has focused almost exclusively on higher organisms capable of at least sentient life. As a part of natural philosophy (11:322b), psychology has no first principles of its own; its basic principles are still matter and form [§16], except that in living things there is a special type of form, called the soul, which so informs primary matter as to render it not only corporeal but also animated in a specific way. Yet psychology is not about the soul only, as its etymology might suggest; rather it is about the composite, the animated body. On this account soul or form is a principle of the science, not its proper subject. Topics discussed in psychology so conceived, usually referred to as *philosophical psychology*, include life in its various manifestations, knowledge, appetition, the human soul and its different powers, and the relationships that exist between man's soul and his body (see also §§72, 73).

## §22. LIFE AND SOUL

1. *Life* (8:734b) may be defined as self-movement *(sui motio)*,

i.e., the capacity of an organism to move itself from potentiality to activity. Perhaps a more obvious defining feature of vital activity is its *immanence* (7:385d), i.e., the type of self-perfecting action that is found in all life functions; thus nourishment perfects the organism nourished and knowledge perfects the one knowing. Such activities whose effects remain in and perfect the agent are termed *immanent*, and the effects themselves usually pertain to one or other species of quality [§9.6]; activities whose effects terminate outside the agent, on the other hand, are called *transient*, and these give rise to the categories of action and passion [§9.8]. The immanent activities characteristic of *plants* (11:426a) include nourishing, growing, maturing, reproducing, and otherwise maintaining a substantial unity or identity over a period of time; *animals* (1:545c), in addition, possess powers of cognition and appetition that enable them to be aware of their environment and respond to it through movements that likewise maintain self-identity and are even more distinctively self-perfective. Both of these characteristics, self-movement and immanence, assure that living things exist and operate at a higher level than do the non-living, for organisms move themselves to full perfection and maturity through their interactions with other bodies, whereas inorganic bodies generally lose their energies and sometimes their existence when they interact with others.

2. The principle of life in living things is called the *soul* (13: 447c). The classical way of defining soul is through a series of distinctions that, for convenience, may be divided into two sets. (I) The first set is as follows: (1) Whatever exists is either (a) a substance or (b) an accident; (2) substance is either (a) matter, which is potency and as such does not exist; or (b) form, which is actuality and as such does not exist; or (c) the composite of the two, the actually existing thing; and (3) actuality is either (a) like knowledge possessed—this is first actuality, or (b) like considering knowledge possessed—this is second actuality. (II) The second set of distinctions: (1) A body is either (a) natural, i.e., both its matter and its form are substantial; or (b) artificial, i.e., an artifact whose matter is substantial but

whose form is merely accidental; and (2) a body is either (a) non-living or (b) living.

3. From these distinctions it is easy to see that a living body (II.2.b) is a natural body (II.1.a) and a substance (I.1.a). Since a living body is an actually existing thing, it is a substance in the sense of a composite (I.2.c). Therefore a living body has a substantial matter and a substantial form: a form that accounts for its being alive, and a matter that is its potentiality for being alive. Thus soul is the form (I.2.b) or actuality of a natural body with a potentiality for being alive. Indeed, soul is the *first actuality* (I.3.a) of such a body—it is actuality in the sense in which knowledge possessed is actuality, for soul is presupposed to life activities. Life activities themselves are actualities in the second sense (I.3.b), i.e., in the sense in which actually considering what one knows presupposes what one knows. To say that soul is the first actuality of such a body is to say that soul is such a body's substantial form [§16.4].

4. But life activities presuppose not only soul. They presuppose also a certain sort of natural body, viz, a body having life potentially in it. Such a body is composed of certain sorts of natural elements and compounds, and is productive of certain others whose natural activities contribute to life activities. Such a body is also an *organized body*, i.e., one with various bodily parts ordered to diverse functions. Functionally ordered parts are organs; and a body with such parts is said to be an organized body or an *organism* (10:757a). Therefore soul is the first actuality or *entelechy* (5:455a) of a natural body having life potentially in it, i.e., of a natural organized body.

5. A second definition of soul may be given in terms of the formal effects it produces in the body, namely, soul is "the *primary* principle whereby we live, sense, move, and understand." Here "primary" differentiates soul from other principles, and the various vital powers that characterize different types of living things. This definition is sometimes referred to as the formal definition, and the one previously given, the material definition. The first demonstration in the science of psychology consists in demon-

strating the first definition from the second, in a manner analogous to showing the connection between the formal and material definitions of motion, which was noted as the first demonstration in natural philosophy [§18.1].

6. There are three *kinds* of soul, all implied in the second or formal definition, which designates soul generally and so includes features of the various kinds. These three types are distinguished in terms of the extent to which activities commonly attributed to living things transcend the activities of matter in its non-living states; or, alternatively, in terms of the extent to which these activities transcend anything found in the makeup of the natural organized body of a living thing. (1) There is an activity of soul that so transcends anything in the makeup of a natural organized body that it is not even performed by a bodily organ; this is the activity of the human or *intellective* soul. (2) Below this, there is an activity of soul performed by a bodily organ, but transcending the natural activities of the elements and compounds that constitute the organ; this is the activity of the animal or *sensitive* soul. (3) Lastly, there is an activity of soul that is performed by a bodily organ and by the activities of certain natural elements and compounds; this is the activity of the plant or *vegetative* soul, whose lowest level of transcendence is yet seen in nourishment and the process of reproduction. (For more details and examples, see 5:788b-d.)

7. Since soul performs different kinds of activity it is often said that soul has different *parts*, a part for each kind of activity. Because soul is not a body, but the first actuality or entelechy of a body, these parts of soul cannot be quantitative parts; hence soul is not quantitatively divisible into them. Such parts are nothing other than the *powers* or potencies the soul has for performing different sorts of life activity; therefore, if one says that soul is divisible into these parts, the meaning is simply that these parts are distinguishable from each other by definition, since each may be defined in terms of its object (see 5:788a).

8. The parts of the soul are often called *power parts*, to distinguish them from quantitative parts; and the soul, a power whole or a potestative whole [§3.8]. The following will make

clear the difference between power parts and quantitative parts: (1) quantitative parts are spread out, as it were, whereas power parts are not; (2) quantitative parts are homogeneous, whereas power parts are heterogeneous—there being as many different kinds of parts as there are different activities; and (3) quantitative parts are intrinsic constituents of the whole, whereas power parts are not, since the soul is something substantial [§9.4] and the powers of the soul are accidents in the second species of quality [§9.6].

## §23. COGNITION

1. *Knowledge* [§38] is variously defined as the act by which one becomes the other in an intentional way, or the act of a power part of the soul by which it is aware of something, or the habit by which one can recall such an act, or the matter that is the object of such an act or habit. In psychology knowledge is studied from the point of view of its being a life activity, indeed a most important life activity, an immanent operation that springs from one of the power parts of the soul and is especially perfective of the agent in which it comes to exist.

2. In this understanding *cognition*, or the knowledge act, is not doing something but becoming something. It is a self-modification brought about by the objective possession of some thing other than oneself. The knower's being is expanded by the addition of a perfection previously not possessed, yet contributed by something else that has lost nothing in the giving. There has been no change such as occurs when matter receives a new form while losing an old one; rather form, itself a perfection, has had new perfection added to it, and thus has been modified and perfected cognitively. Unlike the process by which a stone is heated, receiving the form of heat from another, or wax is imprinted by a seal, receiving the shape of the seal, the form received in a knowledge act is undetectable in the knower and known to be present only by the one knowing. Hence it follows that the form is present in a way unlike the way physical forms come to be

present. This new presence is termed "immaterial," meaning not received in the knower as a simple physical effect. Then, since materiality is the reason two like forms are distinct from each other [§19.6], the immaterial presence of the form in the knower leaves it somehow indistinct from the form in the thing known. Thus the objectivity that is an experiential feature of knowledge acts becomes capable of reasonable explanation.

3. On the foregoing analysis a knower somehow has the power to transcend the real distinction between itself and the others that are found in the natural world, and somehow becomes and is the other that it knows. This it does by way of increase: remaining itself, it becomes also the other. It receives formal determinations not merely as its own, but also as the other's. Thus it receives not only in a subjective manner, as material things receive, but also in an objective and intentional manner. The fullness or perfection of being by which the knower can overcome its own material limitations and its distinctions from other things is known as *immateriality* (7:389b). Immateriality is the root principle of knowledge and intelligibility. By it the knower has a certain preeminence over the potentiality of matter, an amplitude of being and perfection whereby it can come to possess formal determinations in an intentional way, which itself is the vital activity of knowing.

4. The notion of *intentionality* (7:564a) casts fuller light on the knowledge process. A form that is received in a knower, such as the form of yellow or that of a horse, is simply a meaning or a cognition or an intention of the same form in reality. But, unlike the reception of the form of yellow in a physical or material object, which makes the object itself become yellow, the reception of the form of yellow in an intentional way in the knower does not make the one knowing it become physically yellow. Rather, such an intentionally received form is better referred to as a *species*, i.e., something through which the physically existing form is rendered, as it were, perspicuous to the one knowing it. The form that has intentional being in the knower is therefore a likeness, a *similitudo*, of the physical form that exists in the object known. Thus, through the intentionally received form, as

a *similitudo* or an *intentio* of the physically existing form, the latter comes to be known. It is in this sense that the concept, the likeness or the intelligible species in the intellect, is both that "by which" (*id quo*) the intelligible object is known and the meaning or objective content, the "that which" (*id quod*) is cognized in the knowing process [§3.2].

5. The expression *intentional species* (13:555b) similarly designates the immaterial mode of existence an object acquires when it is united to a knowing power such as the intellect or one of the external or internal senses. Intentional species are frequently qualified as "impressed" or "expressed" species to designate the particular manner in which an object is received in the knowing power. Since the external senses are essentially passive with respect to their objects, because the change a sense undergoes is in the order of an impression only, the species that comes to exist in the external sense is said to be an *impressed species* only. In most of the internal senses, on the other hand, since the object is received and expressly understood, both an impressed species and an *expressed species* are said to be required for their knowing processes. Likewise in the intellect there is both an impressed and an expressed species, the former corresponding to what is known as the intelligible species [§25.2] and the latter to the concept already discussed [§3.2].

6. The foregoing purports to be the basic explanation of all acts of knowledge, whether of sensation or of intellection. The difference between these two types of knowing lies in the different ways in which intentional species are received. In sensation the concrete, individual forms of an object, e.g., its visible, palpable, audible features, are received as, being present, they "impress" themselves on the subject, or, as grasped and later recalled, they are "expressed" by the knowing power. In intellection, on the other hand, the mind attains the abstract, and hence universal, ideas drawn from the sensible experience of its objects. Each of these types of knowledge now merits examination in more detail.

## §24. SENSATION AND PERCEPTION

1. *Sensation* (13:84d) may be described as the most elementary cognitive reaction of an organism to its environment. The awareness of green, of warm, of sharp—when not accompanied by the awareness of something green, warm, or sharp—is a simple sensation; the awareness of a particular green leaf, on the other hand, is not a sensation but a perception [§24.11-12]. The act of simple sensation is itself achieved in several stages. First there is the physical stage, wherein an outside stimulus (e.g., electromagnetic or sound waves) originating from some object impinges on a sense organ. This is followed by a physiological stage, wherein a modification is produced by the stimulus in the sense organ. Since the organ is alive and animated, its physiological modification is accompanied by another, or psychic modification, whose production constitutes the psychological stage. The result produced here is the impressed species, or the impressed intentional form already discussed [§23.5]. It is a substitute for the outside object within the sense power, by means of which the object becomes known. Up to this point the sense power can be regarded as passive or receptive. But knowledge, as has been seen, is a vital activity. Hence there is a last stage, the active psychological stage, wherein the sense power turns, as it were, toward the object, grasps it, and knows it. Only when this occurs is there *sense knowledge* (13:89b).

2. It is important, on this account, to stress that the senses know the *object* itself, and not simply its substitute, the impressed species. The reason for this is that the impressed species is a formal sign, not merely an instrumental sign [§3.4]. An instrumental sign must be known in itself before the thing it signifies can be known; a formal sign, on the other hand, is not known in itself, but it is the means whereby the signified object is known. An example of a formal sign is the retinal image, or picture of the perceived object on the retina of the eye; man never sees the image itself, but through it he sees the object. In sensation, more generally, man knows the object itself and not simply the impression made by the object. If he knew only the impression he

would be forever cut off from reality, and he would never have real knowledge. For this reason simple sensation does not require an image or substitute for the object, and thus there is no expressed species in knowledge that derives from the external senses.

3. The *senses* (13:90d) are the immediate principles of sensation. They have an organic structure that is scientifically observable and they are energized by a power of the soul. Both organic structure and vital power are thus required for sensation, and these are linked to make unique realities, viz, the senses. A distinction is usually made between external senses and internal senses, to each of which correspond different powers of the soul. The existence of external senses is obvious; ordinary experience recognizes most of them, and scientific study confirms and completes its findings. The existence and nature of the internal senses, on the other hand, is not obvious and more problematical on that account. The organic structures of external senses are found in the peripheral and central nervous systems. Sensory receptors are anatomically and functionally discernible, and these are specifically affected by different typical stimuli. The peripheral organ's stimulation unleashes nerve impulses that rise to the *brain* (2:748c) along complex routes, intersected by synaptic relays. In the brain these influxes terminate in different zones, where specific centers can be pinpointed for each sensation. The internal senses, without peripheral organs, are all found in the brain or at its base.

4. Five *external senses* are traditionally noted: sight, hearing, smell, taste, and touch. Since the senses are passive powers, they are distinguished from each other in terms of the external *sensibles* (13:93a), i.e., the objects that are capable of affecting them. The differentiation of the external senses, therefore, is a matter of properly understanding various stimulus-objects and receptor-subjects, and of identifying the relationships that obtain between them. Pursuing this, a stimulus is defined as an energy pattern that arouses a sensory receptor; sensory receptors, reacting to specifically distinct stimuli, constitute as many different senses. Beginning with such a distinction of stimuli, one can note a

difference among receptors by considering the proper organs, the nerves linking these organs to the brain, and the zones of the brain where the nerves terminate. In this way *sight* and *hearing* are very clearly distinguished. *Smell* and *taste* are similarly dissociated, despite the close chemical interdependence between them. *Touch* is more difficult to analyze; it is generally seen as made up of the following functions: (1) tactile or cutaneous sensitivity that selectively perceives pressure, pain, warmth, and cold; (2) deep organic sensitivity, viz, kinesthesis or proprioception for muscular sensation, and deep touch for the viscera and internal organs; and (3) vestibular function, located in the semi-circular canals of the ear, for the positioning and movement of the body in equilibrium, a function that works in harmony with kinesthesis and deep touch. (For a discussion of the various physico-chemical factors involved in sensation, see 13:86d-89b.)

5. The *object* of an external sense is called a sensible because it can modify the sense. It appears as a complex ensemble that acts upon the senses in many ways. There are, first of all, qualities such as color (3:1030c) that are capable of specifically stimulating a particular sense, in this case sight, to which they belong as their own immediate or *proper sensibles*. These qualities, however, exist as properties of quantified material realities; thus they are located in space and time, and are subject to movement. They therefore affect also the senses in a way that is related to these quantitative aspects. Because these can act simultaneously upon many senses and are common to all of them, they are designated as *common sensibles*. Finally, these quantitatively conditioned qualities manifest the natures of material realities, as well as their functional values for the knowing subject. Perception of these natures and of these values is made possible by the activity of the senses, but it immediately surpasses simple sensation and requires other principles of knowing, such as the internal senses and the intellect.

6. *Internal senses* are called such because they contact reality only through the intermediary of the external senses. To identify them as principles of knowledge one must investigate functions of sense knowledge that are themselves irreducible to the external

senses. These functions must be grouped around specific objects: whatever functions cannot be referred to the same object must then require distinct principles of operation. Such a methodological principle is commonly used to identify four different internal senses, viz, central sense, imagination, cogitative power, and memory.

7. The *central sense* (3:400b), also known as the *sensus communis*, is necessary for consciousness of sensation, which is impossible for the external senses because their organic structure prohibits reflection on themselves. It is also needed to explain comparisons between sensations of the various senses, comparisons that no sense can make since it does not know the objects of the other senses. To the degree that it implies a loss of consciousness, *sleep* (13:290d) requires a corresponding inhibition of the central sense.

8. The *imagination* (7:372d) registers the impressions unified by the central sense to reproduce these subsequently, sometimes with fanciful elaborations. Its necessity derives from the inability of the central sense to retain its own impressions; functioning in combination with the external senses, the central sense knows reality only when this actually affects the senses, whereas the imagination brings back the image of these realities known in their absence. The image produced by this power of imagining is known as the *phantasm* (11:251a); it is an expressed species that represents the sense object as it is past or absent or otherwise inaccessible to the external senses. Apart from its role in sense knowledge, the phantasm plays an indispensable role in man's knowing process, where it supplies a representation of a concrete reality from which the intellect extricates the concept or essential meaning [§7.5]. The imagination can also cause error, however, since it is the source of *illusion* (7:368d), i.e., the distorted perception of a reality actually present to the senses. Imaginative activity is also involved in the *dream* (4:1053b), the illusory psychic phenomenon that occurs during sleep.

9. The *cogitative power* (3:981a) employs data arriving from the external senses, the central sense, and the imagination to detect values whose perception escapes these lower powers. Such

values include the functional meaning of reality for the knowing
subject, and the existence of this reality as concrete, individual,
and reducible to a general category. Because it acts in a round-
about, discursive way, the cogitative is sometimes referred to as
the *discursive power* (4:897d). This plays a role in human
knowledge similar to that of the *estimative power* (5:558a) in
brute animals, where it is used to account for the purposiveness
or intelligence discernible in animal activity and generally explained by *instinct* (7:546d).

10. The *memory* (9:639d), or memorative power, plays a
role with respect to the cogitative or estimative power analogous
to that played by the imagination with respect to the central
sense. It preserves functional meanings such as estimates of good
or bad so that it can re-experience what has happened before and
recognize this experience as something past. Thus the memory
stores experiences and recalls them, situating them in a type of
temporal continuity that is measured by the projection of perception toward the past. It functions to assure the continuity of
experience lived by the knowing subject and, in man, is indispensable for organizing his personality [§29]. To achieve this result
both the memorative and the cogitative power employ the expressed species produced by the imagination and known as the
phantasm or percept.

11. *Perception* (3:401a; 11:117b) is usually differentiated
from both sensation and intellection [§25]; the term applies to
any immediate experience of objects obtained through the senses,
and so to an experience that is more integrated than sensation
and more concrete and individual than intellection. Although so
distinguished, it is commonly agreed that human perception includes both intellectual and sensory elements. Moreover, the distinction between sensation as an elementary experience and perception as the knowledge of particular objects does not mean that
sensation can be experienced as distinct from perception. Perception is always a unitary and instantaneous awareness of the material object in a sensory way.

12. To explain this *unified knowledge* of sensed objects it is
necessary to resort to the internal senses in general and to the

central sense in particular. The latter sense integrates and amplifies the sensory apprehensions, though the other internal senses, particularly the cogitative and the imagination, also play important roles, and indeed they alone can produce the phantasm or the percept. The need for the central sense is evident from the fact that the awareness of a unified object is neither a proper sensible nor a common sensible that can be known by any of the special senses. The only power by which one can compare and contrast sensations and their objects is the unifying or central sense. It is the cogitative power, however, that gives an immediate experience of the individual object on the basis of the sensory cues available; imagination and memory are also operative in the perception of *space* (13:491), *time* (14:161d), and *motion* (10:27c).

## §25. INTELLECTION

1. Man's *knowledge process* (8:230b) involves both sensation and intellection, and these two elements inevitably go together. Sensation, as has been seen, gives a person knowledge of concrete aspects or qualities of individual, material objects, e.g., colors, sounds, and odors, and when such qualities are organized so as to constitute a unity in space and time, the result is a perception, e.g., of this individual tree. Apart from these instances of sense knowledge, man can also say, "That is a tree," and this is an example of *intellection,* or of intellectual knowledge. The statement implies that the one making it has a concept of tree; even though he applies it only to a particular oak, it can be applied to innumerable other trees, and thus is universal. To affirm of a thing that it is a tree, moreover, is to make a judgment, to state that the objective reality is constituted as it is understood by the knower. The power or faculty that enables man to make such a statement is called the *intellect* (7:554c).

2. The process by which man forms ideas or concepts from sense knowledge is usually explained in terms of *abstraction* [§7.4] as a special intellective function. To understand this one

must be aware that the intellect itself is not purely passive in forming the idea but exercises an active role also. The active power of the intellect is designated by a special name, the agent intellect (*intellectus agens*), and its passive power is correspondingly denominated the passive or possible intellect (*intellectus possibilis*). Through sense knowledge, as already explained, man is in possession of the phantasm or percept of the single, concrete, material object. By a process of illumination the agent intellect extracts from the phantasm the nature or quiddity of the object, leaving aside all the individuating notes that characterize it in its singularity. This process results in an intelligible species which the agent intellect impresses on the possible intellect, and so gives rise there to the abstract, universal idea or concept of the object. The intelligible species originating in the agent intellect is an impressed species, and the concept formed (or conceived, *conceptus*) in the possible intellect is an expressed species. The concept is a formal sign of the nature grasped in the object; like the senses, the intellect does not know the concept as such, but rather knows and understands the object as it is in reality through the concept. Moreover, the concept has a nobler and more immaterial mode of existence in the intellect than the phantasm has in the inner senses. On this account one cannot regard the phantasm as the efficient cause of the concept, for no agent can produce an effect superior to itself. Rather the phantasm is said to be the material cause of intellection, or at best its *instrumental cause* [§35.9], insofar as the phantasm is used by the intellect to generate the intelligible species from which the concept is itself formed.

3. The process of *concept formation*, so understood, is not to be viewed as a mere mechanical functioning or as one that sharply separates the work of the intellect from that of the senses. Man's substantial unity, in fact, implies not only the unity of body and soul but also that of sense and intellect. As the soul is to the body so the intellect is to the senses. The body never acts without being animated by the soul, and similarly, in man, the senses never act without being animated by the intellect. This means that the intellect is already at work with the inner senses,

and particularly with the cogitative power, in the formation of the phantasm. Indeed, the intellect animates this formation and in such activity produces the universal idea. The impressed species of the intellect is thus best understood as a dynamic relationship between the agent intellect and the phantasm from which the passive intellect derives intelligible content.

4. Just as the sensible is the object of the senses, so the *intelligible* (cf. 7:562d) is the object of the intellect [§7.4]. The proper material object of man's intellect comprises every object that can be perceived by the senses—other men, animals, plants, artifacts, all the things he can know naturally and easily. Whereas the senses grasp such objects as sensible, however, the intellect recognizes them for their meaning, for what they are. On this account the "whatness" or *quiddity* (12:25a) of material objects is the proper formal object of the human intellect. Yet the scope of the human intellect extends beyond the realm of material objects. The fact that one speaks of material objects implies obviously that he knows of others that are not material. What is required in any object for it to be knowable by the human intellect is that it *be*, or, at least, that it be *able to be*. Hence, the total or the adequate object of the intellect is *being* [§31], in all its extension, whether corporeal or spiritual. Now the intellect knows such being from the viewpoint of its *truth* [§39], or intelligibility. Accordingly, while the adequate material object of the intellect is being, its adequate formal object is truth or intelligibility.

5. Unlike the senses, the intellect has no material organ or organic structure on which it directly depends for its operation, and on this account is itself an *immaterial* or spiritual faculty. Because of the involvement of the internal and external senses in thought, however, man's brain is required for thinking. Still the brain is not the cause of thinking; it is merely a necessary condition [§35.3]. The brain is a material substance, concrete, visible, tangible, singular, extended, existing in space and time, contingent, and not necessary; its effects must exhibit these characteristics also. And indeed, a brain tumor and a brain wave do. But man's intellectual operations show different characteristics.

.4

His ideas or concepts are universal, not limited to space and time, not extended, not concrete, and many of his judgments are necessary and true at all times, in all places, and in all circumstances. The universality of man's ideas and the necessity of many of his judgments cannot derive from a material organ such as the brain. They require a power that is, to some extent, beyond time and space, free from the contingency of matter. This immaterial, spiritual power is the intellect.

6. Another evidence for the immateriality of the intellect is to be found in man's capability for *reflection* (12:166d). Man not only knows, but he also knows that he knows. In his awareness of being aware, subject and object coincide. This cannot occur in a purely material being. The luminous self-presence of man's act of reflection is thus another indication that he possesses an immaterial, spiritual power of thinking.

## §26. APPETITION

1. Apart from cognitive powers, beings that possess knowledge also have powers that incline them to seek or avoid the objects with which their knowing powers put them in contact. The generic name for such powers is *appetite* (1:703c), deriving from the Latin *appetitus*, which means a seeking for something. Appetite in the strict sense thus designates the capacity of a thing to seek its *good* (6:614b); when used more broadly it includes the actual seeking as well, otherwise known as *appetition*. Appetite therefore means both the fundamental power to seek and the actual exercise of that power. It is closely related to a number of other psychological concepts, such as orexis, conation, urge, drive, feeling, emotion, affectivity, and passion. Orexis is a transliteration of the Greek term for appetite, sometimes signifying appetite in general and at other times the power of the will. Conation, urge, and drive (4:1063b) are terms that are used almost interchangeably to indicate the forceful or impulsive aspect of appetites. Feeling (5:876b) and affectivity are generally used to indicate the felt quality connected with appetitive activity, whereas

emotion (5:308d) and passion (10:1052c) indicate acts of an appetite, frequently including both their feeling and drive aspects.

2. The first *division* of appetite is into natural and elicited appetites. Because things exist as they are and tend to continue in existence for a while, and because they operate as they ought to operate, they are said to have a *natural appetite* to exist and to operate. Such a natural appetite is not conceived as a reality in a thing distinct from its nature [§17.1]; it is rather the nature itself conceived in terms of tendency to be and to operate.

3. *Elicited appetites* are those aroused by cognitive acts, and they are considered to be distinct parts or powers of the nature of a cognitive being. The evidence for elicited appetites is, first, man's own experience and, secondly, his observation of other animals. A person feels impulses and affects aroused in himself by cognitive acts toward various objects, and these impel him to action toward these objects. Animals, moreover, seem to act the same way and are endowed with the same kind of organs that serve man. Thus knowing beings give evidence of having the capacity to be moved by objects as known, and this capacity is, by definition, an elicited appetite.

4. Since, then, there are appetites aroused by cognitive acts, there will be at least as many distinct kinds of elicited appetite as there are distinct orders of knowledge. Knowledge, as we have seen, is divided into sense knowledge and intellectual knowledge; appetites are correspondingly divided into sensitive appetite and will, the appetite that follows on intellection.

## §27.  SENSITIVE APPETITES

1. By definition a *sensitive appetite* is a capacity to be aroused by a concrete object perceived through the senses. It is therefore an operative power, i.e., a power to respond and react. This response or reaction on the part of the possessor of the appetite has a twofold moment. First of all it is a kind of passivity by which the possessor is changed or moved by the impact of the object

sensed. Secondly, since this change is of the nature of a tension produced in the possessor, an inclination to action follows, for the purpose of relieving the tension. Hence appetites tend to provoke action. The actions are designed to obtain or avoid the object that originally aroused the appetite: to obtain it if it is good, or to avoid it if it is evil. Since avoiding evil is itself good, one can define the appetite as ordered simply to the good, either directly or indirectly.

2. The sense appetites therefore arise from the sense knowledge that elicits them. They involve physical changes in the organism, and they result in actions. The physical changes may be greater or less, but they are always present and are recognizable as the emotional components of changes in the circulatory, respiratory, glandular, etc., systems. The actions that result are known as emotions, and these are *classified* into two general kinds, as are the appetites that elicit them, on the basis of the following reasoning. Some emotions in the organism are aroused on the basis of simple pleasure (11:438d) and pain (10:864d), as it seeks out what is pleasing physically and avoids what feels injurious. These reactions constitute the operations of one appetite, the *concupiscible* or *impulse* appetite, whose ultimate object is defined as the simple, sensitive good. Other emotional reactions are not so simply explained, for example, inclinations impelling one toward things that are hard or difficult to attain, or emotional responses impelling the knower to reject or despair of good objects. Such appetitive reactions are therefore assigned to a second sensitive appetite, called the *irascible* or *contending* appetite, whose object is the difficult or arduous sensible good.

3. The *emotions* are further divided into eleven different categories, six of which are impulse emotions and found in the concupiscible appetite, the remaining five contending emotions, found in the irascible appetite. *Love* (8:1039b), the first impulse emotion, is the fundamental reaction that underlies all others: it is defined as the simple tendency toward a good thing. *Desire* (4:800c), which arises from love, is a tendency toward a good thing that is not yet possessed but is presently attainable. *Joy* (7:1133c) follows from desire when the good thing is actually

possessed. *Hatred* (6:946d), the opposite of love, is the turning away from an evil thing. *Aversion* or dislike arises from hatred, as an actual repugnance to an evil thing presenting itself. *Sadness* (12:845a) or sorrow follows after aversion, if the evil thing actually afflicts the knowing subject. These are the six basic impulse emotions. *Hope* (cf. 7:133a) is the name given to the first of the contending emotions; it is the vehement seeking for a good object that is hard to obtain. *Courage* (4:390c) is the energetic attack on evil that is hard to overcome. *Despair* (4:805b) is the giving up of a good object because of difficulties, and *fear* (5:863b) is the urgent avoidance of an evil that is hard to escape. *Anger* (1:521c), finally, is the movement toward an evil that is hard to overcome for the sake of avoiding it. These are the five basic contending emotions. All other emotional reactions, with their various modalities and mixtures and shades of difference, can be comprised without great difficulty under one or other of these eleven basic categories (see 5:310d-317a).

## §28. VOLITION

1. The *will* (14:909d) is the rational or intellectual appetite in man, i.e., the source of *volition* whereby he seeks goods as perceived by the power of the intellect [§25.1]. As the intellect is the supreme cognitive power in man, so the will is the supreme appetite in man, controlling all human behavior; and as the intellect is a spiritual power, so also is the will. Thus all purely spiritual or rational goods are sought by the will alone, and rational and spiritual evils are rejected by the will. It is the will that desires justice, truth, order, immortality, and the like, and hates injustice, deceit, chaos, and death. However, the will's objects are not limited to spiritual things—it seeks also to obtain or avoid physical goods sought by the sensitive appetites; but when the will acts in this sphere it is because it sees reasonableness in these physical goods. Thus, the sight of food might arouse a person's concupiscible appetite because food is pleasant to eat, but he wills to eat it only if he sees that it is reasonable here and

now to do so. Hence a man can also starve himself in spite of a contrary urging from the sensitive appetites, if in the circumstances he judges this is a reasonable thing to do. The will ultimately controls all behavior, as long as man is conscious and sane; even behavior motivated primarily by the sense appetites is not carried out unless the will consents [§52].

2. The will is a free power in man, basically because it is the appetite that follows reason. Because reason can see several alternatives equally feasible as means of reaching one end, the will has freedom (6:95d) to elect from among them. Thus *free will* (6:89a) is an ability characterizing man in the voluntary activity of choosing or not choosing a limited good when this is presented to him. Such voluntary activity is also called free choice (3:620a) or free decision, from the Latin expression *liberum arbitrium* [§50.6-8].

3. Just as the object of the intellect is the true, so the *object* of the will is the good. Because of this the will can be attracted to something only so far as it recognizes it to be good. A good that can satisfy only to a limited extent is called a particular or finite good, whereas one that can satisfy in every conceivable aspect is called the universal or supreme good (6:620c). Now it is commonly held that the human will is strictly determined in its nature toward an object recognized intellectually as the universal good. If this is so, then freedom of choice is exercised only with regard to objects recognized as particular goods. A man is not determined to these because particular goods can be viewed in two opposing ways: (1) they may be seen as good, i.e., according to the proportionate good they possess when compared to the universal good; or (2) they may be seen as lacking in good, i.e., to the extent that they lack goodness when measured against the universal good. Thus, any finite good can be considered under an aspect of desirability or undesirability when compared to the universal good; as desirable, it can attract the will, as undesirable, it cannot. Not being determined by such a good, the will remains radically free to choose it or reject it.

4. The most important of the powers of the soul that *influence* choices of will is obviously the intellect. The will is urged toward

anything that is understood to be in some way satsfying; such understanding is a function of the intellect. On the other hand, since even understanding of an object is a finite good for the person considering it, he may refuse to acquire its complete understanding [§39.5]. Because of this he may be attracted toward an object that here and now he considers good, whereas a more complete understanding of the same object would have presented it as undesirable. The will can also be affected indirectly by objects of the sense powers, insofar as such objects are presented with a vividness rarely found in intellectual activity. Sense impressions and physical states, as a consequence, can influence a person's intellectual deliberation and choice. (For a discussion of other factors that move the will, called *motives*, see 9:39b, also §50.9).

5. The *acts* of the will are often called by the same name as the emotions of the sense appetites, namely, love, hatred, desire, fear, anger, and so on. These, however, are not the names of the will's proper acts. The principal proper acts of the will [§50.8] are to intend an end or purpose, to elect the means to accomplish it, to command the actions that execute it, and to rest content in the purpose accomplished (14:910d-911b). If the purpose is to attain a good, one may call the acts of intention, election, and command acts of love; if they are aimed at destroying evil, one may call them anger; if at escaping an evil, one may call them fear, etc. The best understanding of the acts of the will, however, is attained when they are seen in their complex interplay with the acts of the intellect that go to make up the distinctively *human act* [§50]. The various intellectual acts specify the acts of the will, for what one wills depends on what he knows; on the other hand, each act of the will subsequently moves the intellect to a further act of knowing until the will is brought to some rest in an enjoyment of what was initially desired or, if unsuccessful, to a sadness in not attaining what was initially desired [§50.8].

6. The *relationships* between the acts of the will and those of the sense appetites are complex. One can arouse the sensitive appetites deliberately by willing to think about and imagine the objects that stir them. Moreover, it often happens that a particu-

larly strong act of the will produces a similar passion in the sense appetites, by a kind of overflow or redundance. In their turn, the sense appetites can exert considerable influence on the will. The freedom of the will, for instance, depends on the power of reason to judge a situation calmly, taking into account all possibilities. But when the emotions are strongly aroused the power of reason often fails to judge carefully [§39.5], and a man is precipitated into actions he would not otherwise have performed. The emotions can fix the attention of the mind on the things that stir them and limit its capacity to reflect, and thus indirectly limit the freedom of the will. Moreover, to act contrary to strong passions produces strong feelings of pain and sorrow, and rather than endure these, men often consent to things they would otherwise reject. Thus, although the will is free and in supreme command of the human act, in practice it is often restricted in its freedom by the sense appetites. (For a discussion and evaluation of other accounts of psychological *determinism,* see 4:813c).

## §29. MAN

1. The process of determining the nature of the soul and the various life powers with which it is endowed is the *analytical* part of psychology; the *synthetic* part is the definition of the whole human composite made up of these various elements and the assessment of the resulting structure of man or of human nature. This part of the discipline is sometimes called *philosophical anthropology.*

2. *Man* (9:124d), in the classical definition, is a rational animal, *animal rationalis,* i.e., an animal like other animals, but distinct by having the power of universal, abstract reason, and all that follows from it [§2.1]. Like all living things, man is a union of body and soul, but the human soul differs from all others in being a rational or intellective soul [§22.6]. The body is an essential part of man and it has a positive value; yet the body exists, not in its own right, but in virtue of the human soul, which is a form in the real sense and  the unique substantial form of the

body. (For medieval controversies on this point see 5:1024b and
7:557b.) Since the body is only human through the soul, and the
soul in turn determines the body, the *soul-body relationship*
(13:471d) is not that of a mere juxtaposition of parts but rather
the unity of a substantial being. The essential unity of man is
manifest from the fact that the same concrete man who is
experienced in his bodily presence is also a person who thinks.
The spiritual activity of thinking and the material givenness of
the body are both manifestations of one and the same human
reality. Again, the transcendence of the spirit over material reality
is manifested by the immateriality of intellection [§25.5]; this
means that the human soul, having an activity that is intrinsically
independent of material conditions, cannot have a mode of being
inferior to its mode of operation. In other words, it must be essentially independent of matter. On the other hand, man is really
material, and this not merely accidentally; the body belongs
essentially to his nature. Now the only way in which one can
reconcile all these data is by maintaining that the human soul
informs matter as a substantial form [§16.4]; in so doing, however, it is not dependent on matter in the very fact of existing,
but, on the contrary, man's body is dependent on his soul and
exists in virtue of the soul's existence. Such a special and intimate
ontological relationship between soul and body alone explains
man's substantial unity, the spiritual character of his soul, and
the fact that his body is an essential part of his nature.

3. The *human soul* (13:459d), on this understanding, (1)
is man's substantial form; nonetheless (2) it is immaterial, i.e.,
it is a subsistent form, or a *spirit* (13:568b); but (3) it is not
complete as to species. Moreover, (4) though it is essentially and
quantitatively simple, it is dynamically composed; (5) some of
its powers require habits for their perfection; and (6) even
though it is immaterial it is dependent on the human body for
certain of its operations. Points (1) and (2) should be clear
from man's substantial unity and from the foregoing analysis of
intellection [§25]. With regard to point (3), human nature
is a species [§8.2-3] insofar as man is a composite of body and
soul, and thus man's soul is incomplete in species when not

joined to his body. Point (4) stresses the fact that the only composition in the soul is one of power parts, which are ordered to the diversity of man's life activities, as already explained [§22.8]. Point (5) may be developed as follows: some of the powers of the human soul operate more easily and more efficiently when perfected by a *habit* [§50.3]. Habits are acquired qualities, as opposed to powers, which are innate; science [§13] is a typical habit of the intellect, as justice [§56] is of the will. Point (6) accents that the human soul is dependent on the bodily senses for its phantasms, which it requires for its thought processes, as previously detailed [§25.2].

4. Man is mortal, as is univerally admitted, because his soul can be separated from his body; the human soul, on the other hand, is *immortal* (13:464a) and will endure forever regardless of biological *death* (4:687b, 16:116c). This conclusion follows from the nature of the human soul as incorruptible. Being simple, it lacks any spatial or constitutive parts into which it can break up. Being spiritual, at the death of the body it continues to exist because it does not depend on matter for its existence; indeed, its spiritual operations of intellection and volition give clear indications of its immateriality, for they reveal no intrinsic dependence on matter, only the extrinsic dependence required for the origin of ideas. Other evidences for the immortality of the human soul can be adduced from man's unlimited spiritual capacities and desires, and from the necessity of moral sanctions in an afterlife.

5. The immateriality of the human soul also has important ramifications when examining the problem of its *origin* (13:470a). Just as man's soul is intrinsically independent of matter in its being, so is it intrinsically independent of matter in its becoming. As a consequence the human soul cannot be produced from matter by the generative act of the parents; rather it comes into being by *creation* [§47.2], by being produced directly from nothing [§71.2].

6. From what has been said so far one can gather the essential elements that go to make up human nature, the humanity that is common to all men. While sharing in this nature, each individual man is also a *person* (11:166c). The classical definition of person,

formulated by Boethius, is that it is "an individual substance of a rational nature." In the later development of this definition the expression "individual substance" has come to mean a substance that is complete, subsists by itself, and is separated from others; the expression "of a rational nature" designates the rationality, or capacity for abstract thought, that characterizes such a substance. On this interpretation neither the human soul [§29.3] nor second substance [§9.4] is a person, the first because it is not complete, the second because it can have no existence by itself when separated from the individual; on the other hand an immaterial substance that is complete in species and subsists by itself, such as an angel, is a person (see 1:509c-514a).

7. The ontological basis for a substance being denominated a person is its special dignity, which separates it from a mere *thing* (14:91a); this consists in its entitative sufficiency for independent *subsistence,* its dominion over its own activity, and its spirituality, all conferring on it a perfect and enduring manner of existing [§34.4]. The human person, precisely as spiritual, is free from the limitations of space and time, is endowed with consciousness [§38.3], has responsibility for its actions, and can enter into relationships with other persons, with all that such relationships imply for a moral and social order.

8. All men are persons and have rational souls, and in these respects they are essentially alike; they also have *individual differences* (7:470a), however, and these are the basis for asserting various diversities among men [§34.6]. Some of these differences are inborn, for example, the obvious diversity of *sex* (13:147d) and the inclinations of *temperament* (13:983d) and *disposition* (4:907b) that affect all individuals psychologically as well as physically (see 14:352b). Given these differences in native talent, however, there are also acquired differences—some partly natural, coming from native propensities, others purely acquired, generated by repeated acts. Many of these differences can be explained in terms of habit formation (6:882d-884c), for it is by this means that the intellect and the will, as well as the sense appetites, develop their characteristic modes of activity [§50.3-4]. Strength of will that is acquired through the repeated acts of

virtue, for example, endows a person with *character* (3:457a), which itself is distinctive. Other qualities that serve to distinguish a person, such as his social capabilities, his mannerisms and his peculiar skills, are frequently grouped under the more generic term of *personality* (11:174a). Amidst all this differentiation, finally, man's conscious activity makes him aware of his being a *self* (13:56d), an individual knowing who and what he is, encountering and interacting with others, continually sharing existence with them in the world of matter and in that of spirit, himself situated at the meeting place of both.

# CHAPTER 5.

# METAPHYSICS

## §30. METAPHYSICS

1. *Metaphysics* (9:727b) means literally "beyond physics," and it is usually understood to be the branch of philosophy that comes after natural philosophy [§20.6] and that has for its study not merely mobile being but being as such. Because the Greek word for being is *on* this discipline is also called *ontology* (10:703b), i.e., the study of the meaning, structure, and principles of whatever is and inasmuch as it is or exists. In its material object, or the number of things it studies, metaphysics is all-inclusive, extending to everything and every aspect of whatever is or can exist, whether of a sensible, material, physical nature or of a higher, non-material nature—from which extension to the most perfect and divine it is called *first philosophy* and even *theology* [§41]. Its formal object is being precisely as being (*ens qua ens*), i.e., according to the relation that any thing or aspect of things has to existence, rather than to one of the particular aspects treated in the other branches of philosophy. The unity of this point of view, centered on what is most fundamental to all reality, enables metaphysics to investigate the way in which the many are interrelated to the one in the deepest ontological sense. Further, since things are reflected in knowledge, it enables metaphysics to order and evaluate the various types of speculative and practical knowledge, on which account it is also called *wisdom* [§36].

2. The *subject* of metaphysics is best clarified after one has established in natural philosophy and in psychology the existence

of non-material realities such as the first unmoved mover [§20] and the human soul [§29.3]. Knowing of such immaterial reality, the mind is enabled to make the negative judgment of separation that the real is not necessarily the material. On this account the perfection of metaphysics as a distinct science requires (1) that its subject, whose real definition is the middle term in its demonstrations, be drawn from material things, the quiddity of which is the proper object of man's intellect [§25.4], and (2) that the separation of a meaning for being distinct from that of material being be validated by the witness of actually existing non-material beings. When enabled by such witness to make its judgment of separation the mind can remove a restriction on its understanding of things. Whereas previously, having attained knowledge of all things through the senses, it spoke of reality precisely as sensible, it now is enabled to speak of these distinctively according to that by which they exist as real.

3. From the above it follows that the common notion of being, i.e., being as being or being in general (*ens in commune*), which is the subject of the science of metaphysics, is expressed by "what is," for being affirms in act "what" is and of whatever kind, and does so by the "is" (*esse*), which, as the actuality of all determinations of kind or nature, is the most formal element in being [§33.5]. This subject is attained by an abstraction of the third order properly called a separation [§13.4], whereby the mind leaves aside all the limitations of matter and cognizes an object that is intelligible without reference to matter and so is independent of matter in both meaning and existence.

## §31. BEING

1. *Being* (2:230b) may be defined as "what is," or as that which exists, or simply as *reality* (12:117c). The term being signifies a concept that has the widest extension and the least comprehension [§3.2]. Aside from the fact that being can be said to be the subject of metaphysics, it is also the first thing grasped by the human intellect, the first concept formed by the

mind [§25.4]. If man knows anything at all, he knows being. The concept of being is not only chronologically prior to all others; it is also analytically prior, insofar as every subsequent concept is some modification of this first concept. The recognition of the "thereness" of what is initially grasped in sense experience underlies the formation of the concept of what exists, what is there, what is present to the senses. Through this concept the mind is enabled to embrace in a confused and universal manner whatever can be known in perception. The concept itself tells man the least about anything but it also tells him something of everything; as the first concept and the beginning of his intellectual life it could hardly be otherwise. He attains a more exact and precise knowledge the more he recognizes how one being differs from another. Being as first conceived is not the knowledge of the sensible singular as such, nor is it the knowledge of something that exists apart from sensible singulars. The universality of the concept is in consequence of the way in which sensible things are grasped intellectually [§7.4-6].

2. The being that everybody first knows is not to be identified with the being as being that is the subject of metaphysics, as will become clear from what follows. The term being sometimes designates positive being, sometimes propositional being, sometimes logical being. Consider the following statements: (1) Peter is; (2) Uncle Sam needs you; (3) Definitions abound. Only the subject of (1) can be said to be without qualification; it signifies positive or extramental being. Uncle Sam exists in the sense that he can figure in statements like (2), for if one asked where he could be found the reply would be that he does not "really" exist. So too logical entities like definitions (3) do not enjoy extramental existence. Thus, if there is a sense in which mythical or fictional as well as logical entities exist, in the full sense of the term they do not exist and are not beings. Only what enjoys positive or extramental existence has an *essence* [§33.5], meaning by essence that whereby something can exist in the real order. Since the concern of the metaphysician is with positive being, with what enjoys existence independently of man's knowing, he is concerned with whatever has essence.

3. All real or positive beings, however, do not have essence in the same sense. Although essence is that whereby real being has existence, men, motions, colors, and sizes do not exist in the same manner. Motion, color, and size exist as modifications of a more basic type of existent; their mode of being is one of inherence, of being in a subject. A man, on the other hand, does not exist in a subject; rather he is a subject in which motion, color, and size inhere in order to enjoy the mode of existence that is theirs. In short, the kind of being that has essence, positive or real being, is subdivided into two types, substantial and accidental being, and essence means that whereby a *substance* exists or that whereby an *accident* exists. The doctrine of the *categories of being* [§9] is founded on this distinction.

4. If both substance and accident are instances of real being, the term being is not predicated of them equally. Substance is what is chiefly and obviously meant by "what has essence" and "what exists extramentally"; accident is rather *in* what exists—it is a modification of what *is* in a more fundamental sense. The meaning of being as applied to accident therefore incorporates the meaning that is predicated directly of substance. This peculiarity in the predication of being arises from the fact that being is not a genus [§8.2-3]. If being were a genus, substance and accident would have to differ in something other than being, but only non-being (10:487d) is other than being, and for substance and accident to differ in non-being is no difference at all. Since being is not a genus, it cannot be predicated *univocally* [§3.3] of substance and accident. Nor is the attribution of being to substance and accident merely *equivocal*. Rather being is predicated *analogically* of substance and accident, because its meaning as said of accident includes its meaning as said of substance, but not conversely.

5. *Analogy* (1:461a) is a kind of predication midway between univocation and equivocation; it may be defined as the use of a term to designate a perfection or analogon found in a similar way in two or more subjects or analogates, in each of which the perfection is partly the same and partly different. In univocal predication, predicates have an absolute meaning and can be accurately

and distinctly defined in themselves. But strictly analogous predicates cannot be so defined; their meaning is proportional to the subjects of which they are predicated. The reason for this difference is that univocal terms arise by a complete abstraction from the particular subjects in which the perfection is present, so that the difference in the subjects does not enter into their meaning. Analogous terms, on the other hand, arise by the incomplete abstraction known as separation [§13.4], and on this account they retain a relation to a primary subject. A consequence of this is that there is no single clear meaning for an analogous predicate, since it must always include in its definition a reference to the subject from which it was derived. All terms arrived at by separation are therefore analogous in their major uses, and these are the terms with which the metaphysician is primarily concerned, e.g., being, goodness, and causality. Substance is being in a primary sense; the being of accident is derived from, and proportional to, that of substance. Stated otherwise, accidents are not being by themselves but rather by their relation or reference to substance, and the being attributed to them is the being of substance. So the meaning of being as applied to substance and to accident is partly the same and partly different: partly the same, because the being of substance is attributed to accident; partly different, because accident does not have being in the primary sense verified of it in substance.

6. There are various kinds of analogy, and these have important uses in both philosophy and theology (1:464d-469a). For purposes here it will suffice to indicate two kinds, the analogy of *attribution* and the analogy of *proportionality*. (1) In attribution, which is sometimes referred to as two- or three-term analogy, a perfection is predicated of each analogate, but one analogate is primary with respect to the other(s), and the perfection of the primary is attributed to the others by virtue of some relationship to the primary, usually that of causality. If the perfection is predicated properly and intrinsically of only the primary analogate and not of the other(s), the analogy is called *extrinsic attribution;* an example would be "healthy" as said of man and then attributed to other subjects because of some causal relationship to health

in man, e.g., healthy food, healthy exercise, etc. If the perfection is predicated properly and intrinsically of all analogates, on the other hand, even though one is primary, the analogy is called *intrinsic attribution;* an example would be "is" or being as attributed to substance and accident, for here the being that is primary in substance is predicated properly of accident as dependent upon such substantial being. (2) The analogy of proportionality, sometimes spoken of as four-term analogy, usually takes the form of a proportion (schematically $A:B::C:D$) stating that a perfection found in one analogate is similarly but proportionately found in another analogate. If the perfection is really extrinsic to one of the analogates, the analogy is said to be one of *improper proportionality;* an example would be the metaphor of calling a king a "lion" because the courage in the king is similar to the corresponding quality in the lion. If the perfection is found properly and intrinsically in both analogates, on the other hand, the analogy is called *proper proportionality;* an example would be the proportion, "as vision is to the power of sight, so simple apprehension is to the power of intellect." Similarly, one could say, "as substance is to its being, so accidents are to their being." As can be seen from the latter example, the analogy of proper proportionality can be very similar to that of intrinsic attribution. The difference is that in proper proportionality no direct relationship of dependence between the two analogates need be expressed, and so neither need be seen as primary with respect to the other or defined in terms of it, whereas in the case of intrinsic attribution such a relationship is explicitly recognized. Both types have important applications in natural theology [§42.3-4].

## §32. TRANSCENDENTALS

1. The division of being into substance and accident gives rise to words whose scope is less than that of being itself. For example, while every substance is a being, not every being is a substance. There are other terms, however, whose range and scope are equal to those of being itself. Since what they mean

transcends the division into categories, they are called transcendental attributes of being, or simply *transcendentals* (14:238d).
They are the properties that necessarily accompany being and
thus are found in every being; of these the most commonly discussed are unity (*unum*), truth (*verum*), and goodness (*bonum*).
Some would add beauty (*pulchrum*) to these attributes, and yet
others add thing (*res*) and otherness (*aliquid*).

2. These properties are *coextensive* with being; in them being
manifests itself and reveals what it actually is. Just as being is
never found without such properties, so these are inseparably
bound up with one another in the sense that they include and
interpenetrate each other. Consequently, according to the measure and manner in which a thing possesses being, it partakes of
unity, truth, and goodness; and conversely, according to the measure and manner in which a thing shares in these properties, it
possesses being. This ultimately implies that subsistent being is
also subsistent unity, truth, and goodness [§§44-46].

3. Precisely as essentially given with being, these determinants are called its essential attributes; as transcending all particularities in the order of being, they are called transcendentals; and
as belonging to everything whatsoever, they are designated as
the most common determinants of all things. Finally, their denomination as *properties of being* establishes their connection
with the fourth of the predicables [§8], i.e., property or *proprium*,
with the following consequences: (1) these are not synonyms
for being, but rather characteristics that add something to being
and are of necessity found with it; (2) neither are they accidents,
such as properties usually are, but rather determinants that are
formally identical with being; (3) these properties do not actually arise out of being; being is their foundation, and is otherwise
identical with them—it is not their principle, therefore, and certainly not their cause; and (4) the distinction between being and
its attributes is a distinction of reason reasoned about [§10.8];
although the distinction originates in the mind that understands
or reasons, it has a foundation in reality because the attributes
either manifest what being is or add something to it. Because of
these peculiar characteristics of the properties of being, many

demonstrations in the science of metaphysics employ middle terms that are only rationally distinct from the attributes they demonstrate (4:759c).

4. The connection between the transcendentals follows from their definitions and may be seen as follows. *Unity* (14:448a) is the attribute of a thing whereby it is undivided in itself and yet divided from others [§10.2-3]. *Truth* (14:332c) is the attribute of being whereby it has a relation to a knowing intellect and on this account is intelligible [§25]. *Goodness*, the ontological good (6:614c), is the attribute of being whereby it has a relation to an appetite and on this account is appetible or desirable [§26]. Through being, unity comes directly to an entity; it is given with being directly, without any intermediary, and for this reason can be referred to as a pre-operative attribute of being. Truth and goodness build upon this; they are not merely educed from the unity of being, but rather are given through a type of operation, and so are referred to as operative attributes [cf. §46]. Intrinsic to truth is a relevance to or conformity with a spiritual knower, and this comes to an entity in virtue of its being. In the same way goodness implies a similar accessibility to or conformity with appetite, and this too comes to an entity in virtue of its being. Further, since in knowledge there is only an imperfect or still incomplete union of spirit with being, while in appetition or love this union is complete or perfect, truth is ontologically prior to goodness. What begins in truth therefore finds its completion in goodness. Unity transforms an entity, making it a harmonious whole in which truth is so luminous that it is not merely grasped discursively, but is perceived directly. But the perception of truth embraces goodness, which leads one from the disquiet of appetite to the quiet of pleasure and fruitful enjoyment.

5. *Beauty* (2:202b) is usually included among the transcendentals because it includes unity, truth, and goodness simultaneously and in this sense is their completion and perfect harmony. At least a rudimentary beauty is found in every being, because the complete destruction of harmonious wholeness, which makes contemplation and pleasure possible, is equivalent to the annihilation of being [§58.4]. The two other attributes, thing

and otherness, although transcendental, do not, it appears, stand out as special attributes in contrast to the others, but rather are reducible to these as co-constituted with them. Thus *thing* (14:91a) goes with being because being bespeaks "something" that accompanies being; this "something," or subject of being, is in fact exactly the same as whatness or essence [§33.5]. In a similar manner unity includes otherness (*aliquid*, i.e., *aliud quid*), because what is undivided in itself is necessarily divided from everything else or separate, for which reason unity as separation is already implied in intrinsic unity.

6. Paralleling these various transcendental properties, and expressive of them in the form of judgments of being as possessing these properties, are the *first principles* [§11] of being (5:939b-940a). To being as one there correspond the principle of *contradiction* (4:277c), which states that a thing cannot at the same time be and not be; also the principle of *identity* (7:346b), which states that every being is determined in itself, is one with itself, and is consistent in itself; and, for some, even the principle of the *excluded middle* (5:703d), which holds that there cannot be an intermediate between contradictions, or that of one subject any one predicate must either be affirmed or denied. To being as true there correspond the principle of *intelligibility* (7:562d), which asserts that everything that is, insofar as it is, is intelligible; also the principle of *sufficient reason* (13:777a), which states that everything that exists has a sufficient reason for its existence; or even the related principle of *causality* (3:351b), which holds that whatever comes to be has a cause [§35]. To being as good, finally, there corresponds the principle of *finality* (5:919b), which maintains that every agent acts for an end, or that all beings when acting tend to some definite effect [§35.10].

## §33. PRINCIPLES OF BEING

1. Apart from these transcendental notions, the science of metaphysics also investigates the intrinsic principles of its subject and the external relationships between beings, for such study

enables it to explain how there can be more than one being or how being can be limited and, again, how these many beings, while differing one from another, can still be similar as beings. Among the intrinsic principles of being are usually enumerated potency and act and essence and existence, while among the external relationships are causality and participation, each of which deserves fuller consideration.

2. *Potency* (11:633b) is the capacity or aptitude in a being to receive some perfection or perform some action. The correlate of potency is *act* (1:90c), which expresses the fully present realization or completion of potency. Potency and act are analogical notions, and in the full amplitude of their meaning they divide being as such; being is that which *is* either in potency or in act. The intimate *relationship* between potency and act (11:635b) is found in the context of being that does not exceed the limits of the categories [§9], otherwise known as *finite being* (5:924a), for it is of this being that potency and act are principles. It should be emphasized that potency and act so understood are not things, but simply principles [§16.7]; as such they are essentially incomplete, since neither is able to claim more than an imperfect participation in the form of being. Furthermore, they are naturally corroborative. Potency is the indeterminate and perfectible element that looks to act as its determinate and perfecting complement. Because of their imperfect grasp on the form of being, the two necessarily require mutual assistance to exercise their role as principles of an existent.

3. The *distinction* between potency and act is a real distinction and not merely a distinction of reason [§10]. There are instances where the actual separation of act and potency proves beyond doubt the reality of their distinction. The extensive distance between the concepts of potency and act is also alleged as a proof of their real distinction, for the concept of each stands diametrically opposed to that of the other, and there exists no ground on which this opposition can be resolved. The concept of potency formally signifies capacity or the absence of perfection, whereas that of act signifies perfection (11:123b). Thus potency formally negates the very substance of act. Granting the correct-

ness of each concept, it necessarily follows that the one and the other signify notions that defy identification, and this not only conceptually but also ontologically.

4. In the order of knowledge act has a natural priority over potency. Because potency signifies possibility (11:627d) and the measure of the knowableness of an entity depends on its actuality, potency can be known only through the act that is its fulfillment. In the ontological order, on the other hand, potency usually has a natural and/or a temporal priority over act, in the sense that potency is generally the subject of act and therefore pre-exists it in some way. Viewed absolutely, however, act is prior to potency even in the ontological order, for the only source that can effect a transfer from potency to act is a being that is already in act [§20]. Despite this, potency plays a major role in the constitution of finite being, for it alone can be the principle of act's *limitation* (8:767b). Potency is by its very concept self-limiting; it is a capacity for a definite act. Possessed of this inherent limitation it naturally imposes limitation upon the act it receives; whatever is received must be received according to the measure, or limiting capacity, of the recipient (*quidquid recipitur ad modum recipientis recipitur*).

5. The relationship between *essence and existence* (5:548d), like that between matter and form [§16], is an instance of a potency-act relationship. Neither essence nor existence is a thing, nor is either to be identified with the actually existing thing, even though there could be no such thing without benefit of both. In themselves they are principles of being whence the actual existent thing is constituted. Each of these principles is incapable by itself of producing the total result, the actual existent; to effect this each principle requires what the other contributes. Viewed in isolation from existence, *essence* (5:546a) signifies a mode or manner according to which reality might be fashioned. As a principle of the actual existing thing, it is the element that provides a full explanation of the whatness or quiddity [§3.1] of the existent as being, i.e., as susceptible of the formal act of *esse. Existence* (5:720a), for its part, makes not the smallest addition to that whatness; moreover, there is no need that it should,

since essence provides the complete explanation in its own order. Existence is not simply a factor; it is the primary component of actuality. It is not a form but an act, the act whereby a thing is present in nature or in mind, different from nothing and outside the causes of its becoming. In fact, it is act *par excellence*, the act that perfectly fulfills the notion of act in its most formal sense. For whereas form as act finalizes in a qualified sense, existence finalizes completely. It is the act that effects the release of essence from a most remote hold on actuality; prior to this release, essence's only claim to actuality is its susceptibility to receive it.

6. The *distinction* between essence and existence, like that between potency and act, is more than a distinction of reason [§10]. The two are really distinct, for their otherness is not the result of mind's consideration alone. Reason does not make essence and existence to be two, but discovers that they *are* two. Despite this otherness, neither can survive the dissolution of their unification; once their hold on each other is loosened, no trace of either remains in the order of the actual existent. Reasons that can be given in support of this real distinction include the follow-ing: (1) the argument from the non-inclusion of existence within the comprehensive content of essence; (2) the argument that exist-ence, as the difference distinguishing things that communicate in a generic or specific unity, must be really distinct from essence or quiddity; and (3) the argument, based on the notion of parti-cipation [§35.12], that any perfection which is in itself common and intrinsically unrestricted but is present in things in a limited fashion must be really distinct from the thing in which it is found —and this is true of the perfection of existence.

## §34. SUBSTANCE AND SUBSISTENCE

1. In light of the foregoing it is possible to make further clarifications in the notion of *substance* [§9.4]. Frequently the term substance (13:766c) is used with the same connotation as essence, but this usage fails to spell out the relationship to exist-ence that substance also entails. To see this it should be noted

that substance is the basic and independent source of a thing's unity and the ultimate subject of all predicates ascribed to it. As such, substance has two functions: (1) it properly must subsist and be sustained in itself, and does not require an extrinsic foundation in which it is sustained, and (2) it is itself a foundation sustaining accidents, and for this reason it is said to stand under them. Aquinas focuses on the primary function when he states that "substance is essence to which *per se* existence is proper," though in so doing he also gives the reason why the second function of supporting accidents is possible. Note that in his definition both essence and existence appear. Yet he is explicit that "to exist *per se* is not the definition of substance; because by this we do not manifest its quiddity, but its existence; and in a creature its quiddity is not its existence." The nuances of his terminology thus stand in need of clarification.

2. The proper formality in a finite substance, for Aquinas, may be identified as its capacity for independent or *per se* existence. This formality enables him to distinguish finite substance from (1) God as substance and also from (2) essence, (3) nature, and (4) accident. (1) Finite substance is distinguished from God as substance in that the former has existence as act in relation to which substance is potency, whereas in God alone is substance the same as existence [§44.6-7]. (2) Substance is distinguished from essence in that substance signifies the basic principle in a thing in its reference to an independent mode of existence, whereas essence signifies reference to existence without specifying independent or dependent mode. Hence essence, as such, is applicable both to substance and to accident, though primarily to substance. (3) Substance is distinguished from nature [§17] in that nature signifies the substance as a principle of activity. Hence, in one and the same thing substance, essence, and nature can express the same reality but differ in connotation by a distinction of reason reasoning [§10.7]. (4) Substance is, however, really distinct from accident, which it underlies and sustains. The precise difference between the two is that substance is of such perfection that it can exist independently, whereas accident is so imperfect a principle that it has need to exist in another.

But if substance is other than accident and finite substance is other than its existence, this does not mean that existence is an accident. The substantial existence of a thing is not an accident, but rather the actuality of its form, and this when it is either with or without matter.

3. An *accident* (1:74b) differs from a substance in that its complete definition requires the inclusion of the subject in which it exists; thus it does not have a perfect essence, though it does have some kind of essence. In virtue of its imperfect essence, accident is like substance in having a capacity for existence; what is properly characteristic of accident is its need or aptitude for existence in another. For this reason it is most properly called a being of a being (*ens entis*); it is also said to be a being in a qualified way (*secundum quid*), in contrast to substance, which is a being absolutely (*simpliciter*). Accident and substance are thus distinguished by their differing capacities for different modes of existence, while remaining interrelated as the dependent on the independent. This interrelation may be highlighted by noting that every finite existing substance has need of further perfections, and these are nothing more than its accidents. An accident, in this way of looking at it, is neither a perfect being nor an individually existing being; rather it is a principle that complements substance in much the way that act complements potency. Therefore a finite substance does not simply subsist by itself alone; it needs proper and common accidents for its completion, and because of this the existence (*esse*) of such accidents is an "existence in" (*inesse*) the very substance they complement and perfect.

4. The term *subsistence* (13:763b) is generally used as an abstract noun to denote the order to independent existence that is proper to substances, as distinct from accidents. The same word is also used as a concrete noun to denote a substantial essence in its relationship to proportionate existence, although it is preferable to use another term for this, viz, supposit. A *supposit* (from the Latin *suppositum*, the past participle of *supponere*, meaning to put or to place under) thus signifies that which underlies and supports accidental being, namely, substance with its own order to self-contained being independent of any subject. When a sup-

posit has a rational or intelligent nature it is designated by a special name, viz, *person* [§29.6-7]; so a person is a supposit of a rational nature, and a supposit is an individual substance of a rational or an infra-rational nature.

5. In things composed of matter and form, nature or essence [§46.1] and supposit differ; the difference is real because the supposit adds extraneous elements to the nature or definition, notably individual matter [§19.6]. Similarly in immaterial substances such as angels nature and supposit are not the same because the supposit somehow includes predicable accidents over and above those that pertain to its species [§8]. Again, existence pertains to the supposit in a way in which it does not pertain to nature. The ontological ordering of these concepts is therefore the following: first individual nature, then supposit or subsistence, and finally existence. In this context *subsistence* may be described as really distinct from essence, or nature, in the sense that to nature it adds a real *mode* [§34.6], i.e., a transcendental order or relationship to existence. Abstractly considered, subsistence is this order to existential actuality; concretely considered, it is the essence so ordered. The notion of nature-ordered-to-existence is analogous as applied to different natures, material and immaterial, so that while the relationship is different in each case the common notion is proportionately verified in all substantial natures. In immaterial substances supposit is related to existence as potency is related to act. In material substances the notion is more complex: even prior to ordering nature to existence, subsistence brings to nature a termination making it apt for existential ordination. So the material supposit includes as intrinsic to itself the principles that individualize the nature, real modifications of the material substance, yet distinct from its essence; hence material subsistence has a twofold function of terminating nature and ordering it to existence. (For other accounts of subsistence, see 13:765a-c.)

6. The concept of *mode* (9:989a) is helpful for clarifying the notion of subsistence. A mode may be defined as a limitation or determination produced in some actual reality by a principle or cause extrinsic to itself, e.g., rapidity or slowness of motion and

varying degrees of a virtue or a vice. Modes are pervasive in nature, for all experienced reality involves partial or limited perfection, insofar as whatever is received is limited according to the recipient. The principles proximately producing modes are two, viz, agent and matter, or, more generally, efficient and material causes. The efficient cause effects a form of determinate species and so determines it; the material cause, by its relative aptness, receives this form more or less perfectly and so determines its individual perfection. In the latter case mode resides in both the perfection modified and in the principle that modifies it, though it is more properly in the modifying principle. So *individuality* (7:474c) is a mode of being found in all corporeal things, and arising from their corporeity, since matter exigent of quantity is the root of individuation [§19.6]; yet individuality, more properly in matter, affects the form also, individualizing it through its relation to matter. Modes are further divided into *intrinsic* modes and *extrinsic* modes. Intrinsic modes constitute or complete something because they are requisite to the being, either essential or existential, of the nature. Subsistence is such an intrinsic mode. Extrinsic modes, on the other hand, suppose a nature complete in its interior being, essential and existential, but determine it in non-essentials, relative to other things or natures. Location [§9.10] and its related categories are such extrinsic modes.

## §35. CAUSALITY

1. The foregoing discussion of modes should suffice to indicate that intrinsic principles alone are insufficient to account for the amplitude and diversity to be found in the realm of being. To investigate the many relationships between beings it is further necessary to examine in detail the notion of *causality* (3:342d). A cause is generally defined as that from which something else proceeds with a dependence in being. As such it is distinguished from a *principle* (11:787b), which is that from which something proceeds in any way whatever. It is also to be differentiated from

a condition and from an occasion, as will be clear from what follows. All these concepts further explicate how things are related to each other and so cast fuller light on the structure of being.

2. The essential notion of *cause* is that it is a positive principle exerting some influence on a perfection or thing that is coming to be, i.e., an influx into being. This definition is general and obscure to the extent that cause is an analogous concept, for the precise manner of causing differs in various exercises of causality. The major types of cause, however, may be set out schematically in terms of the general doctrine on potency and act [§33.2]. Since a cause is that upon which the being of another thing depends, this being may be viewed under the aspect either of act or of potency. As act, its cause of being is a *form* by which it is constituted a being-in-act, thus called a *formal cause*. As potency, it further requires two other causes, namely, *matter* that is potential and an *agent* that reduces this matter from potency to act, known as the *material cause* and the *efficient cause* respectively. But the action of an agent tends to something determinate, and that to which it tends is called the *end* or *final cause*. Thus there are four basic types of cause. Each of these can also have subdivisions and various modes of acting, and these will be explained presently.

3. A *condition* (4:129a) is that which makes possible, makes ready, or prepares the way for an efficient cause to act, or for its action to be efficacious. A condition may be referred to the agent or to the patient, and so is intimately related to efficient and material causality; however, its primary referent is the patient or subject that is acted upon [§18.6]. A condition may indicate a state or disposition of a patient or subject that permits the subject to receive the action of an agent; it may also connote the absence or the removal of an obstacle that would otherwise block the agent's activity or render it ineffective. The latter is referred to as a *removens prohibens*; it is not a direct cause of the effect that follows, although it may be viewed as its incidental or *per accidens* cause. If a condition stipulates an absolute requirement that must be met for the cause to function effectively it is termed a necessary condition, a *conditio sine qua non*. Such a condition, like the

removal of an impediment, does not influence the effect so much as it influences the action of the agent, either in itself or in the subject.

4. An *occasion* (10:624b) differs from a condition in that its primary referent is not the subject acted upon but rather the agent that acts; it may be defined as that which affords an opportunity for a cognitive agent to exercise its causality. An occasion may provide a mere opportunity for such an agent to act, or it may serve as a kind of inducement for action, in which case it tends to merge with the act's final cause. Yet, in its proper understanding, an occasion does not strictly cause the agent to act, being related to the agent's activity only incidentally, i.e., in a *per accidens* way.

5. *Formal causality* is best examined under the various meanings of the term *form* (5:1013c). The word form comes from the Latin *forma*, a term signifying figure or shape or "that which is seen" and having many derived meanings, such as kind, nature, and species. In early philosophical usage it came to signify the intrinsic determinant of quantity from which figure or shape results, and then to mean the intrinsic determinant of anything that is determinable. In a stricter sense it is limited to signifying the intrinsic principle of existence in any determinate essence, a definition that applies to both accidental and substantial form [§16.4]. In a further extended usage, every species [§8.3] or nature [§17], whether in itself material or existent as immaterial, is called a form, although it may not be strictly a formal principle. Hence, form is sometimes used as a synonym for essence or nature [§§33.5, 46.1]. Similarly the formal cause is frequently identified with the essence, as that in virtue of which the essence, even of material and composite entities, is precisely what it is. Thus substantial form is what determines or actuates primary matter to become a specific substantial nature or essence; accidental form is what determines a substance to one or other of the accidental modes, such as quantified, qualified, relationed, etc. Forms can also function in the knowing process: thus a concept can be said to be formal, or to be an intelligible form, because it informs man's intellect, even if in a general and abstract way.

Forms of the same kind exclude one another from the same substrate, although many forms not of the same kind can co-exist in it. A material form comes into being when the composite of which it is the form comes into being, and is said to be educed from the potency of its corresponding matter under the action of the efficient cause. It passes out of existence when the whole of which it is the form is destroyed. Such forms are physically inseparable from things, and yet they can be separated intentionally in the knowing process and analyses can be made of their nature, kinds, and characteristics [§23].

6. From these considerations it may be seen that the *causality of form* is that of an intrinsic cause and, as such, one that requires the receptive action of some appropriate matter. Form and matter exercise their special causality by a mutual communication of their own being; their proper effect is the composite that results from their union [§16.7], itself neither matter nor form but an intrinsic mode of being shared by each [§34.6], since each in a manner proper to it determines and modifies the other. Both form and matter obtain their actual existence from the existence of this composite, even though the form may have pre-existed potentially in the matter (and previous composite) from which it was educed. And neither form nor matter can exercise its causality unless there is a proper proportion between them, and unless an efficient cause acts to bring about the composite's formation.

7. *Material causality,* or the causality of *matter* (9:473d), is best understood in relation to that of form, its opposite and correlative principle through which it is normally known. Matter is that of which things are made, the intrinsic determinable principle that receives its actuation and determination from form. There can be as many different kinds of matter as there are kinds of form: primary matter actuated by substantial form, secondary matter actuated by accidental form, and so on. The elements, parts, and components of which a thing is composed [§68.6] are generally viewed as material causes. In its most radical meaning, however, matter is the substrate that persists through change, the intrinsic principle that in itself lacks all determination and as such is purely potential, incapable of existence by itself, and yet emin-

ently capable of receiving the determinations of form, through which it receives existence in the composite effected by both [§§16.3, 42.2].

8. *Efficient causality* (5:184d) may be defined as the productive or transient action initiated by an *agent* (1:201b). If an agent be understood as anything capable of initiating a motion or a change, then the action whereby it first produces such a motion or change is itself the exercise of efficient causality [§20.2]. Every agent moreover acts insofar as it is in act, and according to its form. Yet such an action is attributed to the supposit [§34.5] from which it originates and not to the substantial form; rather the action comes proximately from an accidental form, such as a power [§9.6], whose actuation in turn is effected by prevenient causes. There are as many kinds of efficient causality as there are agents. Some of the more common types are the following: (1) essential and coincidental; (2) total and partial [§47.6]; (3) principal and instrumental [§35.9]; (4) primary and secondary [§47.6]; (5) perfecting and disposing; (6) natural and non-natural—the latter including many other types, such as violent, chance, artificial, and voluntary [§§17, 52]; (7) univocal and equivocal or analogical, depending on whether or not the agent is on the same metaphysical level as the patient [§§47, 69.4]; (8) universal and particular; (9) corporeal and incorporeal; and (10) agents that are causes of being and those that are causes merely of becoming, according as the effect continues to depend on the cause after it is produced or not [§47.4]. Generally, since an agent is most properly denominated a cause only when it is producing an effect, cause and effect are simultaneous [§20.3], being identified with the change or motion that is produced as action and passion respectively [§18.6].

9. Of these types *instrumental causality* (7:549b) requires special explanation. An instrument is something from which an effect flows by reason of its subordination to a principal efficient cause, to which the instrument ministers and by which it is moved, e.g., the pen in the hand of the writer. Such an instrument attains an effect beyond its proper or permanent power, e.g., making legible marks on paper. To attain the former effect it

must receive, after the manner of a motion [§18], a power derived from the principal cause, and it is this transiently received power that elevates it to produce an effect exceeding its normal power. The use of the instrument imposes a mode [§34.6] in the effect produced; the total effect results from the joint action of both principal and instrumental cause, with the latter imposing its particular modality on the operation of the former. Such causality has many interesting applications in philosophy and theology [§47.6]; through its use, for example, one may explain how the agent intellect utilizes the phantasm as an instrument in its process of concept formation [§25.2].

10. *Final causality* (5:915c) is the type of causality exercised by the *end* (5:335d), from the Latin *finis;* it is also referred to as *teleology* (13:979b), from the Greek *telos.* The existence of a thing or of a phenomenon can depend on the end for which it was intended, and this may be of two types: an extrinsic final cause, i.e., another substance for whose sake the thing has been produced, as wheat grown for the nourishment of man; and an intrinsic final cause, the full development of the subtance or the completion of the process itself, as the maturity of the wheat plant. The final cause need not pre-exist the process of which it is the cause, except as a tendency in the efficient cause, as the tendency to mature growth that pre-exists in the grain of wheat [§17.4]. The end itself may be defined as that for the sake of which something exists or is done, or that for which an agent acts or action takes place [§51.1-2]. It is said to be first in the order of intention and last in the order of execution or activity. What is first intended exercises a determining influence over all that follows, and the terminal state completes what the agent does or seeks and brings the movement he initiates to its goal. If it is correct to call a cause anything that influences the becoming or existence of a thing, the end so understood must be said to be a cause; indeed its influence is so pervasive that it is rightfully named the cause of causes (*causa causarum*).

11. Related to the notion of final causality is that of *exemplary causality* (5:715c), i.e., the causal influence exercised by a model or an exemplar (5:712c) on the operation of an agent. As such

it specifies the determination or form of an effect as this is pre-conceived by an intelligent agent. Because of this relation to the agent it is referred to as his operative *idea* (7:337d) and so is conceived as a type of productive or efficient causality; because of the relation to form it is alternatively thought of as an extrinsic formal cause and so is classified as a type of formal causality. However, since the exemplary cause is extrinsic to the effect and exerts its influence mainly as an idea in the intentional order, it would seem to be more proper to view it as a type of final causality.

12. *Participation* (10:1042), finally, is a concept closely related to that of causality; it signifies the derivation of temporal diversity from eternal unity and the structural dependence of the many on the one. In natural theology, where it is best investigated in detail [§42], it is used to explain the complete dependence of creatures on the creator in the order of efficient, exemplary, and final causality. The term itself is obviously analogical, always involving a reference of many to one or one to many. Etymologically it means to share or take part (Latin *pars*, part, and *capere*, take) in some whole; in philosophical usage it means to receive only part of what belongs to another fully and so merely to share in it. Thus man is said to share in animality because he does not have the whole of animality exclusively; for the same reason Socrates shares humanity. Similarly a substance can be said to share accidents, and matter to share form, because substantial and accidental forms, which are common of their very nature, are limited when received in this or that subject. More generally, an effect is said to participate in its cause, particularly when the effect is not equal to its cause; thus the being of an accident participates in the being of substance, since substance possesses existence more fully and directly than does accident.


## §36. WISDOM

1. From this sketch of the scope of metaphysical investigation one can see why this science is spoken of as a natural *wisdom*

(14:967d). It is a habit of mind that enables one to judge of all things in terms of their ultimate causes; from this reference point deep in the interior of being such a habit confers the prerogative and the obligation to defend the first principles of being and knowing and to order all the other human sciences, none of which can discourse ultimately about its own principles. The wise man, in the traditional understanding, must have universal and difficult knowledge, greater than ordinary certitude, and a capacity to identify causes, to seek knowledge for its own sake, and to be able to rule others. Metaphysics possesses all of these characteristics. It is the most universal science, extending even to what most transcends the human mind; yet it has the greatest certitude and elicits the most complete commitment because concerned with being itself; and finally, because it knows the principles of all being, it is able to rule and direct the sciences that are concerned with particular types of beings. Metaphysics, therefore, stands at the culmination of man's knowledge; it derives from a negative judgment based on evidence [§40] from all the sciences [§13], and, as a potential whole, it is present in the exercise of all other intellectual virtues, wherein it is but partially expressed. Since it uses other sciences to enlarge its knowledge, its ordering and architectonic function in their regard is part of the work of wisdom itself.

2. Closely akin to the habit of wisdom is that of *understanding* (14:389b), described by the Latin *intellectus* and by the English *insight* (7:545c), which perfects man's intellect to grasp principles immediately and without discursive reasoning; on this account it is called the habit of first principles [§§11, 32.6]. In its practical function of grasping indemonstrable principles in the order of action this habit is also referred to by its Greek name, *synderesis* [§54.5)]. Metaphysics makes special use of this intellectual virtue, for of all habits of mind metaphysics is most characterized by its intellectuality. Intellectuality is itself a mode according to which all is comprehended in one simple act and idea that attains the full truth of manifold beings and their principles. The human mind, proceeding abstractively and by way of *analysis and synthesis* (1:469a), approaches this ideal im-

perfectly, but truly, to the degree that it is able to unify its knowledge of all things in one formal subject, through which it attains a uniquely simple, immediate, and comprehensive knowledge. This special intellectuality is had by metaphysics inasmuch as its formal subject is being, the common object of the intellect and the source from which its principles are derived immediately and its conclusions most directly.

# CHAPTER 6.

# EPISTEMOLOGY

## §37. EPISTEMOLOGY

1. As part of its sapiential function metaphysics is concerned with the problems posed by knowledge, partly to validate its claims and partly to defend the possibility of their attainment against those who would deny this. The branch of metaphysics devoted to the study of knowledge and its problems is known as *epistemology* (5:492b), from the Greek *epistēmē,* meaning knowledge in the true and certain sense. The study is also called *criteriology* (4:462b), from the Greek *kritērion,* meaning a criterion or rule by which one may test knowledge to distinguish the true from the false; less frequently it is known as *gnoseology* (6:522), from the Greek *gnōsis,* meaning knowledge in a quite general sense. The diversity of names reflects the controversial aspect of the discipline, which, unlike the branches of philosophy already discussed, has not had a long history; there is not even consensus on its subject matter or on the precise problems it attempts to solve. The position adopted in what follows is that the study of knowing cannot be divorced from the study of being, and thus that epistemology is at ground a metaphysical discipline. As such a discipline, moreover, it is not merely negative and defensive, but is concerned with the positive investigation of knowledge and its properties as these reflect the structure of the real.

2. It is frequently taken for granted, particularly since the rise of modern philosophy, that no one can enter the temple of wisdom without first making a critique of knowledge so as to determine, from the beginning, whether or not his ideas correspond

with reality. As it turns out, however, it is impossible to begin all investigation in this way. Man does not first know knowledge; he first knows things. It is only in one's reflective awareness of the knowing process that he can know what it is to know. *Reflection* (12:166d), therefore, is the key to the problem of knowledge; only through its use does man realize that what presents itself to him as sensible is also intelligible and so is understood by his intellect in terms of its proper object, being. Equipped with the first principles of being, themselves neither postulates nor dogmatic assertions but starting points that his mind must and naturally does embrace, he gradually builds up his understanding of things, distinguishing between one and many, being in nature and being in knowledge, whole and part, cause and effect, and so on. Finally, by reflecting on his knowledge of things in the light of intelligible being, itself the universal criterion of truth, he comes to know the conformity between the intellect judging and the thing judged, and so is prepared to address the problems of knowledge in all their complexity.

3. A convenient way of developing a science of knowledge along such lines is to set it out in terms of the four scientific questions first proposed by Aristotle, namely, (1) Does the thing exist (*an sit?*); (2) What is it (*quid sit?*); (3) What are its properties (*an sit talis?* or *quia?*); and (4) Why does it have these properties (*propter quid?*). Each of these questions can be meaningfully asked about knowledge, except the first. With regard to knowledge one need not inquire about its existence, for this is a fact of immediate experience; indeed, if there were no such thing as knowledge, the so-called problem of knowledge would never arise. The remaining three questions, however, provide an adaptable structure for developing the discipline: the answer to (2) involves the nature of knowledge; that to (3), the properties of truth and falsity; and that to (4), the nature of evidence and the certitude it engenders. Each of these will be considered in turn.

## §38. KNOWLEDGE

1. The most important thing to note about *knowledge* (8: 224b) is that it is not the result of a physical or mechanical process; rather it is a perfection found only in living things, a vital and immanent operation whereby one thing (the knower) becomes another (the thing known) in an intentional way [§23]. Once this is seen one can define knowledge generally as the possession of something in an immaterial fashion, or the possession of the form of a thing without its matter [§35.5]. The one knowing or possessing the form is called the *subject* (13:757c) and the thing known or the form possessed is called the *object* (10:607d). Knowledge never occurs except in this framework of subject-object relatedness. Apart from knowledge, the subject has not as yet begun to be a subject but remains only an organism or a person; the object too has not yet begun to be an object, but is simply a thing, sensible or intelligible but not yet known. A being is constituted an object only by some relation that it begins to have to some living thing having the power of knowing, which simultaneously becomes a subject.

2. The correlative reference of subject and object can be stated in another way, namely, by stressing that all knowledge involves an element of interiority or *immanence* (7:385d) and an element of exteriority or *transcendence* (14:233d). The interiority of knowing demands an operation that proceeds from a living thing, an operation having its roots in immateriality [§23.3] and thus completely different from any kind of motion in matter [§18]; the exteriority of knowing, on the other hand, demands a real relation to something other than the self, an object to which the subject becomes related through some type of intentionality [§23.4]. This means that a cognitive power is a living relation to the object that stimulated it and thereby set off the act of cognition [§23]; the object, on the other hand, has neither a real relation to the subject nor any real dependence on it. The difference between being and being known is merely a distinction of reason [§10.6-8].

3. In some theories knowledge is identified with *consciousness*

(4:206d). Despite their close connection the two are not the same. Consciousness is a state of greater or less awareness in a cognitive being; as such, it should not be substantialized and made a reality in itself. Man's conscious act is an act of knowledge that involves knowing one's internal operations and dispositions and oneself as subject to them. These operations may in turn be acts of knowledge, but they may also be non-cognitive acts such as wishing or walking. It is possible also that knowledge occur without consciousness, as happens when one dreams or experiences an external sensation during sleep. Consciousness and knowledge are simultaneous when one knows an object and at the same time is aware of oneself as knowing it.

4. There are many different *kinds* of knowledge. The most fundamental division is that into *sense* knowledge and *intellectual* knowledge, which has already been discussed [§§24-25]. Another division is that between *actual* and *habitual* knowledge. At any given moment the activity of one's cognitive powers is producing in him actual knowledge; yet some of these powers are capable of preserving knowledge and recalling it when the objects previously known are no longer present. Such habitual knowledge is preserved through qualities that are more or less permanent, such as the phantasm on the sensory level [§24.8] and the concept or idea on the intellectual [§25.2]. Yet another distinction is that between knowledge that is immediate or intuitive and that which is mediate or discursive. In the first type, sometimes known as *intuition* (7:598d), the knowledge arises either from the direct contact of a power with its object or the direct intellectual grasp of a proposition whose terms are seen to be necessarily related [§36.2]. In the second, known as *reasoning* [§5.1], there is a progression from one or more propositions to another whose truth is recognized as being based on, and implicated with, the propositions already known.

## §39. TRUTH AND FALSITY

1. The term *truth* (14:327a) means in general some kind of

agreement between thought and its object, between knowledge and that which is known. It is sometimes applied to things, and a thing is said to be true in the sense of ontological truth [§32.4]. In reference to speech, truth is called veracity or truthfulness [§14:335d], and is present when a person expresses what is in his mind. But the primary meaning of the word refers to the truth of the intellect, the truth of thought as opposed to the derived notions of truth of being and truth of speech. In this sense truth is a property of intellectual knowledge and is defined as the adequation of intellect and thing.

2. Since truth in its most general sense is a conformity of knowledge with its object, it is possible to apply the term truth to any knowledge, including simple apprehension [§3] and sensory knowledge [§24], insofar as these are in genuine conformity with their respective objects. The intuitive contact of the senses with their proper objects guarantees the validity of *sense knowledge* (13:89b) and thus its truth. The actual impinging of the object on the senses is the objective grounding of all human knowledge. Only in *experience* (5:750d) can intellectual knowledge be resolved, and since the external senses are ultimate among the cognitive powers, either man contacts reality through them or he never contacts it at all. So the lack of any one of the senses deprives the knower of all the knowledge that particular sense might have apprehended. Aberrations in sense knowledge can arise, of course, but these are traceable either to defective senses, to improper media, or to some disproportion existing between the sense and its object, e.g., when one fails to perceive objects too small for sight. Assuming a normal state for the sense organ, however, and the absence of other aberrations, whenever there is an appearance to the senses there must be a reality appearing. If one senses, he senses something; and if he senses something, he senses it as it is [§24]. The same general evaluation applies to intellectual knowledge in its apprehensive dimension; the intellect, in simply knowing what a thing is through the idea or concept, apprehends what it knows and knows it as it is [§25]. The basic reason for this is that the proper object of the intellect is being, and so intellectual knowing manifests itself in the living

relation of the intellect to being, to the real. Just as color is necessarily perceived by sight, so being is necessarily understood by the intellect. Assuming that the object is properly sensed and perceived, the intellect spontaneously grasps its essential determinations or its meaning and formulates this in the concept [§25.2]. The validity of all *apprehensive knowledge* is thus assured by the necessary relationship that exists between the powers of such knowledge and their respective objects. Truth at this level is necessary and unavoidable; it is built into the cognitive operations themselves, which may not be false. But this type of truth, sometimes called material truth, even though naturally guaranteed, is as imperfect as the apprehensive knowledge of which it is a necessary and infallible property.

3. Truth in its full significance and in a formal sense is found only in the second act of the mind, the *judgment* [§4]. To understand this one must recognize that in apprehension the mind grasps only bits and snatches of the real. Through his concepts man appropriates to himself isolated elements of reality, or single aspects of the things he knows, without putting these aspects and isolated elements together as they are found in nature. Only through a series of judgments does he begin the process of unifying this knowledge to bring it into conformity with the constitution of things in the world [§4.1]. When the intellect makes the unification in a way that corresponds to the actual unity found in the object known, the mind enunciates a proposition that is true and so attains truth. When the enunciation is at variance with the mode of being found in reality, the result is *falsity*. In apprehension the mind simply grasps an object and represents it to itself conceptually; in this function it has no alternative to presenting the object as it has been stimulated by it. But in judgment, the dynamic act of composing and dividing apprehended concepts, the mind no longer depends solely on the object represented but produces something new and original, i.e., a composition or division contributed by itself. It is this original element, a new unity, that opens up the possibility of formal truth or falsity.

4. The validity of judgment poses the key problem in the analysis of truth, and yet this too dissolves when one realizes that

the human mind was made to know truth and spontaneously recognizes it in self-evident principles [§11]; these it neither has to
learn nor assume but simply grasps as soon as it understands the
meaning of their constituent terms. The mind is further rein-
forced in its pursuit of truth by habits that it can acquire [§50.3]
and that perfect it in its search, namely, understanding [§36.2]
whereby it becomes proficient in making primary judgments, and
science [§13] and wisdom [§36] whereby it attains skill in moving from such judgments to conclusions. But the touchstone of
truth, the bridge that closes the gap between the mind and reality,
is the judgment whereby the intellect assents to first indemonstrable principles [§11]. To such principles the mind comes naturally and necessarily in its inspection of reality, whether they
be formulated in terms of the general modes of being common
to everything, or in terms of the special modes of being proper
to the different kinds of things in man's experience. And the
ultimate test of the truth of any other scientific judgment can only
be the analytic resolution of that judgment back to these first
principles. This does not mean that from such principles all
knowledge can be deduced, but only that before anything can
be deduced they must be admitted and correctly applied.

5. Given the mind's natural propensity to attain knowledge,
*falsity* (5:824a) is more difficult to explain than is truth. Like
its opposite the term can be applied to things in the sense of ontological falsity (5:825a), to speech in the sense of lying (8:1107),
and to intellection or judgment in the sense of being an inade-
quation or lack of conformity between intellect and thing. The
latter type of falsity is also known as *error* (5:521a); it is to be
distinguished from *ignorance* [§52.4], which is the lack of knowledge in one naturally capable of having it, and from *nescience*,
a similar lack in one not so capable. The possibility of error or of
falsity of judgment arises, as has been seen, because judging is
not a merely passive reception but an active synthesizing and
interpreting of innumerable and diverse apprehensions at the
level of both sense and intellect. When the intellect judges falsely
it does so because it has not given sufficient attention or has not
reflected adequately on the data of sense, the association of per-

cepts, the reliability of memory, the connecting reasoning, or the validity of its principles. The intellect thus judges precipitately without fully reflecting on these sources and so not withholding its assent until sure it has sufficient evidence for it [§40.4]. In such a condition it asserts as true what only seems to be true, and hence it asserts beyond what it knows. And it makes such an assertion under the influence of other powers, particularly the will. The will, either by reason of its attachment to prejudices, or by its impatience or disinclination to effort, or by not applying its attention, can move the intellect to judge what only seems to be [§28.4]. All falsity lies in this chasm between seeming and being. If something did not seem true, man could not assent to it, since his intellect is a faculty of truth. Yet his intellect can take the seeming true for being true because its judgment is under the influence of the will, the emotions, and other powers [§28.6]. From the point of view of the intellect, no error is inevitable.

6. The foregoing account is sometimes referred to as a *correspondence* theory of truth. There are other accounts, and of these the principal are (1) the *intellectualist* or rationalist, (2) the *coherence* or consistency, and (3) the *pragmatist* or instrumentalist theories (14:331c-332b). (1) The *intellectualist* theory would maintain that whatever man conceives clearly and distinctly must be true, or that something can be true only if the knower cannot conceive the opposite. This theory contains a partial truth, for a clearly perceived nature is the ground for judging the true and so for being unable to conceive the opposite. Yet the latter part of the theory is stated in a negative and misleading way. One does not see judgments as true because he cannot conceive the opposite; rather he is unable to conceive the opposite because he sees his judgments to be necessarily true. (2) The *coherence* theory would maintain that the truth of a proposition must be measured by its consistency with the whole system of knowledge, i.e., by the harmony of all judgments with one another. This too contains a partial truth, for consistency and coherence are a negative criterion in the sense that truth cannot contradict truth; of two contradictories, moreover, one at least must be false. But the fact remains that both may be false and that any series of judgments

may be totally compatible and yet totally untrue. The only sure test, therefore, is that a judgment conform, not to other judgments, but to reality itself. (3) The *pragmatist* theory would hold that truth is something relative and has reference to a changing reality; things are never true in themselves but only in their application to existential situations. In this theory the notion of truth is replaced by that of *verification* [§67.1], either actual or possible. This is also a correspondence theory, but since the adequation is not to being but to becoming, the correspondence is at best operational. While eminently concerned with the practical, the pragmatist theory neglects entirely the intellectual and the speculative on which the practical itself depends, and so offers no substantial base from which the changing and the ephemeral must ultimately be judged [§66.4].

## §40. EVIDENCE AND CERTITUDE

1. The immediate guarantee of the truth of a judgment, and therefore the reason why the intellect ultimately affirms it, is what is called *evidence* (5:662b). Derived from the Latin *evidentia* (*e-videre,* from seeing), evidence means clearness and apparentness; in the context of epistemology, it is the clearness and apparentness of the existing real as apprehended through the light of understanding. The certitude of the principles and conclusions of all human knowledge rest ultimately upon such evidence.

2. Evidence may be distinguished in accord with various manifestations of existing reality as (1) evidence of *facts* or *events,* where it is a question of particulars of sense or reflection; and (2) evidence of *principles,* where it is a question of the intelligible structure of being itself. (1) Some evidence of facts or events is grasped instantly by all, as for example the fact of one's own existence and the existence of the corporeal world. Further evidence of facts or events manifests itself more or less completely according to the degree of careful inspection and the experience and training of the observer. All of science, indeed, depends upon the accumulation of such evidence of facts and events

[§67.1-3]. (2) With regard to the evidence of principles, apart from what has already been said about the self-evidence of first principles [§§11, 32.6, 36.2], the intelligible structure of being is evident to all in a general and confused way. A more precise understanding of the evidence of principles proper to the various sciences is attained only through the concentrated attention of the specialist, whether he be metaphysician, natural philosopher, or scientist [§11.3-6]. But the natural character of such evidence is also reflected at the level of common sense in man's spontaneous striving toward a unified understanding of all of experience, and in his equally spontaneous and constant search for explanations of events in terms of source and purpose.

3. *Certitude* (3:408a) is a term deriving from the Latin *cernere*, which means to resolve or to decide after seeing the evidence. It designates a state of mind of the knower which is characterized positively by his firmness of assent to a given judgment and negatively by his exclusion of all prudent fear of error. It is to be distinguished from other states of mind, such as *doubt* (4:1023a), which is an inability either to affirm or deny, and *opinion* (10:705a), which is the acceptance of a judgment as probable. It is not incompatible, however, with *belief* or faith (5:798b), whereby a person assents to truths that are not seen and cannot be proved but are taken on trust in the reliability of another. Since the intellect is made for knowing truth, and its perfect actuation is had only when the truth is known with evidence, formal certitude is defined as the state of mind that results when what is known presents itself as objectively evident.

4. Of special importance for acquiring this state of mind are the firm assents that are acquired by the natural operations of the mind and are themselves based on the self-manifestation of what is known. Whenever this sort of certitude is had it is characterized by the note of necessity, whether grasped intuitively by immediate assents or discursively by mediate assents. The intuitive grasp of first principles, as has been said repeatedly, is the bedrock of such objective certitudes. But while these principles are grasped with supreme evidence and certitude, it must be admitted that they are very general in content and come far from

satisfying man's desire for truth. Thus it is better to see them as a sort of seedbed wherein truths are contained in an imperfect manner, and which must be brought to flower in the actual and certain knowledge of what is virtually contained in them. In this transition from imperfect to more and more perfect knowledge, doubt can play a positive role in preventing error and in initiating serious inquiry. When cogent evidence in support of a proposition is lacking, for example, one *ought* to suspend judgment lest, under influences extrinsic to objective truth, the simple lack of truth known as ignorance become its positive corruption, error [§39.5]. Doubt can also promote the discovery of truth in view of its association with *wonder* (14:1004b) in the genesis of knowledge. Wonder is a kind of emotional shock, a species of fear that occurs when one confronts an effect, the cause of which he does not know. Out of the initial state of wonder there arises a sort of doubt that is not a symptom of uncertainty but a stimulus to investigation. When this incipient doubt is elaborated into technically formulated difficulties (*dubitabilia*) against some position, the mind is in a state called *aporia* (1:678d). An aporia does not spring from nowhere, but from an imperfect knowledge of things and from the natural curiosity or drive of the mind. Without it one would not know what to look for and whether to stop or to continue the investigation; with it he is better able to judge the truth when it appears. Thus aporia is not a skeptical doubt, nor does it lead to skepticism (13:275d), because it presupposes that one already knows something and hopes to know something more or better. It does not take away certitude, nor does it commit one to an aimless search. Rather it urges him to proceed hopefully in the light of what he already knows toward the solution of a clearly formulated question or problem, and thus ultimately to arrive at the perfection of truth.

# CHAPTER 7.

# NATURAL THEOLOGY

## §41. NATURAL THEOLOGY

1. Metaphysics, as has been seen, takes its rise from the recognition that there is a realm of beings, of substances, beyond the physical [§30.2]. Does this mean that metaphysics can have God for its subject? In terms of what has already been said about the object of any human science, i.e., that it must have prior principles and also parts or attributes that belong to it *per se* [§13.3], the answer must be in the negative. Metaphysics has being *qua* being or common being as its subject [§30.3]. As such it studies all beings that do not depend on matter for their existence, either (1) because they are never in matter or (2) because they are sometimes in matter and sometimes not (2:232a-c). To the second group belong the subjects already investigated, viz, substance, potency, act, essence, existence, etc.; it is to the consideration of these that the mind must turn when it wishes to attain natural knowledge of the divine, the being pre-eminent in the first group. Thus if metaphysics is to be a theology, it can be this only indirectly. Even though the intellect of man has all of being as its adequate object, its proper object remains the quiddity of the material thing [§25.4]. This accents what has been called the grandeur and the misery of metaphysics: though its scope is broad enough to reach to God, it is most familiar with, and can best understand, material substance. Not being able to know God directly, it can seek knowledge of him only as he is related to material things as their principle or first cause. When meta-

physics turns itself to this task it takes on the name of "first philosophy" or *natural theology* (14:61a).

2. The basic steps whereby philosophy transforms itself into natural theology may be detailed roughly as follows (6:546b-d). The first step is the discovery of being as an intelligible value of the experienced real, one that is not attained properly in *natural philosophy* with its consideration of the things of experience as merely changeable [§15]. With this initial discovery comes the realization that things need to be evaluated as they are existents, and further that through this distinctive grade of intelligibility something of the nature of any reality whatsoever can be known and expressed [§30]. At this point *metaphysics* is already conscious of its status as a *first philosophy*, of its being an ultimate and absolute account of all reality. In its apprehension of being as such, moreover, it is already on the way to being self-vindicating through its awareness of being's own evidence, made clear in *epistemology* [§37]. On the basis of the distinctive character of its subject metaphysics then proceeds to evaluate the beings of experience, those at the level of the corporeal and the human. Through study of the ways in which these are beings it discovers composition, imperfection, and limitation [§33]; with them comes the knowledge that such beings are not self-explanatory. It is at this juncture that the inquiry for an explanation leads to the affirmation of their dependence on a first cause. This very dependence demands that the first cause be free of the same dependence; as cause, it must be a being not composed of essence and existence as really distinct principles. From this vantage point, metaphysics, already become *natural theology*, is in a position to demonstrate that being in every other case is so composed, and thus must necessarily manifest all the aspects of limitation that started the inquiry in the first place.

3. The foregoing way of locating natural theology within the domain of philosophy offers the advantage that it does not require presuppositions of a non-philosophical nature. No nominal definition of God need be assumed or tailored to fit such pre-suppositions. The knowledge of God it provides is really the knowledge of the dependence of all being upon him. The Christian's recog-

nition of God in this discovery does not have to be incorporated into the philosophical enterprise, as it usually is in Christian philosophy [§1.8]. And the basis and vindication of natural theology as the perfection of metaphysics are autonomous, relying only on the self-assurance afforded by being, the subject of the science.

4. There are other ways of conceiving the nature of natural theology and its relation to metaphysics, and these will now be briefly detailed (14:62d). Some hold that the question of God's existence should be treated at the outset of a unified science of metaphysics, following Aquinas' procedure of treating this question at the beginning of his *Summa theologiae*. Others hold that this is an introductory question that establishes the subject of special metaphysics, which is distinguished from general metaphysics in that it is concerned with uncreated being. Yet others hold that the question of God's existence is a terminal one in the study of ontology or general metaphysics, and thus is prior to the development of a special metaphysics, called *theodicy* (14:14b), another name for natural theology. And still others hold that the question is a terminal one in the science of metaphysics itself, which is one science that admits of no division into general and special. This last position is implicit in what has already been said and in much of the subsequent development of this chapter. (For a fuller account, see 14:62d-64d).

## §42. PARTICIPATION AND THE ACT OF BEING

1. The crucial juncture in the development already sketched [§41.2] is the metaphysician's discovery of composition, imperfection, and limitation in the beings of experience and of their consequent dependence on a first cause. This discovery and its implications are best explained in terms of Aquinas' insight into the being of experience as "that which finitely participates existence" (2:232c) and in terms of the subtle dialectic whereby he attains that insight. To grasp this one must recall that there is a being that is common, an *esse commune* that is shared by substance and accident analogically [§31, 34]. Now the possibility

is further suggested that there might be a being that is common in another sense—not predicably common as existence is to substance and accident, but common in the sense of a unity whose causality extends to all other beings and whose perfection is only partially shared by them [§7.2]. This commonality of being is most readily conceptualized under the aspect of existence known in Latin as *esse* and anglicized as the "to be," the act of being or of existing discerned only through metaphysical analysis [§33.5]; this is not given immediately in experience, as is the "is" that is simply predicated of substance and accident. Such existence under the aspect of *esse*, the act of being, now requires examination in light of Aquinas' teaching on participation [§35.12], and in this light will be seen to demand the existence of a subsistent being, a first cause known as *ipsum esse subsistens*, the study of whose existence and attributes pertains to natural theology.

2. Aquinas' analysis of participation (10:1043c-1044b) develops from the notion of being as ultimate act and is built on four basic concepts: (1) that of act, (2) that of the unicity of the substantial form, (3) that of the personal individuality of the human soul, and (4) that of the real distinction between essence and existence. (1) The concept of *act* signifies perfection *in se* and *per se*, and thus is prior to potency whether it is understood as potency or as form [§33.2-4]. Act itself is thus the affirmation of being, whereas potency is the capacity to receive perfection. As a consequence (a) potency is not a univocal concept signifying primary matter [§16.3] alone, but an analogical concept embracing all the ways a thing can be a subject of act, and (b) primary matter, being exclusively a subject, can have no act of its own: not even an omnipotent being could make such matter exist without form. (2) Since act confers being, which comes through form [§33.5], a corporeal substance can have but one substantial form [§16.4]; rather than admit the possibility of a plurality of forms, Aquinas insisted on the unicity of the substantial form in each substance (5:1024c). In the case of man, who performs vegetative and sensitive functions as well as rational, the intellectual soul is his unique substantial form, and this, including lower

forms virtually through its powers [§22.7], controls all his lower functions also. (3) The human soul is personal and individual [§§29, 34], and has an immaterial *esse* proper to it and inseparable from it, which accounts for its immortality [§29.4]. Again, *esse* properly belongs to form, which is act, and it is impossible that a form be separated from itself; therefore a subsistent form cannot cease to be. (4) In all substances that come under man's experience, including man himself, there is a real distinction between essence and existence or *esse* [§33.6]. But essence is itself a subject, a potentiality for *esse*. Thus even in man his existence or *esse* is a received perfection, and he is only a being by participation. Moreover, since being or *esse* is the first perfection and the act of all acts, man and all other beings that are such by participation must receive their being from a being that is pure perfection. But pure perfection cannot be anything but unique, since it offers no basis for being individuated or multiplied. It must therefore be a subsisting being whose essence is to be. This subsistent being itself (*ipsum esse subsistens*) is being by essence (*per essentiam*); all others are being by participation (*per participationem*).

3. The explication of the foregoing analysis entails the entire development of natural theology, viz, the proofs for the existence of *ipsum esse subsistens*, the determination of the divine nature and attributes, and the complexity of the many relationships of that nature to other beings. For the moment it will suffice to spell out some of the implications of this doctrine of participation for the analogy of being (10:1045c-1046a). The analogy of *proper proportionality*, as has already been noted [§31.6], may be expressed as a proportion, e.g., accidents are to their being as substance is to its being. Despite the radical difference between substance and accident, there is a proportional similarity that allows one predicate, "is," to be said of both analogically. The basis of this proportional similarity, as has also been noted [§34.3], is that accidents participate in the *esse* of substance. Thus, while the formal structure of this kind of analogy simply states relations of similarity, its root is actual dependence and participation. The dependence and participation of accidental being on the being of

substance, moreover, does nothing to prejudice the fact that all beings, substances and accidents as well, have their *esse* by participation from *ipsum esse subsistens*. But the formal or static analogy of proportionality, without mentioning such dependencies, serves to explain how beings obtain the proper consistency of *esse*, each in its own way, since each being is actuated by the proper act of participated *esse*.

4. In contrast to the formal or static analogy of proportions, the analogy of *intrinsic attribution* [§31.6] is dynamic in that it is based explicitly on causality and dependency. To extend the example of the existence of substance and accidents to that of subsistent being, *esse* belongs properly to *ipsum esse subsistens* alone, but it is predicated of other beings because they receive their *esse* in dependence on subsistent being itself. Such analogy is called intrinsic attribution because each being really does have *esse* intrinsically, even though it is from another. Again, the accident has its *inesse*, even though this is dependent on the *esse* of substance. Despite this "inner" or intrinsic aspect, however, whenever analogy of attribution is used it also emphasizes the "otherness" of the characteristic participated. Accidents are beings by participation in the *esse* of substance, and all beings are such by participation in the *esse* of subsistent being. In this way the analogy of proper proportionality can be seen to be related to, and to presuppose, the analogy of intrinsic attribution in the order of being. The use of both allows subsistent being to be transcendent or "other," when compared to other beings, and at the same time it allows *esse* to be participated and thus to be immanent or "within" other beings. So the doctrine of participation can cast light on the analogy of being, and in doing this explain how immanence and transcendence can be applied to being itself [§§38.2, 44.1, 45.4].

## §43. PROOFS OF GOD'S EXISTENCE

1. The argument implicit in §42.2 can be cast in the form of an *a posteriori* demonstration [§12.5] of the existence of an un-

caused cause (14:62a). The middle term of this demonstration is an effect, the act of existing of the beings of experience or the *esse* of material, sensible things, and the demonstration concludes to the existence of their proper cause. Granted that middle term, the proof proceeds thus. "Whatever belongs to a being is either caused by the principles of its nature or comes to be from some extrinsic principle. But it is impossible that the act of existing (*esse*) be caused by a thing's form or essence or quiddity, for then something would be the cause of itself and would bring itself into existence—which is impossible. Everything, then, which is such that its act of existing is other than its nature must needs have its act of existing from something else. And since every being that exists through another is reduced, as to its first cause, to one existing in virtue of itself, there must be some being that is the cause of the existing of all things, because it itself is the act of existing alone." In sum, if the act of existing cannot come from the nature of any being as from its source, it follows that the act of existing must come from a cause whose nature it is to be.

2. Note that the word God does not appear either in §42.2 or in the foregoing demonstration. This defect can be easily remedied by substituting "God" for *ipsum esse subsistens* or for the being "existing in virtue of itself" in the respective arguments. Such a substitution is commonly made in books on natural theology, and its basis usually is the Catholic teaching that God can be proved to exist by the resources of reason alone, and therefore in philosophy. There is nothing objectionable in this procedure, provided that it be noted that the identification of Subsistent Being or First Cause with the God of Revelation is, from the point of view of philosophy, a pre-supposition. (The pre-supposition may be known to be true by faith, or it may be provable in theology, but either source is outside the pale of philosophy.) Somewhat more objectionable is a procedure that is frequently adopted in the name of Christian philosophy [§1.8], namely, to maintain that the Christian experience of God is a valid basis for philosophy and therefore should be frankly admitted from the outset. On this basis the philosophical proof for God's existence must lead ultimately to the Biblical concept of God as "He Who

Is." Here, of course, it is a much simpler matter to identify *Ipsum Esse Subsistens* with the "I Am Who Am" of Exodus. The difference between this and the first procedure is that a religious assumption is here made explicit, whereas in the first procedure it is only implicit; in either case it is difficult to see, however, how the resulting demonstration can remain purely philosophical [cf. §47.3].

3. On the supposition that the existence of the God of Revelation is proved in natural theology, the word God will be used here (and hereafter) in discoursing on the existence and nature of the divine being. Proofs for the existence of God, in this context, are understood as answers to the question: Does God exist? What is required, therefore, is a proof rising from effect to cause. The conclusion of the proof is a proposition, "God exists," wherein "God" is the subject and "exists" is the predicate. In such a proof the middle term of the demonstration is a nominal definition of the subject, i.e., one that merely expresses what the term "God" means. The proofs most commonly developed are those employed by Aquinas in his *Summa theologiae*, where they are known as the *quinque viae* or "five ways" (6:563b). In these ways a different nominal definition is employed for each, respectively: (1) God is a First Unmoved Mover, (2) God is an Uncaused First Cause, (3) God is a First Necessary Being, (4) God is a Most Perfect Being, and (5) God is the Governor of the Universe. Under these nominal definitions are subsumed minor premises stating that a being corresponding to each (or one, or more, or all) of the definitions so stated exist(s). The burden of the proof(s) consists in establishing the second, or minor premise, and this is done through an analysis of the dependencies found in the beings of experience, dependencies that the definitions themselves suggest. So each starts from an existential fact given directly in experience, namely, (1) motion or change, (2) caused existence, (3) corruptibility, (4) composition and imperfection, and (5) finality, and then argues to the existence of the ultimate cause or explanation of that particular datum as expressed in the corresponding definition. (The essential contents of the first way and the fourth way have already been sketched in

§20 and in §43.1 respectively; for details of each way, see 6:563b-568c.) The conclusion in each case signifies God under all these "names," and from its implications the rest of the philosophical discoveries about the divine nature and attributes are derived, as will be explained presently [§44].

4. Other formulations of proofs for the existence of God are known as the ontological, the ideological, and the cosmological arguments respectively. (1) The *ontological argument* (10:699b) has been presented in various ways: one variety would reason that, from the concept of God, who is a being greater than which none can be conceived, his existence in reality follows with *a priori* necessity; for unless he actually existed, he would not be a being greater than which none can be conceived. A related argument, though not strictly ontological, would maintain that an idea that one has of the infinite cannot be caused by finite things, but only by an infinite being, which therefore exists. Yet another argument would maintain that man's natural knowledge of God is direct and intuitive (6:562c) and so God's existence is self-evident to all. None of these arguments has received broad acceptance among philosophers; the usual claim against them is that they make an illicit passage from the logical to the real order. (2) The *ideological argument* (6:552b) is similar to the onto-logical, but is based on intelligibles such as eternal truths and possible essences, and may be stated as follows. There are intrin-sically possible beings whose essence and essential principles are necessary, immutable, and eternal; but such beings demand as their ultimate foundation an actually existing being that is abso-lutely necessary, immutable, and eternal; therefore such a being exists. If this argument has validity, it would seem to be as a development and refinement of Aquinas' fourth way. (3) The *cosmological argument* (16:105d) is any type of reasoning where-by one argues from observable aspects of the universe, or cosmos, to the existence of God. The reasoning is explicitly *a posteriori* and thus the reverse of that of the ontological argument. Though used in the singular, the term actually refers to several arguments, the number depending on the particular observable aspects of the universe that are taken as starting points of the proofs. So

Aquinas' first three ways, and particularly the third, are commonly regarded as cosmological. Some would include the fifth way also, as arguing from the fact of design in the cosmos to the existence of a Supreme Intelligence who has planned and guides the universe in its complex processes; others would make of this a special proof that invokes finality or teleology and so more aptly label it the *teleological argument* [§69.5].

5. Subsidiary evidences that may be seen as confirmatory proofs of God's existence include arguments from (1) moral obligation or conscience, (2) the need for sanctions, (3) man's desire for happiness, and (4) the universal consensus of mankind (6:551c-552a). (1) Man perceives within himself a law commanding him to do certain acts because they are good and avoid others because they are evil; since there is no law without a lawgiver, such a natural law owes its origin to a supreme lawgiver, God, as the author of human nature. (2) Since perfect justice and adequate rewards and punishments as sanctions for the observance of the natural law are not found in this life, there must be a future life where adequate justice is done by a supremely wise and all-powerful judge, namely, God. (3) Man is so constituted that he always strives for happiness but never completely attains it; since this tendency cannot be fully satisfied in this life, where all goods are limited and imperfect, a supreme good must exist that completely satisfies man's aspirations, and that is God. (4) The human race as a whole has always recognized the existence of a superior Being on whom man and the world depend; but mankind and the human mind cannot be universally wrong in a matter of such importance; therefore God must exist. All four of these arguments, it may be noted, lack the cogency of the traditional metaphysical proofs, but by and large they have greater appeal to the philosophically untrained and deserve attention in view of their persuasive force.

## §44. GOD'S ESSENCE AND ATTRIBUTES

1. The proofs for God's existence, each in its own way, lead one to knowledge of God as first on all levels of existence, as *Ipsum Esse Subsistens*. There now remains the task of making explicit what is implicitly contained in that concept (6:556d). One may well wonder to what extent explicit knowledge of this kind is possible. God is transcendent, and though man can "name" him, he clearly cannot comprehend him in a real definition: the only possibility for a genus would be being, and yet being is not a genus, since no specific difference can be added to it that is not already included in its concept [§31.4]. But this does not mean that man can know nothing of God by reason alone: he can know God philosophically, if only in an imperfect way. To attain such knowledge two means are available to him, negation and eminence.

2. The way of negation (*via negationis*) consists in denying of God anything that belongs to a contingent being as such. On this account to know God through this way is not to show what he is, but rather what he is not [cf. §20.5]. Instead of beginning with an inaccessible essence to which are added positive differences leading to better and better understanding, one collects rather a series of negative differences that indicate what this essence is not. The resulting knowledge is imperfect in the sense that it is not positive: God is known, e.g., as incorporeal, immaterial, immutable, and so on. Yet, by denying all the limitations found in creatures, it allows one to say with ever greater precision what God is not and what he cannot possibly be. So, by distinguishing God from what is not God, one attains some knowledge of his essence.

3. The way of eminence (*via eminentiae*) or of analogy consists in attributing to God in an eminent degree everything that can be considered a perfection pure and simple, i.e., a perfection that is without trace of imperfection. To describe the nature of God is to name him variously as just, powerful, wise, etc. The principle behind such predication is this: because God is First Cause, he must possess to an eminent degree all the per-

fections found in creatures. The problem is to discover how these perfections may be predicated of God. It is here that the teaching on analogy proves important, particularly the analogy of proper proportionality [§§31.6, 42.3]. This kind of analogy permits one to say, for example, that in God there is something that bears the same kind of relationship to the divine nature as intelligence does to human nature. In other words, it can express a parallel or proportional relationship between divine nature and divine intelligence on the one hand, and between human nature and human intelligence on the other. Note that such a relationship must be stated in the form of a strict proportion: a perfection that is realized in a finite being to the degree consonant with its proper mode of being is similar to that found in God according to his mode of being. Such an analogy, as has been seen, is legitimated by the foregoing analysis of participation [§42.3]: since any being or perfection that can be assigned to a creature must have its root in God, any perfection that denotes a positive reality in creatures (e.g., life, intelligence, will, justice, wisdom) must be found also in God. Consequently, one cannot remove from God the positive value of this perfection, no matter what the form (or lack of form) it may take in God.

4. The foregoing furnishes a basis for understanding what is meant by a *divine attribute*. In general, a divine attribute may be defined as an absolutely simple perfection that exists in God necessarily and formally, and that, according to man's imperfect mode of knowing, either constitutes the essence of the Divine Being or is deduced from this essence. Divine attributes that do not constitute the divine essence are further divided into entitative attributes [§45] and operative attributes [§46]. Entitative attributes relate to the very being of God; they are perfections such as unicity, truth, goodness, infinity, immensity, simplicity, and eternity that in themselves bespeak no relation to contingent being. Operative attributes, on the other hand, relate to the divine operations, i.e., to the immanent operations of God's intellect and will, from which proceed effects that are extrinsic to God, namely, creation and conservation [§47].

5. The divine attributes do not designate perfections really

distinct from one another; rather there is only a distinction of reason among them, in the sense that each perfection explicitly states what is implied in the others [§10.6]. All the divine attributes designate one and the same, absolutely unique, Entity, but as understood under multiple and diverse intelligible contents: hence the distinction between them is that of reason reasoned about [§10.8]. Moreover, such multiplicity does not impair the divine perfection, because if God appears to human reason as simultaneously one and many, this is owing only to the limitations of man's intellect.

6. Among the divine attributes it is possible to isolate one or more that can be said to be the formal constituent of the *divine essence*. This manner of speaking refers only to a logical determination of the divine essence, for in God all reality is his very essence. The formal constituent, in this sense, is the fundamental perfection from which all others can be demonstrated. Such a perfection must appear to man as absolutely first, prior to any other attribute, and should be the basis for his distinguishing God from what is not God. In view of what has just been said about the distinction of divine attributes, *propter quid* demonstrations [§12.4] in natural theology do not assign the cause of a particular attribute, but rather a prior reason that is only rationally distinct from the attribute it serves to explain.

7. It is commonly taught that God is Being Itself, subsistent by itself, and that this *aseitas,* anglicized as *aseity* (1:945b), or "by-itself-ness," is the constitutive perfection of God. Aseity is fundamental, for God's basic perfection consists in being absolutely independent, self-sufficient, and self-existent. Everything else is said of God precisely because he exists of himself. The perfection of aseity, furthermore, properly belongs to God and distinguishes him clearly from creatures. Though all other divine perfections can be imitated analogically, only existence of himself is absolutely proper to God. Finally, it can be said that the divine attributes are implied in the other only because each contains being. Infinity, for example, implies intelligence, eternity, etc., because infinity is nothing more than an infinity of being. In this sense God is indeed *Ipsum Esse Subsistens,*

"He Who Is," the Being in whom essence and existence are one. It should be noted, however, that this teaching on aseity is not universally accepted, for some hold that *infinity* itself is the formal constituent of the divine essence, others that *subsistent intellection* or intelligence is the perfection in God (as in man) upon which all others depend [cf. §46.1-2].

## §45. ENTITATIVE ATTRIBUTES

1. Among the attributes relating to the very being of God, simplicity and infinity give man direct knowledge of God's personal nature and also can serve to cast light on his other entitative attributes. By the *simplicity of God* (13:229d) is meant the attribute whereby he is absolutely one in himself and perfectly simple, that is to say, it excludes any composition from him, whether physical, metaphysical, or logical. (1) Since God is *Pure Act* (11:1031b) he cannot, on the physical level, be composed of matter and form [§16], both of which necessarily imply potentiality and essential imperfection. A fortiori he is not composed of quantitative parts [§9.5], since these indicate indetermination and passivity. (2) On the metaphysical level, God cannot be composed of essence and existence [§33.5], since he is Being of himself (*Esse per se*); neither can he be composed of substance and accident [§34], since he is fully act and thus not in potency to further determination. Lacking composition at both the physical and the metaphysical level, God cannot change in any way; this changeless and unchangeable character is what is expressed in the attribute of the *immutability* of God (7:393b). (3) On the logical level, God is not contained in a genus or a species [§8.3] because, as universal principle, he transcends all genera and all differences of being.

2. The *unicity of God* (14:394b) is a necessary result of the absolutely divine simplicity. If divinity were multiple, one would have to distinguish, in divine beings, the divinity common to all as well as their individual differences. In consequence, one would find in these beings a composition of genus and differ-

ences; thus, no one of them could be termed *Ipsum Esse Subsistens* and no one would be God. Moreover, since God is his very nature he has no reason to multiply himself. If a man were what he is by reason of human nature rather than by reason of the individuation that distinguishes him from other men [§19.6], he would be humanity itself; thus, there could be no other men besides him. The same reasoning applies to God: he is his very nature, thus there can be only one God.

3. *Infinity* (7:504c) means the same as "without limits." But there are different ways of being without limits. Thus, matter and motion are infinite in a privative sense, they cannot be completed by themselves [§18.8]; in this sense infinity connotes indefiniteness or basic indetermination, and therefore essential imperfection. In a contrary sense, the infinite can also bespeak something that is without limits by reason of its very perfection. From this point of view, one can distinguish (1) the relative infinite, which has no limits within the genus of a certain perfection, and (2) the absolute infinite, which has no limits within the genus of all perfections possible. It is the latter infinity of perfection that is attributed to God when one speaks of the *infinity of God* (7:508b). In fact, God is infinitely perfect insofar as he is *Esse per se,* and for this reason can be spoken of as *divine perfection* (11:124c) itself. In him, existence is not received as in an essence capable of existing; God is unreceived, and therefore absolutely unlimited existence. Alternatively, if God had limitations he would be susceptible to some new perfection; he would be composed of act and potency, which is a contradiction, for then he could not be Pure Act. God is therefore infinite by his essence and with the fullness of infinity, which implies the total and perfect actuality of all perfections.

4. Related to the infinity of God are his eternity and his immensity or omnipresence. By the *eternity of God* (5:565c) is meant his duration, different from that of time and without beginning or end, and thus a direct consequence of his complete interminability and immutability. By his *omnipresence* (10:689c) is meant that God is immanent in all things everywhere; this is

not to be understood in the sense of a dimensional or spatial presence, since God is utterly simple and infinite, and thus free of all spatial limitations. Rather he is present as an agent is in his effects. In light of this it is preferable, when discussing entitative attributes, to speak of God's immensity rather than his omnipresence: *immensity* is the infinite plenitude of subsistent being that is free from all spatial limitations and so is *able* to be present in all things. Omnipresence, as opposed to this, is the actual exercise of that ability to be everywhere. Since omnipresence, in this sense, is said relative to created being, it is better enumerated among God's operative attributes.

## §46. OPERATIVE ATTRIBUTES

1. The operative attributes refer to God's immanent operations, or, in other words, to the *divine life* (8:738b) as this is known to natural reason. Main consideration is given here to God's intellect and will, for these attributes enable one to conceive of God as a personal being and also to understand the effects that proceed from him to creatures. The *divine intelligence*, also known as God's *omniscience* (10:690a), can be deduced from his infinite perfection and supreme actuality. Since God possesses all perfections to an absolute degree, science, the perfection of the intellect, is his first operative attribute; as such it specifies the divine nature, which is the principle of divine operation. (In this sense *nature* [§17] is the source of a being's operations, whereas *essence* [§33.5] is its definition considered in itself; the two, as has been seen, are only rationally distinct [§34.2] by a distinction of reason reasoning.) Again, God is known to be immaterial from his excluding all potentiality. Now knowledge is proportionate to the degree of immateriality [§23.3], and a being is intelligent to the degree that its being is pure. God, the Pure Spirit, therefore possesses supreme and absolute knowledge. Furthermore, since the act of knowing is essentially immanent [§22.1], and since whatever is in God is the divine essence, divine intelligence is identified with the

divine essence; it is, properly speaking, subsistent intellection.

2. To say that divine intelligence is subsistent intellection is to affirm that God understands himself perfectly, that he is Thought Thinking Itself. Knowing that the degree of a being's intelligibility increases with its immateriality, one may conclude that any being that is fully immaterial is fully intelligible. In God the supreme degree of knowledge and the ultimate degree of intelligibility merge within his essence. Again, to know a thing perfectly is to be fully aware of its power, and consequently, to grasp fully the effects to which this power extends [§46.8]. In knowing himself, God knows everything else. He knows things in his essence, which he understands to be imitable to different degrees of participation. He knows all singular beings, since whatever shares in being finds its origins in himself as *Ipsum Esse Subsistens*.

3. To clarify further the field of objects comprehended by divine knowledge, one may inquire whether God knows (1) *possibles*, that is to say, things that do not actually exist but can exist (11:627d), and (2) *future contingents*, namely, the things that can be made to exist or not, at will (4:266b). (1) As to the first type of objects, it is commonly held that since God is the source of all existence, and knows everything that exists, whatever the kind of existence it may possess, he does know possibles. (2) The teaching with regard to contingents is more complicated. Since God is by nature outside of time [§19.4], his knowledge bespeaks a relation to eternity (5:563c). Now eternity embraces all of time in an immobile present. God, therefore, knows future contingents as actually present and realized; yet the *necessity* (10:292a) of God's knowledge of them does not in any way affect their contingent character. (For a discussion of God's knowledge of the future and its relation to man's freedom and predestination, see 10: 692a-694d).

4. From the fact that God has intellection in the highest degree, one may conclude that he also has volition, commonly known as the *will of God* (14:914a). Indeed, since the good as known constitutes the proper object of the will, once any

good becomes known it must also come to be desired; thus, a being that knows the good must be endowed with a will. Now God, as perfectly intelligent, knows being under its formality of goodness; from the very fact that he so knows, he also wills. And just as God's intellect is identical with his essence, so too is his will, since he wills insofar as he is intelligent. The will of God is his very being.

5. Since the object of the will is the good as apprehended by the intellect and since the divine intellect apprehends the divine essence directly, this essence is in consequence the primary object of God's will. Further, every being endowed with a will naturally tends to communicate to others the good it possesses. But if natural beings communicate to others their own proper good, with greater reason does the divine will communicate its perfection to others, to the extent that such perfection is communicable. To say this is to assert that God loves all being, for love (8:1039b) is nothing other than the first movement of the will in its tendency toward the good. Again, for God to love his creatures is for him to love himself. For creatures possess goodness only to a degree proportionate to their being, i.e., a degree that corresponds to their perfection.

6. Thus is God's *freedom* (6:99a) manifested. In fact, God is supremely free: on the one hand, God is free relative to all contingent beings, for divinity as the absolute good is sufficient unto itself; on the other hand, God is free regarding the means he uses to achieve the goals of his infinite wisdom. One could say that God is bound only by his science, by his wisdom, and by the natural *necessity* (10:292a) of things. God's science and wisdom, however, are not something foreign or superior to him, for they are his very self. In like manner, the natural necessity of things cannot limit God's liberty, for this necessity flows from his perfection and from his free decision. God is therefore not only supremely free, he is freedom, for this also is his very being.

7. The divine intellect and will are the source of God's operations with respect to creatures: primary among these is the act, which pertains both to his intellection and to his volition,

whereby he causes, cares for, and directs all creatures to their particular ends, in attaining which each one contributes to the final purpose of the universe. This is known as the *providence of God* (11:917b). This act, like all else in God, is infinite and eternal, not limited and temporal. It exists in God's intelligence and presupposes his will, yet it is not multiple or successive, but one simple act identified with his essence. God is the first cause of all things, and in causing them he also disposes them to the end that he intends; again, since everything is eternally in him, he cares for them immediately also. This is the meaning of providence in the strict sense. The execution of God's plan, of course, takes place in time, and this is usually known by another name, viz, divine governance [§§48.8, 54.4].

8. The power or active potency in God whereby he operates in things is known as the divine *omnipotence* (10:688c). By this power God has dominion over all things other than himself; by it he confers existence on them and also continues to hold them in existence. Omnipotence follows upon God's existence as Pure Act, having within himself the fullness of actuality. Since one thing is able to cause another insofar as it itself is in act, God alone is capable of giving existence to created things. Like all other divine attributes, God's omnipotence is in reality completely identified with his essence. It extends to everything that does not involve a contradiction, i.e., that has the inherent possibility of existence. So God cannot make a square circle, not because his power is limited, but because there is an inherent limitation, in this case a contradiction, in the idea of the thing itself.

## §47. DIVINE CAUSALITY

1. God, however conceived by those who speak of him, is generally regarded in some way as the cause of the world. The *divine causality* (3:347a) has in fact been expressed in terms of all four causes, pantheists seeing God as immanent in and identical with the world, others seeing him as an extrinsic source

affecting the universe through efficient causality and final causality. In truth God is the efficient cause of all, including matter; he is the exemplar [§35.11] above whom there is no further model; and he is the final cause of all (6:514d). Every being apart from God must come from him, for God is Subsistent *Esse; esse* is uniquely an effect of God, and therefore all other beings must participate in *esse* from him. In light of this truth one gains an insight into the meaning of God as *Ipsum Esse Subsistens* and the implications of this concept for an understanding of divine causality. In what follows attention will be restricted to philosophical problems associated with God's influence as the agent, or efficient cause [§35.8] of the existence and activity of his creation and the relationship of secondary causes to his primary causality. Here God's causality, as productive, is required on three counts: the initial production of the universe, the conservation of all things in their existence, and the actual exercise of causality by all agent causes.

2. *Creation* (4:417c) is the production of the total being of the universe from nothingness, i.e., from no subject that exists anteriorly. This total production is not a necessary emanation (5:291d); rather it is a free act accomplished by the divine fiat. It is not eternal but takes place in time. The implications of this for clarifying what is meant by God's own perfection and causality are many. The very being of things is conferred on them from God as from a primal source; whereas there formerly was God and nothing else, other beings suddenly began to exist. God as the source is the fullness of being: his own as unreceived, limitless being; the being of all else as an effect that he produces. Thus what the divine causality explains is the very fact of existence. This means that God alone is the first and proper cause of *esse*. It means that the divine causality does not work physically on pre-existent matter, that God's causality does not require his physical contact or his complete immanence in creation. Rather this causality is a pure communication: the *First Cause* (3:352b) is perfective of its effects without being itself perfected or changed in any way. On the other hand, the creature is totally dependent on such divine causality;

this dependence makes all the difference between its existing and its not existing.

3. It should be noted here that it was the concept of creation that enabled Aquinas to see the full import of God's being the unique Subsistent *Esse,* to appreciate the subordination of all creation to him in being and in action, and so to develop his distinctive teaching on being as *esse* and on God as "He Who Is." Apparently, therefore, it was only with the revelation of Moses, including the fact of creation and its taking place in time, that the tentative insights of philosophers such as Aristotle actually received their full understanding and application. This explains why some insist [§104.3] that natural theology in its full elaboration must rightly be seen as a Christian philosophy [§§1.8, 43.2].

4. Since *esse* is the proper effect of God, wherever it is found outside of God it is just that, an effect, and one that God alone can produce. Every existent, as a consequence, actually and continually depends on God. This continuation of creation is known as *divine conservation* (4:212c). Any effect that is dependent on its cause not only for its coming-to-be but also for its actual being is continually dependent on such a cause. All creatures, because they exist and for as long as they exist, actually and continually receive their existence from God.

5. The teaching that *esse* is the proper effect of God need not entail a rejection of creatural causality. The production of creatures should be understood as the communication of being in various and limited ways. Since God willed to create, his creatures must be limited and cannot themselves be Subsistent Being. Their limitation is in their essence, which is made to be actualized by *esse;* in this way God is the cause of the entire being of his creatures. But the perfection of the divine causality precisely as communicative embraces the production of certain creatures more perfect than others in that the former can contribute actively to the development of creatures, whereas the others cannot. Stated somewhat differently, God makes at least some things to be efficient causes.

6. Not only does God's causality not eliminate the causality

of secondary causes, but rather it causes them to be themselves causes actually causing. Efficient causality [§35.8] is always the active communication of existence to an effect. Because *esse* is the proper effect of God, every other agent in causing must participate in the influence of divine causality. Not only does it do this in view of its essence and its power to operate, received initially from God, but also in actual subordination to God's influx in the very exercise of its causality. The power actually to share in God's proper causality is communicated as a passing force, one that can be received only transiently and subordinately to God. But it is this power that is the ultimate completion of every created cause and renders it capable of actually causing. Only through this power can it impress its proper likeness on its effect, thus functioning on its own level of causality. The completion of its power to cause enables it to make its effect exist, since it communicates *esse*, the ultimate actuality of all perfections. The particular kind of existence is made actual by *esse*, and the power received from God to enter into this communication makes the secondary cause actually the cause of its own effect. Because this ultimate power derives from its subordination to God, both God and the secondary causes are total causes of the entire reality of the effect: God as primary, the created agent as secondary, cause [§35.8-9].

7. Aquinas explains the subordination of secondary causes to God by teaching also that God "applies" the power of the secondary cause to its exercise. This point has become the occasion of controversy among theologians dealing with the problems of grace, free-will, and predestination [§95.7]. Aquinas means simply that God applies all causes to their actual operation because they are moved movers and he is the First Mover [§20]. Yet even this is but another facet of the dependence of the creature, as composed of essence and existence, on the unique Subsistent *Esse*. It is because, in their ontological structure as substances, created causes are so composed that they cannot be identical with their own operation. Their exercise of operation is the acquisition of a new accidental *esse* to which, as created,

they are merely in potency. This potentiality cannot be actualized unless through the intervention of God, who is First Mover and Pure Act precisely because he is *Ipsum Esse Subsistens*. The communication of motion by God, called by some a *premotion* (11:741b) or a *predetermination* (11:722b) and by others a *concursus* or *concurrence* (4:125a), is not the bestowal of a reality distinct from the transient power by which the created agent participates in the production of *esse*. It is simply another facet of the dependence of creatural causality on God's causality.

## §48. THE PROBLEM OF EVIL

1. In explaining the rightness and goodness of the divine causality as it extends to every single entity and to every mode of being, it becomes necessary to treat of the *problem of evil*. If God exists, whence comes evil? How is it possible to explain that an infinitely good and wise God has, if not willed, at least caused ʻ(and as primary cause at that) so much evil in the world? Since he is all-powerful, could he not have prevented the existence of such evil? These questions, which are among the most difficult to answer in all of philosophy, pose the problem of evil. To respond to them it will be convenient to treat of the nature ʻand kinds of evil, the subject of evil, and the causality involved in its production.

2. *Evil* (5:665b) is opposed to good [§32.4], which is the integrity or perfection of being in all orders: material, moral, and spiritual. Evil is sometimes taken concretely as the thing that is evil, i.e., the subject affected by evil; at other times it is taken formally or abstractly to designate the ill affecting the subject. Taken in itself evil is a negation of the perfection due to a nature or to a being. As such, however, it is not a simple negation; rather evil consists in a *privation* [§16.5] i.e., in the fact that a certain being lacks a good it requires to enjoy the integrity of its nature. While this implies that evil is non-being, it does not imply that evil is non-existent. Blindness truly exists, but to say

that "Peter is blind" is not to attribute blindness to him as a thing possessed; the predicate here does not signify being, but simply the reality of a lack or of a defect.

3. There are many *kinds* of evil: a common division is that into (1) metaphysical, (2) physical, and (3) moral. (1) *Metaphysical* evil is associated by some philosophers with the mere *finitude* of created beings, i.e., the absence of a perfection not required for the natural integrity of creatures. This usage is generally regarded as improper, since finitude in itself is not an evil. It is indeed the negation of a higher perfection, in the sense that a dog is not a man, but this is not as a privation, since a dog is not deprived of the perfections proper to a man. (2) *Physical* evil is that affecting a nature, whether this be corporeal or spiritual, whose integrity it alters. *Pain* (*malum poenae*) and *sorrow* are physical evils, as are psychoses and neuroses, in that they deprive the soul of its natural equilibrium, just as blindness deprives the body of its natural integrity. Cataclysms such as earthquakes and epidemics are sometimes listed as physical evils, although this again is not a proper usage; evil rather lies in the physical defects and *suffering*, often great and terrible, that accidentally follow in the wake of such phenomena. (3) *Moral* evil (*malum culpae*) consists essentially in the disorder of the will, and is called *fault* or *sin* (13:241a). This is the primary evil in the universe, and is best elaborated in the context of its proper subject [§48.6].

4. Since evil is a privation it can exist only in a *subject* or in a being that, as such, is good. Evil presupposes good, both as the subject that it affects and as the perfection that it negates. From this point of view evil can never be total or absolute; if it were a denial of the subject in its totality, evil would annihilate itself for lack of something to affect. Negation or non-being cannot exist as such; they can only "exist" in some being that is good in itself and whose integrity they limit or alter.

5. The *subject of physical evil* is the material universe in general, but especially living beings who are able to undergo physical or moral suffering. A wine may go sour, or a substance may turn out to be a poison, but properly speaking evil is not

in such things; it is man who classifies them or makes them evil because of his needs or the uses he puts them to. *Suffering*, on the other hand, is a physical evil, though it affects men and animals differently. Man is able to suffer more than animals because he is aware of his suffering, and this serves to intensify the evil. The problem becomes particularly acute in the context of *death*, for man alone knows that he will die and is capable of anguish as he faces death. Yet even death is not an absolute evil, for the soul survives the body and all its defects; should a person, on the other hand, not believe in an afterlife, then death takes away the problem: the evil annihilates itself in its very realization.

6. In contrast to physical evil, *moral evil* is found in a rational and free nature as such. Properly the *soul* is its immediate subject, or, more precisely, the *will*, with its power of obeying or disobeying the norms of conscience and the natural law [§54]. Moral evil is therefore a privation of rectitude required by the natural law, a privation affecting a free will, which through its own fault lacks the perfection it ought to have. Physical evil, as has been seen, is always an evil suffered, whether this affects a corporeal or a spiritual nature; moral evil, just the opposite, results from the voluntary activity of an agent who, in depriving himself of a perfection to which he is obliged by nature, inflicts upon himself a self-mutilation. Moral evil is thus properly constituted by this very activity. Being a voluntary privation, a refusal to enter here and now on the path to right action for the purpose of a good that is not *the* good, evil is a consequence of freedom. Such a "negative positivity," such placing of a refusal or a negation, makes the will disordered and defines evil properly so-called.

7. God is not and cannot be in any way the *cause* of evil, for he is infinite goodness and desires only to communicate good. Yet in the physical order there are undeniably pain and suffering, and were these to no good purpose they would be unmitigated evil. But God, through his divine providence, orders even these to the good and to the happiness of man; in other words, he permits such evils so that out of them a greater good may come.

Seen in this way they do not merit being called evil in the strict sense, since from this perspective they are not privations, but rather accidental negations of a greater good, namely, the spiritual good of man. Moral evil presents more of a problem. As we have seen, it results ultimately from the *fallible liberty* of a free agent [§48.6]. Is God to be reproached for the gift of free-will because this turns out to be fallible? It would seem not, for free-will is undeniably a perfection. And even if man makes ill use of his freedom, God is still good in giving him this perfection. For it is a perfection to possess self-determination, to conform the self by a decision of the will to the order desired by God, and thus to collaborate in God's creative activity. Moreover, fallibility can explain the possibility of evil but not its reality; its reality is absolutely contingent and has no other cause than the free decision of an intelligent agent. In this sense, evil itself has no *per se* cause; to search for a cause is to postulate an antecedent evil, and hence to institute an unending inquiry. Voluntary evil is therefore a sort of absolute: the primary negation and refusal of a liberty, which is such only because of the mysterious power of refusal and negation.

8. *God's providence* governs the whole of the created order as well as its parts. Proceeding from the infinite knowledge of God and from his absolutely perfect will, it never takes on a capricious aspect but acts always in a way consonant with the nature of each creature. Therefore, in reference to man, this action will respect man's freedom, even his power of refusal. Granted that God has given man freedom, in a sense he is powerless to take that freedom away, just as he is powerless to make a square circle. It is also true that, when man places a sinful act, God is the primary cause of the *being* of the act. The *disordination* or privation of rectitude in the act that constitutes its sinfulness, however, comes not from God but from the sinner, whose choice it uniquely is [§50.6-8]. Because of God's respect for human nature and its prerogative of freedom, evil thus insinuates itself in the plan of providence. God *allows evil* to enter into this order—not as essential to order, since evil is not directly willed by him—but *accidentally*, in virtue of the needs of mercy,

of wisdom, and of divine power. God, as has been said, makes suffering serve a purpose, and even in the case of moral evil he offers the sinner the possibility of good. For by sin, man can know his misery, acknowledge his dependence on God, and will to seek his help. This too is the greater good. In any event, divine providence and governance cannot be blamed for the evil in the world. If there is mystery here, nonetheless there is no injustice.

9. At a philosophical level, one cannot penetrate into the intimacies of the divine nature or the mysteries of the divine plan. It would seem that the more man penetrates into the infinite, the better he understands that it is beyond him. What little he knows of God by his natural reason can therefore be but a small fraction of all there is to know. And yet man's intellect, in its philosophical search, neither destroys nor diminishes the *mystery*, but rather serves to deepen it. This, it would appear, is sufficient justification for his intellectual efforts: the wisdom he attains by ever deeper and deeper reflection is itself a springboard to higher truth.

# CHAPTER 8.

# ETHICS

## §49. MORAL PHILOSOPHY

1. *Ethics* (5:570c) is the philosophical study of voluntary human action, with the purpose of determining what types of activity are good, right, and to be done, or bad, wrong, and not to be done, so that man may live well. As a philosophical study, ethics is a science [§13] or intellectual habit that treats information derived from man's natural experience of the problems of human living, from the point of view of natural reasoning. The term ethics is etymologically connected with the Greek *ethōs,* meaning custom or conduct, and is equivalent in meaning to moral philosophy, which is similarly connected with the Latin *mores,* meaning customs or behavior. It is generally regarded as a practical science [§13.6], in the sense that the objective of the study is not simply to know, but to know which actions should be done and which should be avoided, so as properly to translate knowledge into action.

2. The *subject* of ethics is voluntary human conduct; this includes all actions, and also omissions, over which man exercises personal control, because he understands and wills these actions (and omissions) in relation to some end he has in view. Included within the scope of ethics, however, are somewhat involuntary activities that are performed with repugnance yet involve a degree of personal approval [§52]. What is aimed at in ethics is a reflective, well-considered, and reasonable set of conclusions concerning the kinds of voluntary activities that may be judged good or suitable (or evil and unsuitable) for a

human agent in the context of man's life as a whole, including his relations to other beings whom his actions influence in some significant way. It also includes the relation of human actions to some overall goal of living: the knowing and loving of the perfect good, the higher welfare of the person or of his society, happiness or pleasure, or some such highest end.

3. The distinctive character of ethics may be seen by considering the various kinds of *order* that man can discern among beings and that require different habits of mind to be understood. (1) The habits of speculative philosophy, say, of natural philosophy [§15] and metaphysics [§30], enable one to consider the order to be found among all real beings, apart from any effect of man's activity. (2) The habit of logic [§14] enables man to order his own thinking. (3) Similarly, the habit of art [§58.1] enables him to order the production of useful or beautiful artifacts. (4) Finally, moral philosophy enables him to put order in his voluntary activities, i.e., activities proceeding from man's will according to the ordering of reason and so properly directed to an end. From this it can be seen that ethics is a practical or productive science and that it is also *normative*: it is concerned with what man "ought" to do, not merely with "how" he operates. Although practical, however, it also has a speculative aspect, in the sense that action follows on being (*agere sequitur esse*) and that human actions are right when they are in conformity with human nature. Thus ethics requires a knowledge of psychology [§21] and metaphysics for its proper elaboration. Some thinkers, e.g., Kant, claim that ethics is impossible unless one postulates man's freedom, his immortality, and the existence of God; the viewpoint here is that these are not mere suppositions but truths already demonstrated in speculative philosophy.

4. Like natural theology [§41], ethics encounters a problem in its relations with faith, for it can be argued that a moral science based on reason alone is an inadequate guide for the actual decisions of man's life, neglecting as it must original sin and man's *de facto* elevation to the supernatural order. Because of this some would propose a *Christian ethics*, similar to Chris-

tian philosophy [§1.8] generally, that would be subalternated to theology and thus provide a more adequate and practical guide to Christian living. Granted the value of such a mixed moral science, what will be developed here is an ethics based on the natural life of reason alone; although incomplete, this provides a reasonable foundation on which a moral theology can later be built. (The student should be warned, however, that many of the articles in the *New Catholic Encyclopedia* to which reference will be made intermingle theological and philosophical considerations, and thus special care is required to isolate the matters that are purely philosophical.)

5. Ethics can be *divided* in various ways. Some would make only the basic distinction between voluntary actions as they are related to the private good of the person, which would be the subject matter of *individual* ethics, and such actions as they are related to the common good [§54.1], which would count as the domain of *social* ethics [§75.1]. Others would propose finer divisions on the basis of the scope of the good that is envisaged. Thus individual ethics deals with the private good; domestic ethics with the good of the family; political ethics with the common good of a society, state, or nation; and international ethics with the broadest natural common good, that of mankind. In what follows main attention will be centered on individual ethics. Matters relating to social and political ethics will be considered in the chapters devoted to social [§75] and political [§81] philosophies.

## §50. THE HUMAN ACT

1. Since the subject of ethics is voluntary human activity, it is necessary to clarify at the outset what is meant by a distinctively human act. A *human act* (7:206a) is defined as an act that is performed only by a human being and so is proper to man [§29]. Some acts that humans perform are done also by animals, e.g., vegetative acts and acts of perception and of emotion. When a person does such acts they are called acts of man,

but not human acts. What makes an act performed by a human being be distinctively human is that it is voluntary in character, i.e., an act in some way under the control or direction of the will, which is proper to man. A voluntary act proceeds either from the will itself, such as an act of love or of choice, called an act *elicited* from the will, or from some other power that can in some way be moved by the will, called an act *imperated* by the will. So an act of the intellect, of sense cognition, or of emotion, or an act of some bodily member as commanded by the will can be a voluntary act in the imperated sense.

2. From the foregoing it is clear that there are principles from which the human act springs and which can aid in its understanding. These principles are either *intrinsic*, in the sense that they pertain in some way to man's being, or they are *extrinsic* to man, such as law [§54], which as known can exert an influence on his voluntary activity. The intrinsic principles of human acts include the intellect, the will, and the sense appetites, and the habits, both virtues and vices, with which these powers of his soul can be endowed. Since the first three have already been treated under psychology [§§25-28], only an exposition of habits and their various kinds need be given here.

3. A *habit* (6:880d) can be understood initially as a disposing of a power [§21.7] to act in a determinate way. Man is able to perform a variety of acts through his various powers, but without the disposing influence of habit most of his distinctively human acts would be done haphazardly. A habit develops and strengthens a human power, enabling the power to operate more effectively and with more facility. So understood, a habit may be defined as a firm *disposition* (4:907b) of a power to act in a determinate way. As the actualization of a power or potency it may be seen as a perfection. A habit, moreover, far from being merely mechanical in operation and somehow alien to good human action, actually enters into the performing of human acts so intrinsically that it may be regarded as a *second nature*: habit makes its distinctive act a kind of natural act just as a power is the first source of a natural act.

4. The notion of habit as perfecting or bettering human

action is not in conflict with the division of habit into good and bad, that is, into *virtue* and *vice*. Any habit permits man to operate better than he otherwise would, but whether a habit is good or bad is a moral consideration, distinct from the psychological explanation of how a habit develops a power more fully. In general terms, the distinction between virtue as a good habit and vice as a bad habit turns on whether the habit produces acts conducive to promoting man's moral good or evil. Acts of virtue are those that are suitable to human nature, i.e., they are acts habitually performed according to the rule of reason. Acts of vice are opposed to human nature inasmuch as they are habitually opposed to the direction of reason. More precisely, a *virtue* may be defined as a good habit by which one lives righteously, or, alternatively, as a habit inclining one to choose the relative mean between the extremes of excess and defect. *Vice*, as the contrary habit, would incline one to choose either of the extremes, both morally evil.

5. The foregoing definitions apply primarily to the four *cardinal virtues*, viz, prudence, justice, temperance, and fortitude. In a broader sense, human virtues may be either intellectual or moral, depending on whether they perfect the intellect or the will, the two basic principles of human action. Good habits of thinking perfect the human intellect either in its speculative dimension with the intellectual virtues of understanding [§36.2], science [§13], and wisdom [§36.1], or in its practical dimension with the habits of art [§58.1] and *prudence* [§54.7], although the latter is also moral to the extent that it requires right appetite for its proper operation [§55.6]. Good habits of desiring perfect the appetite, either the will by means of the virtue of *justice* [§56.1], or the sense appetites by means of the virtue of *temperance* [§55.3] in the concupiscible appetite and the virtue of *fortitude* [§55.4] in the irascible appetite. There will be corresponding vices for each of these virtues by way of contrary habits.

6. An alternative exposition of the human act may be given by explaining how such an act is *free*. Here it becomes necessary to distinguish between a voluntary act and a free act; for

although every free act is necessarily a voluntary act, not every voluntary act is strictly a free act. A free act, most properly speaking, is an act of *choice* (3:620a). There are occasions, however, when it makes sense to say that man has no choice and that what he wills to do he must will to do [§28.3]. Such acts are voluntary in that they proceed from the will as a principle, but they are not free, at least in the usual and proper sense of the term.

7. There are two types of free act, corresponding to two types of *freedom*: exercise and specification. (1) Freedom of *exercise* is that between contradictory alternatives; it is the freedom of an agent to act or not to act in an absolute sense. In any given situation, a man who is at all rational can will to act or not. This sort of freedom man as a voluntary agent always has; and as related to the interior act of willing or not willing, the voluntary act and the free act, for all practical purposes, are identical. (2) Freedom of *specification* presupposes freedom of exercise and looks further to some object specifying the act to be done by the agent. It is the choice of this alternative rather than that or, more precisely, the choice of this means in relation to a desired end. The free act as choice, therefore, is concerned with means properly, not with ends as ends. To will an end as an end is not a matter of choice but a matter of simple willing; an act of the will centering precisely on the means is the act of choice. When reference is made to human freedom in moral contexts, it is usually this freedom of specification that is meant.

8. In light of the foregoing, one may distinguish the *component parts* or specific acts that make up the complex human act, which is always concerned in some way with ends and means. The list below analyzes the human act in terms of its various steps.

Intellect                                   Will

Concerning the end

1. Apprehending an end      2. Willing an end
3. Judgment about an end    4. Intending an end

Concerning the means

5. Deliberating about means   6. Consent to means
7. Judgment about choice      8. Choice of means

Concerning execution

9. Command to execute choice  10. Use of powers to execute
11. Judgment of end attained  12. Enjoyment of end attained

Not every human act man performs involves all these individual steps, nor need the steps occur in exactly this sequence, but every human act in the practical order does involve seeking some end, a judgment and a choice of means, and a consequent decision to attain to the desired end by carrying out the chosen course of action. The steps, particularly 7 and 8, are also helpful for showing how man's free act, or what is sometimes called his free will [§28.2], is actually a joint product of intellect and will. The intellect, in its practical judgment with regard to means (7), is a determining cause of the will's choosing one action rather than another (8). But this is a determination coming from knowledge; and hence the will, in exercising the act of choice, is still choosing freely what is proposed on the part of the intellect. Even though one knows what one should do, freely choosing to do it or not is a freedom of specification inseparably connected with appetite, with the will in its act of choice.

9. The structure of the human act, so detailed, explains how the intellect moves the will in a general way; a more exact determination of the movement of the will pertains to a discussion of *motive* (10:39a). In the order of specification, of final caus-

ality [§35.10], the will can be moved by the intellect and also
by the emotions and the sense faculties as these awaken a
response to the apprehended good. In the order of exercise, of
efficient causality [§35.8], however, the will holds the place of
first mover in man and so is itself unmoved by any other power.
As far as man is concerned, the will simply moves itself. This
need not preclude, however, that the will be moved in its exercise by the First Unmoved Mover who is Pure Act. As already
explained, the efficacy of the First Cause is such that his power
extends not only to the production of all things, including the
will-act, but also to the mode or manner in which such things
are effected [§48.8]. Experience, moreover, is the best proof
that the will is an agent that acts freely. But as a secondary
cause in the ontological sense [§47.6], even the will must be
moved to its proper operation according to the nature of its being
as a participation of Being itself. Since its nature is to operate
freely, it is moved freely by the sole cause of its nature.


## §51. THE ENDS OF HUMAN ACTION

1. The *end* (5:335d) is the cause of causes, and nowhere is
this axiom more applicable than in the study of human action,
for a knowledge of the ends of man's activity confers the greatest intelligibility on the human act itself. The end may be
defined as the object by virtue of which an event or series of
events happens or is said to take place. In this sense it is the
same as a *final cause* [§35.10], that for the sake of which something exists or is done, that for which an agent acts or action
takes place.

2. Four elements contribute to an understanding of the
concept of end in moral philosophy: its terminal nature, its
causal aspect, its identity with the good, and its relation to
means. (1) As *terminal* the end is simply the outcome or goal
of what an agent does or seeks, and as such it terminates his
movement toward that goal. Even when the goal aimed at is
action, as when one plays simply for the action involved in

playing, the end, in this case the action itself, completes the agent's striving. (2) As causal, the end is what is first intended and so exercises a determining influence over the actions leading up to the goal. When a patient dies in the midst of an operation, death is for him an end in the sense of a terminus; but the patient's death is not the end in the sense of the cause or reason for the operation, since it is not what the surgeon intends. The intended end, health, is responsible for each step taken by the surgeon in preparing for and carrying out the operation. If health were not intended, they would not be. Somewhat paradoxically, that which is final in the sphere of action is the cause of all the activity leading up to it; hence, the name final cause. (3) As *good,* the end gives the reason why the agent tends to it or wills it; thus end and good necessarily involve each other. Its desirability is the very reason why the good is a cause: good is said correlatively to appetite [§26.1]; whatever satisfies appetite and perfects it is suitable to it, and is therefore desirable. Such a concept of good is obviously wider than that of moral good. Man has different levels of appetite, and an object will be morally good only if it fulfills and is suitable to the whole person; it must benefit man as man, not simply as he is a sensitive or a living being [see §62.2]. End, final cause, and good on this accounting can be seen as identical. One and the same thing is called end because it is the term of an agent's striving, final cause because it influences the agent to act to begin with, and good because it indicates why the agent is so moved. (4) As *related to means,* the end specifies why something else exists or is done; the "something else" referred to is the means. A means cannot be understood without referring it to the end in view of which it is chosen. What attracts the agent to the means is not so much its nature as a particular kind of thing as it is its value for achieving the end; put otherwise, what the agent sees and seeks in the means is basically the goodness of the end itself.

3. While the distinction between ends and means is clear, the reality these terms describe is not so simple. Sometimes a thing may be an end in one respect and a means in another.

To deal more precisely with the complexities of the concrete situation, philosophers make various *divisions* of end. (1) Related ends in a given series may be distinguished on the basis of their order of achievement. A *proximate* end is that for the sake of which something is done directly or immediately. An *intermediate* end is that in view of which the proximate end is sought and which itself is desired for something else. Both proximate and intermediate ends are also means, each often being referred to as means-ends. The last end in the series is called the *ultimate* end. This may only be *relatively* ultimate, as when the series of which it is last is subordinate to a higher end or ends. The *absolutely* ultimate end, the supreme end, is that to which all of an agent's actions are directed and which is sought for its own sake alone. In this sense the supreme end of man is said to be happiness [§51.4]. (2) Another division of end is that into *objective* end (*finis qui*), the good or object itself that is sought, e.g., money or knowledge; *personal* end (*finis cui*), the person for whom the good is desired, e.g., health is sought for Peter; and *formal* end (*finis quo*), the act in which the good is possessed or enjoyed, e.g., the enjoyment of food is in the eating. (3) The end of the *work* (*finis operis*), sometimes called the end of the *act*, is the normal purpose or function of a thing or action, or the result normally achieved; e.g., cutting is the normal function of a knife. The end of the *agent* (*finis operantis*) is what the agent actually intends when acting, be it identical or not with the end of the work; so a person may use a knife for cutting or as a screwdriver.

4. The problem of man's *ultimate end* is not easily solved philosophically (9:132c). Yet there is an overall good of human action, an ultimate end, that is only an end and must be loved and sought by itself alone. Philosophers are in verbal agreement concerning the comprehensive good sought by man: all men seek *happiness* (6:918b). This is intended to be a purely factual or descriptive statement, viz, to be a human agent is to direct oneself toward some end as perfective and as constitutive of happiness. Unanimity is far from complete, however, concerning where human happiness is to be found [§86.6]. The classic

statement is Aristotle's, who held that, from the vantage point of philosophy, there is only one ultimate end that truly perfects the human agent. His argument may be summarized as follows. Only a good commensurate with the agent can be perfective of the agent. For this reason the human good, human happiness, cannot consist in the activity of the vegetative powers or in that of the sensitive powers as such. The specifically human function is rational activity, and the human good consists in the excellence of that activity. Consequently, Aristotle observes, the human good must consist in *excellent*, or *virtuous rational activity*. And since "rational activity" is ambiguous, covering both the activity of reason itself and the acts of other faculties insofar as they can be brought under the sway of reason, the excellences, or virtues, that constitute the good perfective of the human agent are both intellectual and moral. In the context of the moral virtues, therefore, man is not free to choose whether or not his happiness or perfection consists in prudence, justice, temperance, and fortitude. These are so many articulations of the end that, in the natural dispensation, is given man as alone perfective of him as a human agent. But the highest excellence of reason is wisdom [§36.1], and so the truest human happiness lies in the *contemplation* of the truths that can be known about the highest realities. Such a life is godlike, since it belongs to man only because he has intelligence like that of immaterial beings.

5. A Christian ethics would complement Aristotle's teaching by emphasizing that God is the true final cause and ultimate end of all of man's activity [§47.1], that God alone is the supreme good (6:620c), and that man's happiness must therefore consist in the contemplation of God himself, given in the *beatific vision* (2:186a) and attained only in an afterlife.

## §52. VOLUNTARITY AND INVOLUNTARITY

1. *Voluntarity* (14:747c) is the character of a human act that is free, i.e., performed willingly with adequate knowledge

of the circumstances and without necessitation from external forces. This characterization arises in the context of man having an ultimate end, and requiring deliberation and choice so as to select the means whereby to achieve, or realize, this end in particular acts. Once more, man is not free to choose just any end as perfective of the kind of agent he is, any more than he can constitute his own nature otherwise than as it is [§17.4]. But, unlike other cosmic agents, man must direct himself to the end he recognizes as his. He must choose, in the various and fluctuating circumstances in which he finds himself, the way in which he can achieve his good, or perfection. In order so to choose, he must be aware of his circumstances so that, given these, he can deliberate about and assess the best way to act here and now. The voluntary act is one that proceeds from such deliberation and involves a choice that is not necessitated by any external force.

2. The voluntary act is deliberate, flowing knowingly from a principle intrinsic to the agent. The "knowingly" is important, for actions done out of ignorance usually do not satisfy this definition, and thus are called *non-voluntary*. The "principle intrinsic to the agent" is the will, in the case of elicited acts, or a power that comes under the sway of the will, in the case of imperated acts [§50.1]. Thus, just as acts can be rational either essentially or by way of participation, so too acts can be denominated voluntary either essentially or by way of participation. Again, it should be noted that sometimes *inaction* or not willing is said to be voluntary. A mark of the voluntary agent is that he has it within his power both to act and not to act; and although it is positive action that first comes to mind when one speaks of the voluntary, the refusal to act, the refusal to will, can be praiseworthy or culpable—itself a sign that not acting too is sometimes voluntary.

3. The nature of the voluntary act can better be seen by examining cases in which the voluntarity of an act is seemingly or really, wholly or partially, impeded, and thereby gives rise to what is known as *involuntarity* (7:604d). (1) An act done

whose source is outside the agent and to which the agent contributes nothing [§17.6]. One who is seized and borne away against his wishes, who is compelled to go where his captors take him, does not go voluntarily and is not held responsible for such activity. Note that the only actions that can be forced, however, are those that are normally imperated or commanded by the will; elicited acts are voluntary by their nature and can never be forced [§50.1]. (2) Actions done out of *fear* (5:864a) combine elements of voluntarity and involuntarity. For something to be done because of fear, there must be at least some consent on the part of the will, since the agent is led to what he does, not because of the fear itself, but in order to avoid the evil that is feared. Yet what is done out of fear is also involuntary, in the sense that it is contrary to what would be the will's inclination apart from the circumstances that evoke the fear. To put the matter generally, actions done because of fear remain voluntary and responsible absolutely speaking (*simpliciter*), although they become involuntary in a certain respect (*secundum quid*), and thus lessen responsibility [§53.7] to that extent. (3) Actions performed under the influence of *emotion* (5:317a) can stand in a twofold relationship to the intellect and will, and so are evaluated differently depending on whether the emotion is antecedent or consequent. (a) Emotion is said to be *antecedent* if it arises independently of any stimulation or encouragement on the part of the will. It is thus not a voluntary excitement of the sense appetite, but one that is set off spontaneously on a subvolitional level. It is called antecedent because it arises prior to any act of the will causing or approving it. Since emotion of this kind is not subject to voluntary control, it cannot be accounted voluntary. The person thus impassioned is not responsible for the emotion until it is possible for the will to assume control of it. At the moment when the will deliberately consents to the emotion, or neglects to subdue it when it can and should, it becomes voluntary and hence ceases to be antecedent emotion. (b) *Consequent* emotion is voluntary, whether indirectly, as when the will neglects to subdue it, or directly, as happens under compulsion or *force* (5:1004c) may be defined as one when the emotion itself is the object of direct desire either for its own sake or as a means to something else.

4. Not every *ignorance* (7:356d) deprives an act of its voluntarity [§52.2]. In its moral aspect ignorance is generally considered as being of three types. (1) *Invincible* or *antecedent* ignorance precedes the action and effectively makes it non-voluntary. It is said to be invincible when it cannot be dispelled by the reasonable diligence a prudent man would be expected to exercise in a given situation. (2) *Vincible* or *consequent* ignorance is that which could be dispelled by the application of reasonable diligence. To the degree that the agent culpably neglects to make the effort necessary to become better informed his ignorance is effectively willed, and to that degree, the resulting action is voluntary. (3) *Concomitant* ignorance is that of an agent who does something he is not aware of doing, and who yet would be quite willing to do the same thing even if he were not ignorant. For example, a man unwittingly insults another person whom he happens to dislike and would be only too happy to insult if the occasion presented itself. His act is not involuntary in the sense that it is opposed to his will; neither is it voluntary in this particular case because he does not know what he is doing. He acts, therefore, with ignorance but not out of ignorance, and the action is best described as non-voluntary. The external act is not imputable [§53.7] to the agent, but he is not free of fault because of his habitual malicious disposition toward his neighbor.

## §53. MORALITY AND RESPONSIBILITY

1. *Morality* (9:1129b) is the quality attributable to human action by reason of its conformity or lack of conformity to the standard or rule according to which it should be regulated. This supposes, on the one hand, that human actions are voluntary and responsible and, on the other, that there is a standard or rule by which human conduct can be measured. From what has

already been said, such a standard is provided by the end or supreme good of man, which consists in action that is most in accord with his nature, viz, virtuous living as specified by right reason. Another norm is more extrinsic to man, namely, law; how these two norms or standards are related will be explained presently [§54]. For the moment it will suffice to say generally that man's end sets the norm against which the morality of his actions is to be judged, and in terms of which the species of morality can be determined [§51.4-5].

2. The relation of any act to man's end may be threefold: (1) if the choice promotes the attainment of the end, the act is morally *good;* (2) if the choice defeats the end, the act is morally *bad* or *evil* [§48]; and (3) if the choice does neither, the act is morally *indifferent.* The third category presents a special problem, whose discussion will be postponed on that account [§53.6]. The more fundamental distinction is between actions that are good and those that are bad, and the problem of morality is that of determining what makes the one good and the other bad.

3. The morality of a human act is specified by three determinants of the action: the object, the end, and the circumstances. (1) The *object* is that which is actually done or projected as a possible human accomplishment. It is also that about which the choice is concerned, or alternatively, the *finis operis* to which the action tends by its very nature. For example, the object of murder is the taking of the life of an innocent person. It is the object, so understood, that primarily specifies an action as morally good or bad. (2) The *end* is the purpose or motive for which the agent acts. An act, otherwise good, might be vitiated by being performed for an evil purpose. On the other hand, an act that is evil by its object, such as murder, cannot be made good because the murderer has a good intention; hence the axiom, the end does not justify the means (5:337c). (3) The *circumstances* (3:880d) are individuating conditions that, although in themselves not part of the nature of the action, nevertheless modify in some real way its moral quality. Some circumstances affect the very doing of the action, i.e., when, where,

and how; others relate to the causes that bring about the action, i.e., who, by what means, with whose help; and yet another, how much, concerns the effect with regard to its quantitative aspect. Some moralists list the motive or purpose of the act, its why, among the circumstances, but this is usually counted as a special determinant, the end already mentioned (2).

4. Just as a being is good only when it has all the perfections or goods belonging to its nature, so an action is good only when all the determinants of its morality are good. A morally good object must be chosen, the motive that prompts the action must be good, and the attendant circumstances must also be good. Thus the general rule is that a human action warrants the qualification of goodness only when all the determinants are in accord with the norm of right reason and therefore good; when any single element among these determinants departs from the norm and is lacking in goodness, the action is characterized as morally bad, even though bad in a qualified sense. Hence the Latin axiom: *bonum ex integra causa, malum ex quocumque defectu.*

5. The *consequences* of an action normally do not affect its morality, except insofar as they are known and willed and thus become part of the nature of the act itself. Yet bad consequences, which, though unintended, are foreseen as following from what is directly intended, may be reason for forbidding an act innocent in itself. Difficult cases are generally adjudicated in terms of the principle of the *double effect* (4:1020d). The principle enumerates four conditions that must be verified for one to perform an action from which at least two effects or consequences will follow, one good and the other bad. (1) The action as determined by its object must be morally good or at least indifferent. (2) The agent must not positively will the bad effect but must merely permit it; if he could attain the good effect without the bad, he should do so. The bad effect is sometimes said to be only *indirectly* voluntary. (3) The good effect must be produced directly by the action, not by the bad effect; otherwise the agent would be using a bad means to a good end, which is not allowed. (4) There must be a proper proportion

between the good achieved and the evil tolerated because of it.

6. The problem as to whether or not a human act can be morally *indifferent* [§53.2] is generally solved as follows (7: 468b). The object of an act is the primary determinant of its morality, but since it concerns the general nature of the act it is expressed in an abstract way, such as exercising, working, speaking. Yet a human act is never actually placed in the abstract, but rather in the concrete conditions of its existence. Viewed in the first way an act can be indifferent, for some acts according to their nature neither imply something pertaining to the order of reason nor something contrary to this order. Seen in the second way, however, every human act is morally good or bad, for in the concrete it is always performed for some end and is surrounded by a host of circumstances. These, being good or evil, will remove the indifference of the act as abstractly conceived and make it either good or bad for the person who performs it for this purpose, at that time, and so on.

7. *Responsibility* (12:392d) designates a person's moral accountability for his actions; the same general idea is expressed by the related term, *imputability* (7:407d). More precisely, imputability is a quality of actions, facts, or consequences by which they are attributable to an agent, and responsibility is a quality of the agent to which they are attributed. The term responsibility is used in three ways. (1) Employed descriptively, it simply expresses a cause-effect relationship between an agent and an action or a consequence, without implying anything with regard to the ethical character of the act. (2) Used prescriptively, it indicates a moral obligation (10:614c) binding one to do or to avoid doing something, as in the statement, "It is a man's responsibility to care for his children." This is responsibility in an *objective* sense. (3) Used ascriptively, the term attributes blame or credit to an agent who acts with or without due conformity to moral norms of conduct. This is responsibility in a *subjective* sense. The last is the more common meaning among moralists, for they are concerned not only with the objective moral character of what is done, but also with whether or not the objectively good or bad act can be imputed

to an agent in the particular state of consciousness or of feeling with which he acts. (For a full discussion of the legal and moral aspects of responsibility, see 12:393b-399a).

8. In connection with responsibility a special problem arises when two or more agents cooperate in the production of an evil action and the degree of their responsibility must be ascertained. This is known generally as the problem of *cooperation* (13: 245d), meaning by this the action of aiding another in carrying out an evil act. It is common to distinguish between cooperation that is formal and that which is material. (1) *Formal* cooperation occurs when the cooperator shares in some way in the intention and purpose of the one whom he assists; this is always evil because it involves, virtually at least, a sharing in an evil purpose. (2) *Material* cooperation avoids participation in the evil intention; the cooperator in this case does not want the evil action to take place, and there is an ambiguity about what he actually does. His assistance may in fact contribute to the evil act, but it is not of its nature or in the circumstances exclusively ordained to the commission of the act. Material cooperation is considered permissible under certain conditions, viz, that the action of the material cooperator is not evil in itself, that his intention is good, and that he has a proportionately grave reason for doing something that may contribute in some way to the evil action of another.

## §54. LAW AND RIGHT REASON

1. Among the internal principles of human acts, virtue is the primary means of directing man to the good of human happiness; among the external principles, law enjoys a similar status in enabling him to lead the good life. As is evident from experience, the *common good* [§76.4] is the end or purpose of all law, and without an understanding of what the common good properly is, the nature and function of law in directing human acts cannot be appreciated. A common good is clearly distinct from a *private* good, the latter being the good of one person only, to the

exclusion of its being possessed by any other. A common good is distinct also from a *collective* good, which, though possessed by all of a group, is not really participated in by the members of the group; as divided up, a collective good becomes respectively private goods of the members. A true *common* good is universal, not singular or collective, and is distributive in character, being communicable to many without becoming anyone's private good. Moreover, each person participates in the whole common good, not merely in a part of it, nor can any one person possess it wholly. The distinctive common good to which human law is ordered is the civil, or political, good of peace and order. Such direction of human acts by law is clearly indispensable for human development and perfection.

2. The classic definition of *law* (8:545a) is based on the foregoing notion of the common good: law is a certain ordination of reason for the common good, promulgated by one who has care of the community. This common definition of law applies proportionately or analogously to the different kinds of law. According to man's mode of knowing, civil, or human positive, law primarily realizes the common definition of law. Hence law is first understood to be an ordinance of reason by one who has authority to direct the political society and its members to the common civil good, a happiness consisting primarily in peace and order. *Civil law* directly concerns the external acts of human beings, presupposing the interior principles and acts [§84]. Although civil law therefore does not directly aim to make men virtuous in their actions, it does command certain acts that dispose men to become virtuous and forbid other acts that lead to vice and tend to make life in society impossible.

3. Every civil law, insofar as it aims at the common good and is accordingly a just law, carries an obligation to be obeyed. Yet this obligation rests on more than civil law itself. It derives from a law more fundamental than civil law and its political sanction, viz, what is called *natural law* (10:251c). This is the "unwritten law" that, in its most common precepts, is fundamentally the same for all. The natural law expresses, in universal form primarily, the fundamental inclinations of human

reason formulated by reason in a judgment naturally made, that is, with little or no discursive reasoning. Such law, then, is natural on two scores: (1) it is not law made by reason so much as discovered by reason; and (2) all men thus naturally know the most universal precepts expressed in natural law. Natural law, so understood, is clearly a fundamental principle for directing human acts.

4. One other kind of law must still be mentioned: *eternal law*. It is even more fundamental than natural law, being the law in which even natural law participates. Eternal law refers to the idea of the government of things that exists in the mind of God [§46.7]; it is the plan of God's wisdom by which all action and motion of the universe is directed. It directs the universe as a whole to the common good of God himself. This is not the law given through revelation. The knowledge about eternal law can be arrived at by reason alone, though usually indirectly. Eternal law is therefore the ultimate source of all law and the ultimate directive principle of all acts and motions of creatures to their proper ends.

5. The habit or innate ability in man to recognize the first principles of the moral order and so of natural law without recourse to discursive reasoning is known as *synderesis* (13: 881d). This is a natural habit basically the same as that of understanding [§36.2]. The principles at which it arrives are not themselves natural or innate, for like all intellectual knowledge they have their origin in sense experience; yet each man does have the innate or natural capacity to grasp their truth once he understands the concepts presupposed to their judgment. One man may have greater insight into their meaning than another, however, if he has greater capacity of intellect; this in turn will depend upon the state of refinement of his internal and external sense powers.

6. Synderesis is the internal source from which springs man's knowledge of the natural law. Since the most general concept inducing man to action is that of the good, the *first principle* of the practical order must be: Good is to be done—together with its necessary complement: Evil is to be avoided. This therefore

is the basic principle for natural moral law. Following immediately from it, and thus known also by synderesis, are the simple or *primary precepts* of the natural law: A being must act according to its nature, a reasonable being must act reasonably, etc. The natural law prescribes those acts that are morally good for man, i.e., in accord with his natural inclinations: namely, (1) in common with all beings and living things, to maintain his being and his life; (2) in common with animals, to ensure continuation of his race by reproducing and caring properly for offspring; then, (3) properly as human, to pursue truth, exercise freedom, and cultivate virtue. These are the basic natural inclinations of all men, at all times, everywhere. However, man's understanding of them increases with experience and with intellectual development.

7. Synderesis assures possession of the most general and universal knowledge of the principles of the practical order; to discover reasonable rules of acting in more specific detail another habit of mind is needed, and this is known as *prudence* (11: 925d) or practical wisdom. Unlike synderesis prudence is an acquired virtue whereby man discerns the correct means to achieve the goals set by synderesis in his individual actions; for this reason it is known as *right reason* concerning what is to be done (*recta ratio agibilium*). Although, like synderesis, a habit of the intellect, prudence is counted as a moral virtue because it forms the link connecting the activities of the other cardinal virtues, discerning for them the proper means whereby they can achieve their natural, and therefore good, inclinations. Its key role in enabling man to achieve his goal of virtuous living in accordance with right reason is explained in what follows [§55. 5-6].

8. Unlike synderesis and prudence, which are habits, *conscience* (4:196b) is an act of judgment; it is the knowledge that accompanies an action and notifies the agent of its rightness or wrongness. Because of this accompanying role conscience is referred to as the subjective norm of morality, since it provides a personal evaluation of the goodness or badness of each individual action. Unfortunately conscience in itself is fallible and so not

a sure guide to objective morality; to become this it must be under the influence of practical wisdom or prudence, and when such is the case it is known as a *right conscience*. As such it is effectively the last practical judgment of the prudent man, itself expressed as the conclusion of a practical syllogism whose major premise is provided by synderesis, informing him proximately and surely of the morality of a particular action to be done or to be avoided.

## §55. THE LIFE OF VIRTUE

1. With this all the elements are at hand to explain how man achieves his natural end in this life by the activity of virtuous living according to right reason. A *virtue* (14:704d), as already noted, is a good habit [§50.4]; more specifically it is a habitual, well-established readiness or disposition of man's powers directing them to some specific goodness of action. As such it is not the approval given an action after it has been performed, but the source of action, a modification over and above a native power, inclining it toward its full realization in action. Just as there is a diversity of powers in man, so there is a diversity of virtues, and indeed a greater diversity than that of powers. For whenever there is a different human value [§62.2], a specific kind or dimension of goodness, to be realized in human action, a different virtue is necessary to equip man to achieve it.

2. The power that is perfected by a virtue is called its *subject*. Those powers of the soul that are fixed and determined by nature, e.g., vegetative and sensory powers, are not susceptible to development by habit. Only those powers in which originates activity that is the expression of man's controlled self-realization —activity that is humanly determinable—can be the subjects of virtue. The emotive powers, the sensitive appetites, are so determinable by the virtues of temperance and fortitude, and this because they are subject to control by reason and will. Likewise the intellect itself is perfectible by the virtue of prudence in its ability to discern rectitude in action, and the will is perfectible

by the virtue of justice to pursue goods not immediately and obviously identifiable as its own. None of these virtues, moreover, are natural in the sense that they are innate; rather they are acquired by repeated acts, and so can exist only in consequence of deliberate, human activity. All human habits, in fact, are generated and developed, and these are either good or bad, virtues or vices, depending on the kind of action that brings them into being. The development of virtue, then, is not incidental to human activity: it is one of two necessary alternatives.

3. *Temperance* (13:985d) is the virtue of moderation in desires and pleasures, especially those of the impulse emotions, and as such is seated in the concupiscible appetite. Its role is not to repress emotion but rather to temper it, so as to attain a reasonable sensibility that strikes the note between immaturity and insensibility. As a special virtue it moderates the pleasures of food, drink, and sex arising from the sense of touch. It has many parts or component virtues, each of which confers a special skill, e.g., in restraining greediness for food, in achieving sobriety with intoxicating drink, in becoming chaste in matters of sex, in developing unwillingness for the infliction of pain, in seeking moderation and restraint about luxuries, and so forth.

4. *Fortitude* (5:1034b) is the corresponding virtue for the contending emotions and so is seated in the irascible appetite. It is a type of courage of soul that enables a person to adopt and adhere to a reasonable course of action when faced by danger and particularly by the danger of death. It also moderates by controlling the impulse of fear, on the one hand, and of foolhardiness, on the other. It too has many parts or component virtues, enabling its possessor to strike vigorously and aggressively against evil, to endure it when necessary, to be patient in adversity, to persevere in achieving a difficult task, and so on.

5. Both temperance and fortitude are virtues of moderation, and as such they achieve their perfection by seeking the mean between excess and defect. To do this they must work and develop together with prudence so that their activities are regulated under the control of reason. Each of their initial acts must be deliberate and proper, and so in conformity with "right

reason." The latter expression means only that the control of reason must be in conformity with man's nature, and thus conduce to the development of the good and perfect man, who is eventually endowed with all the human virtues and lives according to them. The repetition of such morally good acts gradually rectifies the appetites, producing in them habits of action by which they become more and more responsive to the direction of reason ordered to man's perfection, which itself becomes habitual. The latter habit is the virtue of prudence, the *recta ratio agibilium*, while the habits of action in the appetites are the moral virtues of temperance and fortitude. Each appetite is consequently said to be right, or rectified, insofar as it is in conformity with reason, and reason itself is said to be right, insofar as it, in turn, is in conformity with the right appetite.

6. This way of speaking, it should be noted, does not involve a vicious circle. The judgment of prudence is said to be right insofar as it is in conformity with the *end* to which the appetites naturally incline, which is the good of the individual man with his own bodily dispositions [§29.8]. The appetites themselves, on the other hand, are said to be right insofar as they are in conformity with the *means* found for them by the judgment of right reason, thenceforth become the act of the virtue of prudence itself. Although both reason and appetite are therefore said to be right with reference to one another, their individual rectitudes are judged according to different standards that become consecutively available in the generation of moral virtues, and in no way involve a circular process.


## §56. JUSTICE AND RIGHTS

1. The remaining moral virtue is that of justice. *Justice* (8:68d) may be defined as the strong and firm will to give to each his due. So understood it is a habitual disposition whose *subject* is the will; in a broader context the notion also includes the objective right that is owed to each person [§29.6] and community [§76.1], on the basis of either natural law or the just

legislation of the state [§82], and, sometimes, the laws or statutes in which consequent obligations are expressed [§84.4-5]. As has been noted, basic moral insight and the virtue of prudence are involved in determining what is due to another, the mean not only of reason but of reality, and this not only abstractly and universally but also concretely, here and now. The precise role of the virtue of justice is to facilitate the unbiased search for objective right and so to determine the will to acknowledge and fulfill that right as known.

2. Generally the legislation provided by *positive law* is necessary to assure justice in a society [§80], partly to corroborate what is known to be due on the basis of natural law [§56.5], partly to further determine the requirements that answer to the nature and calling of man in a given historical or governmental situation [§83]. Yet a positive law can entail *injustice*, either (1) if it violates the demands of natural law, in which case compliance is not allowed, or (2) if it is basically neither necessary nor actually useful, in which case prudence determines— with the good of the community and of the person in mind— whether compliance or non-compliance is better. Again, a law may be initially just but, because of altered circumstances, become useless and unjust; whenever there is doubt in such matters, however, one's decision should favor the law. Apart from prudence, the virtue of *epikeia* (5:476d) plays a special role (1) in safeguarding the higher values of the natural law in the face of the imperfections of positive law, and (2) in determining particular circumstances, unforeseen by the legislator and thus falling outside his purview, when one need not observe the letter of the law.

3. Although justice requires that each be given his due, this does not imply that to each exactly the same is due. Apart from private interchanges between equals, where complete parity between what is given and what is due in return is the rule, justice also demands an equality of proportion. This consideration gives rise to the various *kinds* or species of justice: (1) *Commutative* justice is that which obtains between equals, normally between persons but also between a person and a group con-

sidered as a moral person [§76.6]; its aim is the utility of both parties who exchange their goods or services. Commutative justice demands that one strive for a fair standard of giving and receiving in return, and forbids encroaching on the rights of others, e.g., by theft, fraud, or unjust damage. (2) *General*, or *legal*, justice seeks the common good, and here the community is the bearer of rights; it is attained in the promulgation of laws that further the common good and in the individual's obeying such legislation so as to achieve that good [§80.1]. (3) *Distributive* justice intends the good of each individual as a member of the community; it is related to legal justice in the sense that, the more the individual devotes his efforts to the common good, the more the community should also devote to his good. Yet this basic proportion must not be exaggerated, nor should it be considered in terms of commutative justice, for the relation between community and individual is not that of mere service and reward. Rather, as in an organism, special care is due to the weak member. And the more favored are obliged to renounce any privileges, however they may have been obtained, that infringe on the basic rights and the true good of the other members of the community.

4. A *right* (12:496d) is a person's moral claim to the means of reaching an end that is his and that he is objectively responsible for reaching. Considered subjectively and personally, rights are founded upon the objective fact of man's nature and end. As a rational and free being, a person has the moral responsibility [§53.7] to choose those means that will lead to his natural and ultimate end [§51.4-5]; if he is effectively to choose those means he must have access to them, and his personal rights are precisely his claim to access to such means. Men have a right to do what it is right for them to do. And since a man is born (*natus*) with this nature and with these ends, such rights or claims can be called natural rights.

5. Among man's *natural rights* (7:209d), that to life is basic, for without it none of the others can be securely exercised; and since the right to life is a right to a properly human life, other natural rights are implicitly included in this first one. Man has

a right, then, to freedom of conscience, to worship God, and to work toward his final end according to his own convictions. He has a right to follow his own vocation in life as he sees it. If married, he has a right to educate his children as he thinks best [§79.4]. Man needs and hence has a right to sufficient material wealth to make possible a properly human domestic life. For this purpose he needs and has a right to employment, to an adequate family income, and to the private possession of wealth [§80.3]. He has the right of association with other men in the pursuit of common interests, and a right to his good name in the various communities to which he belongs. He has a right to an education [§61] and to the opportunity for spiritual and cultural development. He has a right to good government and to equality before the law, and to freedom of expression and of action within the bounds set by law.

6. Even a cursory examination of the foregoing list shows that there is a *hierarchy of rights,* that some are less connected with man's nature than others, that some appear to clash with others, and that thus there is the ever-present problem of the assessment and precedence of rights in disputed cases. Some generalizations that require prudent application are the following: (1) Rights to spiritual goods take precedence over all rights to purely natural goods. (2) When the rights concerned are on the temporal level, the common good takes precedence over the individual good, since the part, as part, exists for the whole. (3) Though natural rights are inalienable, people can voluntarily surrender the exercise of some of those rights. (4) Existing situations make impossible the full exercise of all human rights (see 7:209d). Relative poverty, for example, in either the domestic or the political society, restricts man's freedom to exercise such rights as those to education and gainful employment, and thus restricts their opportunity for fully human lives.

# PART TWO

# SYSTEMATIC PHILOSOPHY

## SPECIAL DISCIPLINES

*The knowledge contained in Part I is based largely on ordinary experience and common sense and has been available for centuries, well before the rise of the modern era. Most of the disciplines covered in this second part, on the other hand, have come into existence since the scientific revolution and require specialized knowledge to be understood. Of necessity, therefore, the treatment here is more schematic than in the first part and more training is presupposed on the part of the student. References to the* New Catholic Encyclopedia *are continued throughout, but it should be noted that this is not a general encyclopedia and that its coverage is restricted to matters of special interest to Catholics. For fuller details relating to the disciplines covered the reader is referred to the 15th edition of the* Encyclopedia Britannica, *particularly to the* Propaedia *volume, which gives an admirable outline of all of knowledge together with indications where fuller expositions may be found in the volumes of the* Micropaedia *and the* Macropaedia.

# CHAPTER 9.

# PHILOSOPHY OF THE HUMANITIES

## §57. PHILOSOPHY OF LANGUAGE

1. *Language* (8:365c) is a systematic means of human communication, particularly by arrangement of vocal sounds conventionally representing concepts, feelings, objects, etc. Like eating and sleeping it is common to all mankind; unlike them it is not instinctive but must be learned by every individual from other members of the social group to which he belongs. It is a kind of behavior that is man's alone, that he shares with no other living creature. Without it, man's uniquely complex knowledge and control of his environment would be inconceivable. The study of language, traditionally a concern of philosophers, has since the 19th century developed along empirical lines as the science of *linguistics* (8:775b), and since the mid-20th century has come to be pursued by psychologists as *psycholinguistics* (11:957a). The science of linguistics (8:365d-373d) is concerned with the ways by which sounds are organized, the patterns whereby meanings are selected and arranged, how sounds and meanings are linked, how languages change and are differentiated into families throughout time, and how they serve as vehicles for the communication of culture. Philosophers are concerned about language in general [§§101, 103] as well as about the language of philosophy (8:373d-376c). It is regarded by them as a sign [§3.4], i.e., as that which, being known, leads one to the knowledge of something else. Realists favor a triadic theory of signification of which the elements are the word, the concept, and the thing; the relation of concept to thing is natural and that of concept to word is a matter of convention [§§3.3,

25.2]. What makes the vocal sound a word and an element of language is its connection with the meaning or concept.

2. *Semantics* (13:66b) is an effort to solve philosophical problems by making language more precise. It is a modern form of nominalism to the extent that it regards language as arbitrary and erects its theory of metalanguage on its base; for most semanticists names have no intrinsic relation to the objects they denote. Topics discussed in semantics include *antinomies* (1:621d) and formalized languages, called metalanguages; definitions of truth in terms of denotation and connotation, leading to a distinction between semantic truth and analytical truth; *ambiguity* (1:371a); how descriptions can be said to be true; and the meaning of meaning. A related study is *semiotics* (13:75a), or general theory of signs.

3. *Linguistic analysis* [§101.3] is a part of the movement known generally as analytical philosophy [§101.2], which attemps to delimit the sphere of meaningful propositions without becoming involved in the metaphysical and epistemological commitments of traditional philosophers. Thus it proposes to use a "neutral" philosophical method that will serve critical and therapeutic goals. Linguistic analysts tend to associate the meaning of a concept with the role it performs in man's ways of acting and to deny that propositions can map reality because they share its structure. Much of their discourse has been anti-metaphysical, as shown in repeated attempts to establish empiricist principles of *verification* (14:615d) that can also be used as criteria of meaning. Linguistic analysis is a style of philosophizing rather than a doctrine, however, and its methods have proved useful in varying degrees to members of diverse philosophical schools [§101.4].

4. Whereas the analysis of language is mainly an Anglo-Saxon movement, *hermeneutics* (16:347b), or the interpretation of language, has been developed mainly on the Continent. In the past hermeneutics was limited to the study of particular texts, most notably those of the Bible, but in recent times it has taken on a broader philosophical significance (16:206b). It proposes that the meaning of a text can be grasped only to the extent

that it can be integrated into the personal life of its author, and that the humanities, in particular, being refractory to the methods of the empirical sciences, require interpretative understanding for their comprehension. A recent focus is on the resources of language as a means of transcending subjectivity and the acknowledged finitude of the individual's outlook; this is possible because language transmits, in a concealed way, an understanding of the world that is conditioned by social and political factors that transcend the individual and that can be revealed through proper interpretation. Thus language, properly speaking, provides a truly universal dimension to hermeneutics [§103.5]. (See also *metaphor*, 9:724d.)

## §58. PHILOSOPHY OF ART

1. *Art* is sometimes used in a narrow sense to mean only the visual arts (1:854a), sometimes in a sense so broad that it is difficult to find a common definition (1:867a). Its original meaning was skill in making; from this the notion was refined to mean the capacity to make in accordance with sound reason; then it was extended from making products immediately necessary for living to making things ordered to knowledge and enjoyment. Art was early noted as being akin to prudence: prudence [§§54.7,55.5] uses knowledge to act well (*recta ratio agibilium*), whereas art uses knowledge to produce objects well (*recta ratio factibilium*). On the basis of work or product, art is divided into *liberal* and *servile*: the latter makes an object from external physical matter and is the result of bodily effort on the part of the maker; the former is an immanent activity whose object is immaterial and is found primarily in the mind or imagination of the artist [§61.3]. From the standpoint of purpose art is further divided into *useful* and *fine*: the former produce things to be enjoyed not in and for themselves but for some other good; the latter produce objects that are contemplated and enjoyed for their own sake, generally because they contain some element of beauty [§58.4].

2. The classical analysis of fine art is contained in Aristotle's *Poetics* (11:455d), where application is made to the field of drama. In his view, what sets off fine art from either liberal or servile art is *mimesis*, i.e., imitation or representation: all art imitates nature, sometimes in appearance, sometimes in operation; but what is peculiar to fine art is that imitation (and delight in imitation) is the immediate end sought and is not merely a means, as in other kinds of art. Basic also to artistic enjoyment and appreciation is *catharsis*, i.e., purging or purifying, whereby the emotions receive an orderly subjection to reason as shaped by artistic form. Yet catharsis serves only as an instrument, for the proper end of art is *contemplation* (4:258c) and the ensuing delight that results from aesthetic response to the beautiful.

3. *Aesthetics* (1:160d) is the modern term for the philosophy of art, being concerned generally with questions about art, its nature, conditions, and consequences. Answers to the question, What is art?, can usually be placed in three main categories: (1) *referentalism*, which holds that art is basically *mimesis*, and so involves some kind of reference of the work produced to the outside world by means of an important similarity between them, though with something left out or added; (2) *expressionism*, which views art as expressive of emotion or feeling, and thus as a creative manifestation or objectification of its creator's impressions; and (3) *formalism*, which concentrates on the inner unity, order, and beauty in the aesthetic object, and thus accents the self-containedness and self-sufficiency of works of art themselves. Other topics treated are aesthetic *value* and aesthetic *experience*, both of central importance in art *criticism* (1:861d). Typical questions are whether aesthetic value is the same as beauty, whether it is natural or non-natural, objective or subjective, relative or non-relative, and whether it is merely a capacity to provide aesthetic experience. Granted that such experience is characterized at least by an unusually intense absorption in a phenomenal object, aestheticians differ on what makes for the "moving" quality of art, what accounts for its intensity, and whether it can be described as a type of detachment associated with aesthetic *distance* (1:160c). Thomists usually

accent the intellectual aspect of aesthetic enjoyment by working out the implications of Aquinas's definition of beauty as *id quod visum placet*: the perception of beauty, the exquisite intelligibility of the object, its possession of a form proportionate to the intellect itself, all afford that delight mixed with exaltation that characterizes a true aesthetic experience.

4. *Beauty* (2:207d) as studied in aesthetics is different from the ontological perfection studied in metaphysics and commonly listed among the transcendentals [§32.5]. It may be defined as a quality constituting the non-utilitarian value of a form, inhering in it as a subtle and hazardous union of the quantitative and qualitative elements, and discovered with increasing interest and adherence of the mind. As a concept it has had a long history (2:202b-205b) and there is little agreement in the present day on its formal constituent. Yet it does appear to be something that qualifies structure, i.e., that is not imposed on matter as form is, but rather qualifies form itself. Again, it is both objective and subjective: it inheres in objects and, being distinguishable, can also provide an objective criterion; yet beauty depends on the mind, since it is the mind that renders relations actual. (See also *ugliness*, 14:368b.)

## §59. PHILOSOPHY OF HISTORY

1. *History* (7:13d) as a term means either (1) the past of men, i.e., everything that has happened to men in the flow of time (in German, *Geschichte*), or (2) the study of the past in an attempt to discover and understand what happened (in German, *Historie*). The two are not identical because it is practically impossible to recover the past as it actually was, either because ancient surviving records are scanty, or those of the recent past (though partial and incomplete) are too vast, or because the records themselves were created by men who may have given inaccurate or incomplete accounts, or because the historian is biased by his own times and culture and so cannot fully project himself back into the past to understand it on its own terms.

*Historicity* (7:31b), from the German *Geschichtlichkeit*, is a term reserved for something apart from the factually historical; it designates the historically significant, whether factually established or not, and may be described approximately as the full, authentic, active, and durative expression of a belief or movement in terms of personal participation and in relation to a given time. *Historiography* (7:5c) is the writing of history or the methodology used to study the past so as to understand and record it properly.

2. The *philosophy of history* (7:22c) may be described generally as interpretative history; it deals with the basic or ultimate causes of the historical process as a whole, and attempts to see a discernible purposive plan in the multitude of events. Some would equate it with *metahistory* (9:723d), which is concerned with the nature of history, its meaning, and the cause and significance of historical change, and so would see its end as the determination of laws regulating historical facts and the place of such facts in an explanatory view of the world.

3. There is no one philosophy of history; the main positions may be grouped under the following headings: (1) *classical cyclicism,* which envisions an eternal universe featuring a continuous recurrence of historical experience; (2) *providential history,* which sees the historical process as initiated by a divine creative act and proceeding meaningfully to a conclusion—being theological in character, this is better named *theology of history* (7:26b); (3) *explanatory laws,* which claims the existence of laws or keys revealing the metaphysic of the historical process, among which might be mentioned destiny, factors such as race, geography, or economics, and apocalyptic events such as the invention of printing; (4) *interpretative history,* which recognizes the unpredictable character of free human choice and so is non-deterministic, yet discerns patterns or trends in the historical process as a whole; (5) *philosophically oriented history,* which concentrates on relations and causes, epistemological problems, and a philosophy of man with emphasis on human freedom; and (6) *progressivist theories,* which are based on the idea that *progress* (11:834a) is a law of nature which finds application

in the cultural development of man. Christian thinkers do not reject the possibility of progress but they question its inevitability; they see the endless cyclic recurrences as finally meaningless; and they favor an interpretative history that discerns a linear, teleological development toward an eternal goal that is beyond the temporal order and so is metahistorical.

## §60. PHILOSOPHY OF RELIGION

1. *Religion* (12:240b) is difficult to define for, although a universal and unique phenomenon, each person tends to define it in terms of his own religious experience. For Catholics, viewed subjectively religion is a *virtue* that leads man to render to God the homage that is due to him; as an objective manner of behavior and concrete manifestation of virtue, it comprises belief in one God, personal and infinite in his attributes, an attitude of absolute respect and submission, exterior acts that express this belief and this attitude in worship, and, as required by all exterior human activity, institutions to regulate that activity. For anthropologists and others concerned with the history of religion these notions are broadened to include, more or less pragmatically, any beliefs, rites, and institutions that occupy, in a group, the place that revelation reserves for religion. The central core of religious experience, however, is commonly regarded as the *sacred* (12: 816a), as opposed to the profane. This represents an order of reality whose presence commands man's attention and at times escapes him; it is simultaneously desired and regarded with awe. In other words it possesses an essentially ambivalent character, that of the *mysterium fascinans et tremendum,* which makes man feel at once irresistibly attracted by its grandeur and frightened by its superiority. In this context religion is usually studied along with *magic* (9:65b), because their opposition can clarify what phenomena are properly religious.

2. *Myth* (10:185c) is the normal form for expressing the content of religion before the elaboration of philosophical definitions, and even side by side with them. Myth is also rite, although

it is not always the explanation of a rite nor does every rite postulate a myth. The recitation of the myth itself is a rite, as is shown by the conditions, e.g., of secrecy and of ceremony, for communicating it. The myth seeks to give expression to religious experience without separating it from the concrete elements of that experience. To maintain this connection is properly the function of symbols. Only the myth projects this experience beyond actual and profane time in order to emphasize the absolute value attributable to it [§103.2-3].

3. A *symbol* (13:860c) is a particular type of sign [§3.4]: a sensible reality, e.g., a word, gesture, or artifact, that betokens something that cannot be directly perceived, properly described, or adequately defined by abstract concepts. The symbol, by its suggestive capacity, thus discloses something that man could not otherwise know, at least with the same richness and power. Because it communicates levels of meaning and reality that are not accessible in immediate experience or conceptual thought, the symbol as such is in some sense revelatory. Thus it is ideal for expressing religious truths that cannot be pictured in any literal way.

4. There is no unanimity as to what constitutes the *philosophy of religion* (12:255a), as opposed to the study of religion described in the preceding paragraphs. The term is of relatively recent origin, and is variously used to designate (1) natural theology [§41], or (2) more precisely a post-Kantian idealistic substitute for what was natural theology in pre-Kantian realism, or (3) simply a curricular category that covers a variety of topics ranging from the history, sociology (12:261b), and psychology (12:258d) of religion to problems in epistemology and metaphysics. It is possible, however, to distinguish the philosophy of religion from natural theology on the following basis (16: 349a): natural theology is concerned only with the philosopher's inquiry into man's knowledge of God through natural reason, whereas the philosophy of religion takes into account all aspects of religious experience and relationships, focusing on the meaning of religion and its role in man's personal and social existence [§101.4]. Although it considers religion in a context broad

enough to include the Judeo-Christian tradition, it does so in a philosophical spirit that does not itself serve a theological purpose; it is intent merely to seek out the properly human significance of religion as it can be grasped and lived cooperatively by all men. To accomplish this goal it must view Christianity as a sort of abstract dialectic, and this puts it under much the same tensions as are found in Christian philosophy [§1.8].

## §61. PHILOSOPHY OF EDUCATION

1. The *philosophy of education* (5:162a) is an expression popularized by pragmatists [§100.1] to signify a study of the fundamental principles of the theory of education, as distinguished from the *science* of education, i.e., the empirical study of the educational process, and from the *art* of education, i.e., the techniques or methods of educational practice. For pragmatists the philosophy of education deals principally with the values [§62] or goals of education. A broader vision would include (1) the nature of man as he is capable of being educated, (2) the goal or the character of the truly educated man, (3) the trained abilities that man acquires in achieving this goal, and (4) the agents by which man is educated. In this context the term education should not be limited to merely academic training, but rather taken in its widest sense of the development of all facets of human personality—physical, moral, and intellectual —in their individual and social aspects.

2. Various philosophies of education have been implicit in the development of educational *theories* from antiquity to the present (5:162b-166b). These include *humanism,* which sees service to the community of man as an essential end of education; *naturalism,* which sees man as inherently good and construes the task of education as that of returning him to his state of unfettered innocence; *scientism,* which would apply the methods of science, and particularly psychology, to educational practice; *nationalism,* which, like *communism,* would subordinate the individual to the good of the nation or state; *progressivism,* which

values freedom and sees education as a never-ending process, as the continuous reconstruction of experience in order to direct future action; *social reconstructionism,* which sees the primary task of education as addressing current problems and inaugurating drastic social reform; and *traditionalism,* which holds that the school should refrain from social involvement and plans for the future and concentrate instead on intellectual development while drawing from the traditions of all ages. A Thomistic philosophy of education would see its goal as virtuous living and the contemplation of truth; moreover, it is a lifelong process of self-activity, self-direction, and self-realization that nonetheless requires mature guidance, for the learner is the principal agent in the educational process while the educator is essentially an instrumental cause [§35.9] who brings potentialities to realization by giving extrinsic aid to the natural reason.

3. The *liberal arts* (8:696c) have long been seen as ideal preparatory studies for philosophy and detailed scientific investigation. They are usually counted seven in number and include what the medievals called the *trivium,* i.e., grammar, rhetoric, and logic, and the *quadrivium,* i.e., arithmetic, geometry, music, and astronomy. They are designated liberal because they pertain to the contemplative rather than to the productive life of man, and so liberate him to contemplate the higher things. The *trivium* prepares the learner to think and speak correctly, and so to communicate well with others, whereas the *quadrivium* disciplines him in the use of logically rigorous quantitative techniques that also have application in the sciences.

## §62. PHILOSOPHY OF VALUE

1. The *philosophy of value* (14:527b) is an expression used to describe various attempts, from the late 19th century onward, to develop the notion of value into a distinct branch of philosophy, and sometimes into a complete philosophy by itself. An alternate name is *axiology* (1:1139d), or theory of value. Most philosophies of value start with the human experience of wanting

something or other and thus with the fact of desiring or seeking. The experience of seeking is then limited to conscious or deliberate valuing, which raises the general question of valuation. This is generally answered in terms of the value situation and the value judgment: a value situation is one involving a subject seeking, i.e., a valuer, an object sought, i.e., the valued something, and a relation existing between them; a value judgment (14:531b), on the other hand, is either an objective or a subjective appraisal of the worth of the object to the subject. As a consequence of this approach values are variously defined and classified, and different norms or standards are used to discern them, e.g., natural law, the democratic process, or the sheer relativism of time and place proposed by some anthropologists.

2. *Value* may be regarded as a somewhat more current and manageable surrogate for the term *good* (6:620b). Thus one could not convey what is meant by a value judgment, as opposed to a judgment of fact, by calling it a good judgment. Again, goods are now obsolete except when designating articles of commerce, whereas values can appropriately cover the entire field of human desires. Thus understood, a value can mean a pleasant reaction to experience, a subjective state like a *delectable* good (*bonum delectabile*). Values can also have an objective character, however, and so can be divided into instrumental and intrinsic values corresponding to *useful* and *perfective* goods (*bonum utile* and *bonum honestum*, respectively). Among the latter may be listed truth, beauty, talent, meaning, health, rest, play, morality, and religion. A value then represents a wide area of interest and desire, and not merely single acts or single objects of desire. But it refers to fewer things than good; for value belongs only to persons capable of appreciating and distinguishing subhuman, human, and moral values.

# CHAPTER 10.

# PHILOSOPHY OF MATHEMATICS

## §63. PHILOSOPHY OF MATHEMATICS

1. Among modern mathematicians there is no general agreement on the scope and limitations of *mathematics*, nor is there a universally accepted definition of its nature (9:456b). As a discipline it is concerned with the concepts of set, group, function, number, and space; with the generalization, idealization, axiomatization, and abstraction of these concepts; and with their interrelation, interpretation, application, and unification. It can be divided into the following general fields: logic and foundations, which includes set theory; algebra, which includes the theory of numbers and group theory; analysis, which includes calculus and real and complex function theory; geometry, which includes topology; probability and statistics; and applied mathematics.

2. *Philosophy of mathematics* (9:458b) is a broad term including any theory on the nature of mathematics as a whole or on the nature of any part or aspect of mathematics. As a specialized branch of learning it deals not only with a critical evaluation of theories relating to the nature of mathematics but also with the origin of mathematical knowledge and its relation to the real world, and with the nature and type of existence peculiar to mathematical entities. It takes its origin from the Greeks, who early thought that the principles of mathematics, number and form, were the principles and basic reality of all things, and that mathematical entities differ from the objects of sense in being eternal and unchangeable. The Greeks were largely responsible also for the division of mathematics into arithmetic (and music,

as applied arithmetic) and geometry (and astronomy, as applied geometry).

3. In Aristotelian and medieval thought, mathematics is one of the three speculative sciences and arises from sense data by means of an abstraction of the second order [§13.4]; it deals with being as *quantified*, i.e., as discrete or numbered, whence arise the arithmetical branches, and as continuous or figured, whence arise the geometrical branches. Mathematics is but one way of fulfilling man's ability to know reality; it has pedagogical value as a liberal art [§61.3] and useful value in that it can be applied to nature to yield a mathematical physics [§§13.5, 17.7]. But it is not a knowledge necessary for, or leading to, an other-worldly contemplation. In common with other speculative sciences mathematics is based on ordinary knowledge and experience of the quantitative aspects of things; this must include at least a vague understanding of the terms with which one expresses quantity (one, two; circle, square). After adding to these pre-reflective data an explicit understanding of logical procedure, one establishes axioms and postulates, defines mathematical objects (e.g., a square), and then proceeds to deduce the properties of those objects that are necessarily implied in the given definition (e.g., that a square is equiangular). The conclusions that are thereby reached are restricted only by the scope of man's *imagination*. Mathematics is the most exact and certain of the three speculative sciences, and the science in which the general methods of logic have their simplest contraction and so can be learned with the greatest facility.

4. In contemporary thought there are three competing foundational theories on the nature of mathematics: (1) *logicism*, which holds that mathematics is a branch of logic and which is directly tied to the development of mathematical or symbolic logic [§65]; (2) *formalism*, which holds that mathematics is an axiomatic system constructed of meaningless symbols, which system acquires meaning when applied to objects by some type of metamathematics; and (3) *intuitionism*, which holds that mathematics is basically dependent on intuition and requires

constructibility in terms of intuition alone as the sole method of mathematical proof.

5. The traditional view of mathematics as a pure or speculative science dealing with quantity [§9.5] that has a practical, or applied, aspect can be enriched by insights from the history of mathematics (9:447d) and from current theories concerning its foundations. Thus mathematics can still be considered a highly abstract science having both pure and applied branches. As the intuitionists have partly shown, however, there are two ways in which *pure mathematics* originates from sense data. (1) Before the mind actually "abstracts" the notion of circle or number, it must have previously generalized from sense experience such basic notions as structure, correspondence, singularity and group, and sequence and order. (2) It is only in this potentially prepared mathematical world that mind can "abstract" and then "localize" such mathematical entities as group, aggregate, circle, or number. When equipped with these concepts, it is to the credit of logicism and formalism to have shown that one can "mathematicize" in three ways. (a) Aided by creative imagination and by renewed recourse to sense imagery, the mind can tend to purify and perfect the entities, or to embellish and create new instances of them. (b) The mind can neglect the basic mathematical paradigms themselves and concentrate on their arrangement, i.e., their relations of priority and posteriority or of simplicity and complexity. With this done, one can reintroduce mathematical entities to see if they can be made conformable to this new structural arrangement. Here the formalist school is content if no contradiction is shown, while the intuitionists require that each new mathematical entity must be "shown" or constructed. (c) Another way of manipulating mathematical entities is to consider them as relatively moveable and changeable and to determine their laws of generation and their mutual reducibility. It is here that the import of such mathematical operations as squaring and differentiating is made clear, and the possibility of the infinitely small and the infinitely large is seen to be consistent.

6. A final way of considering mathematical entities is that

proper to *applied mathematics*. This is the "projective" technique of matching such entities with, or imposing mathematical structure upon, the world of experience. The fact of alternative geometries and algebras having valid applications in the sciences shows that there is no *unique* geometry or algebra of the real world: whatever mathematical system works best for the problem at hand can be regarded as true. Granted the methods used in mathematical abstraction, however, one can hold that mathematics is still a science of reality. To say that mathematics studies *quantity* (12:7c) is a traditional but inexact shorthand for stating that it studies any ordering or structuring of the parts of quantified being. The speculative mathematical universe, then, is the world of the traditional intelligible or imaginable matter [§13.4] within which the mind engages in any of the various types of mathematical activity outlined above.

### §64. NUMBER AND THE CONTINUUM

1. *Number* (10:561a) has been variously defined as a species of discrete quantity [§9.5], i.e., a plurality measurable by unity, and as the class of all classes that can be placed in one-to-one correspondence with one another. The first definition applies to the numbers of ordinary experience, whereas the second is a highly refined and determinate concept related only analogously to the first. Number, in the second sense, arises from two sources: algebraically, it is the result of operating mathematically on two or more numbers and obtaining another number as a result; or it arises from geometric considerations on the assumption that to every point in a line (or in space, generally) there should correspond some number. As the concept develops in this way number grows more abstract, and yet the appreciation of number is enabled to grow more clear, precise, and certain.

2. It is generally held that the notion of class correspondence, from which the concept of *cardinal number* derives, is more basic in the psychology of number than the notion of sequence, from which the concept of *ordinal number* derives. Yet there are

even more basic concepts that man possesses before he achieves the number concept; among these should be enumerated the notions of unity, multitude, measure, and order. (1) For an object to be regarded under the aspect of *unity* [§32.4] it is suffi-cient that it be seen as distinct and as separately identifiable from other objects. Such unity or singularity, as perceived in sensible experience, is sufficient to achieve the concept of "one" that forms the basis for number. (2) The correlative to this notion of unity is that of *multitude* (10:68d), i.e., a collection, set, or aggregate of objects, which is seen not merely as a plurality but as a type of unity itself, a single whole composed of units. Such a knowledge of multitudes or collections gives rise, in turn, to the notion of *correspondence* or matching between the elements of one group and those of another. (3) Associated with the concept of unity is also that of *measure*. To function as a measure the unity must be some minimum within the required process of counting (how many?) or of measuring (how much?). (4) Finally, in order to develop numbers, the notion of *order* is required: this gives priority and posteriority to a collection or multitude, so that number signifies a certain position or rank of one thing with respect to another.

3. With these notions one can approach the problem of the *nature* and the *reality* of number. First the concept of number must be distinguished from the numerals that are symbols indica-tive of number, just as words are from concepts generally [§3. 1-3]. Then it should be separated from the objects that are num-bered; this can be done, for, given any collection of objects and some unity that can function as a measure, the number of the collection can be known by a process either of correspondence or of counting. The number arrived at designates a genuine prop-erty of the group or collection of things, such that changing the color or the arrangement of the group would not alter its number. Moreover, number designates the relationship of a group to a unity of human origin and determination, e.g., five fruits, or two apples and three oranges. Thus number is a concept truly indicative and expressive of the observable distinction [§10] be-tween sensible things and, analogously, between beings in gen-

eral. The numbers of ordinary experience are real in the sense that they are universal (though at this level, vague) concepts representing man's ability to cope with the quantified aspects of things—their plurality, their magnitude, and their intensity. Mathematical numbers are real also, but in a refined and more abstract sense: they are the measure and the means of ordering the parts of the continuum (as in odd and even; positive and negative; open, closed, and dense sets, etc.) depending on the basic unity that the mathematician chooses as a measure.

4. Broadly speaking, a *continuum* (4:268b) is a manifold whole whose parts, having continuity, are intrinsically differentiated by their relation to the whole. The various analogical uses of the term *continuity*, which cover both physical and mathematical domains and encompass extensive and non-extensive manifolds, give breadth to this description. Relative to the primary analogate, which is the extensive continuum, the parts may be understood under two formalities: as analytic parts or as compositive parts. Thus there are two common definitions of the continuum: (1) a manifold whole that is divisible without end into analytic parts, of which there is no smallest; and (2) a manifold whole, the extremities of whose compositive parts are one.

5. The origin of the notion of continuum is most readily traced to the sensible experience of physical *extension* (5:766d), which is the first formal effect of dimensive quantification, manifesting factual material unity but remaining subject to division. In addition to the static continuity of extensive magnitudes, however, there are also non-static or flowing continua, viz, motion [§18.7] and time [§19.5]. Continuity is logically related to *contiguity* and *consecutiveness*, all three referring to extension but constituting a different ordering of parts. A manifold is consecutive if some element of a different nature intervenes between any part and any other part ordered to the former. The parts are contiguous when nothing of a different nature intervenes, though the parts are bounded; they are continuous when they have a common boundary. A continuum is essentially one, though it has distinguishable parts, whereas both contiguous entities and consecutive manifolds are pluralities, the former

with parts distinguished and bounded, the latter with parts separated.

6. According to the definition given, all continua are divisible into parts that are themselves divisible continua; and since such division does not add anything, the positions of the divisions must be marked by pre-contained *indivisibles* (7:478c). Again, since indivisibles are non-extended an extensive continuum cannot be composed of indivisibles, although it can be terminated by them, as a line segment is by points.

7. With the invention of analytic geometry the notion of continuity has been extended to the realm of the *discrete*. By a pure convention the integers may be placed in one-to-one correspondence with points in a linear continuum marking unit segments; hence, by extension, there should be correspondence between the points within each segment and some numerical value less than one. The genetic development of fractional, irrational, and other analogates to natural numbers chronologically followed the requirements for solutions of various algebraic equations of increasing complexity, and ultimately involved variables that should assume numerical values continuously according to some functional rule. The assumption of *continuous variability* was founded first on the intuitive notions of the calculus and theory of limits, later upon the more rigorous developments in analysis and the theory of functions and series, where the transcendental and transfinite numbers (10:563d) also come to be explored. (For a discussion of physical continua, see 4:270b.)

## §65. SYMBOLIC LOGIC

1. *Symbolic logic* (8:962b) is generally viewed as a modern version of formal logic [§2.4] and is referred to variously as mathematical logic, logistic, and the algebra of logic. (Some dispute whether it is actually an extension of traditional logic, because it is not concerned with second intentions and seems to be only a method of calculation; in this view the two are spoken of as logics only equivocally—see 8:957c.) In any event

symbolic logic differs from traditional logic in its extensive use of symbols similar to those used in mathematics, and in its concern with *formalism* (5:1023d), much of which has evolved from research into the nature of mathematics. Symbolic logicians attempt to deduce logical laws from the smallest possible number of principles, i.e., axioms and rules of inference, and to do this with no hidden assumptions or unexpressed steps in the deductive process, following the ideal of an *axiomatic system* (1:1140a).

2. A fundamental distinction in symbolic logic is that between constants and variables. A *variable* is a symbol that can be replaced by a *constant* or by a complex formula. If a constant is replaced by a variable in a sentence or proposition, the result is a *function;* this is a schema for a sentence or proposition and in itself is neither true nor false. Functions may be transformed back into sentences or propositions by prefixing a *quantifier* to them. There are two types of quantifiers: the universal quantifier, "for all *x*," and the existential quantifier, "there is at least one *x* such that."

3. Symbols are generally divided into two types: *functors* (or predicates) and *arguments;* the general rule is that functors determine arguments. Arguments are either names (substantives) or sentences. Functors may be of three general types: (1) name-forming and sentence-forming functors; (2) name-determining and sentence-determining functors; and (3) functors that determine different numbers of arguments, viz, one-place, two-place, three-place, or, in general, *n*-place functors. In accordance with these principles of division, symbolic logic may itself be seen as divided into three main parts: (1) *propositional* logic, in which all functors are sentence-determining; (2) the logic of *predicates* and *classes,* which treats of name-determining functors; and (3) the logic of *relations,* which is concerned with special properties of functors that determine two or more arguments. In what follows attention will be restricted to propositional logic only.

4. *Propositional logic* is concerned exclusively with sentences or propositions that may be constructed by means of so-called truth functors. Truth functors are sentence-forming, sentence-

determining, generally one- and two-place functors that can be used to form sentences whose truth value depends exclusively on the truth value of their arguments and not on their meanings. *Truth value* in propositional logic is twofold (on which account it is called a two-valued logic): it may be either the value of truth (T or 1) or the value of falsity (F or 0). An example of a truth functor is *negation*, since the value of a negated true sentence is falsity and the value of a negated false sentence is truth, and this independently of the sentences' meanings. The most widely employed truth functors, apart from negation ("it is not the case that ...") are the *logical sum* ("either ... or ..." in the sense of "either or both"), the *logical product* ("... and ..."), *material implication* ("if..., then ..."), *equivalence* ("if and only if ..., then ..."), and *disjunction* ("either ... or ..." in the sense of "not both ... and ..."). Much of propositional logic is concerned with showing equivalences and other relationships that obtain between truth functors of the various types and in various combinations.

    5. The truth functor known as *material implication* is most important for understanding how symbolic logic differs from traditional formal logic. This functor determines two sentences, $p$ and $q$, written as its arguments in the form "if $p$, then $q$," in such a way that the functor is true for all possible truth values of $p$ and $q$ except the one where $p$ is true and $q$ is false, in which event the functor is false. When this stipulation is taken as a definition of "if ..., then ...,"the resulting implication has a different significance from the conditional compound of ordinary discourse [§4.7]. This arises from the fact that its involvement with truth value alone abstracts from, ignores, or leaves behind some of the ordinary elements of meaning of the conditional compound. Some authors make this abstraction the central point of their evaluation of material implication, arguing that it cannot express the intentional character of the conditional, which must lie in the relation of meaning between the component propositions, viz, the antecedent and the consequent [§5.10]. Others, while recognizing differences between material implication and the conditional of ordinary discourse, argue that material impli-

cation expresses a partial meaning of this conditional. Every conditional whose antecedent is true and whose consequent is false must be considered a false compound proposition; it is this element of the conditional that is expressed by material implication. Since material implication has a "weaker" meaning than the conditional compound, material implication can always be asserted when a strict conditional obtains, although the converse is not true. This "weaker" type of inference, however, has the value that it makes possible a purely mechanical process resembling, in its results, a deductive process based on the recognition of meanings of what is stated in the antecedent and the consequent. Using it, moreover, one may derive all propositional logic, and indeed verify most of traditional formal logic, from very few axioms and rules. It is for this reason that mathematical logicians regard propositional logic as the simplest and most basic part of their science, which provides the framework, so to speak, for all other types of logical analyses and deduction. (See also *computing machines,* 4:96d, *cybernetics,* 4:557d, and *game theory,* 6:276d.)

# CHAPTER 11.

# PHILOSOPHY OF THE NATURAL SCIENCES

## §66. PHILOSOPHY OF SCIENCE

1. *Science* in its modern understanding (12:1192c) does not have precisely the same signification as the earlier term from which it derives, *scientia,* which denotes mediate intellectual knowledge that is true and certain because acquired through a prior knowledge of principles or causes [§13]. There is no full agreement on the definition of science in the modern sense, although most are agreed that some intellectual knowledge is scientific and some non-scientific, and that the scientific enterprise is an effort to find the order of things and to assign reasons for this order. The term is generally applied to the result of systematically using a hypothetico-deductive method in a field of inquiry, which yields conclusions with a high degree of probability that yet fall short of certitude [§67.1]. Science has thus become an analogical term legitimately but diversely applicable to many differing disciplines in a set wherein perfectly demonstrated knowledge ranks as the prime analogate.

2. *Philosophy of science* (12:1215b) is a discipline concerned with the philosophical problems associated with modern science, such as the meaning and interpretation of scientific concepts, laws, and theories, the logical structure of science, and the methodology by which it attains its results. Much of the material for the study of the philosophy of science is drawn from the history of science (12:1193a-1212c); in some areas of investigation, moreover, where the interpretation of mathematical results assumes critical importance, the discipline makes contact with,

and overlaps with, the philosophy of mathematics in its applied aspects [§63]. Definitions of the philosophy of science vary widely depending on the philosophical orientation of its practitioners, most of whom are logical positivists or empiricists [§101.1], but an increasing number of whom identify themselves with Kantian or realist traditions. The general tendency among the former is to see the scientist as engaged in explicitly formulating laws and theories, frequently in mathematical form because based on experiments involving measurement, and the philosopher of science as concerned explicitly with understanding their meaning. Others see the philosopher of science as practicing the logic, or the epistemology, or even the metaphysics of science, and so describe the discipline as a second-order criteriology [§37.1] The more traditional view would locate philosophy of science among the disciplines that function within the first order of abstraction and so study the world of nature or material being [§13.4]. Its practice presupposes a knowledge of logic and epistemology, but it itself is not concerned with second intentions or with the validity of knowledge as such. Rather it is concerned with man's understanding of nature [§17] as this is attained using the special methodology and the conceptual apparatus of modern science. As such, it is a specialization within the domain of science and natural philosophy that is concerned with an evaluation of man's attempts to understand nature, using all the means at his disposal, both scientific and philosophical.

3. Recent work on the structure of *scientific revolutions* (16: 402d) has stressed the importance of the *sociology of science* in understanding the scientific enterprise generally. According to one theory, normal science has associated with it certain *paradigms* or model solutions to problems that are agreed upon and accepted in the scientific community. Such paradigms account for the coherence of scientific investigation by assuring its unity and its intelligibility, and they also exercise a control over normal science by determining what counts as a fact or as a problem, the method to be used to investigate it, and how to interpret the result. When sufficient anomalies are uncovered that resist resolution by prevailing paradigms, then science moves into an extra-

ordinary state different from that of normal science, and a scientific revolution is in progress. This is not over until a new paradigm has been discovered and adopted, which then becomes the model for setting up new problems and solutions, and a new stage of normal science sets in. Since paradigms themselves are basically different ways of looking at things, such that a succession of them is equivalent to a series of Gestalt switches, there is no cumulative growth of scientific knowledge as a consequence of revolutions. Revolutions themselves are simply non-cumulative developmental episodes in which an older paradigm is replaced in whole or in part by an incompatible new one.

4. The foregoing thesis stresses an important social aspect of science that has hitherto been largely overlooked. Its critics, however, point out the variety and inconsistency of its uses of the term paradigm, the vagueness of the term and the circularity this permits in its use, and the complete *relativism* that it engenders with regard to the results of science as a whole. For those adhering to the thesis there is effectively no *truth* in science, either in what is presently attained or in what the scientific enterprise is tending toward as a limit. Stated otherwise, science itself is lacking in *objectivity*, perhaps even in rationality. This is obviously too extreme a position. Yet it is difficult for anyone who holds that science can yield *only* probable knowledge to make strong claims for objectivity and certitude. Moreover, in reducing scientific method itself to a type of dialectics [§ 12.1], such a position leaves unexplained the lasting contributions made by scientists to man's knowledge of the universe. Thus a more accurate characterization seems to be that science can attain *some* truths with certitude, even though these are frequently buried in the great mass of theories and hypothetical constructions with which scientists surround their work. To the extent that truth and certitude are attained, moreover, they may be accounted for by an occasional realization of the ideal of *scientia*, granted that this accomplishment is rarely claimed, or even acknowledged, by the practicing scientist.

## §67. METHODOLOGICAL CONCEPTS

1. Although one frequently hears the expression "*the* scientific method," it is increasingly recognized that there is no one distinctive *methodology* (9:747a) that characterizes the natural sciences. Most are agreed that science consists in more than a simple collection of *facts*, and must go beyond these at least to the formulation of generalizations or *laws;* in seeking the explanations for laws, moreover, scientists commonly formulate hypotheses and erect these into a coherent system of principles, called a *theory*, from which laws can be deduced. Although laws are based directly on facts, theories generally are not, and so they can only be verified indirectly through their consequences, a process known as *verification* (14:615d) or confirmation. The general procedure that this involves is commonly referred to as hypothetico-deductive methodology, since it consists in formulating an *hypothesis* (7:307d) and deducing from this one or more consequents that can be tested empirically. If the consequent is not verified in experience, then the hypothesis is said to be falsified and rejected, according to the valid mood *tollens* of the conditional syllogism, viz, "if *p*, then *q;* but non-*q;* therefore non-*p*" [§5.10]. If the consequent is verified, on the other hand, one cannot conclude that the hypothesis is true (the fallacy of "affirming the consequent"), but only that it enjoys some degree of probability or verisimilitude. The fact that hypotheses, by their conjectural nature, cannot be directly certified in experience, precludes the use of the only other valid mood of the conditional syllogism, *ponens*—which goes "if *p*, then *q;* but *p;* therefore *q*"—and so creates the general methodological problem. This, it should be noted, is essentially a logical view of the problem and even as such is over-simplified, but since it expresses a common notion of scientific *explanation* (5:762b) it offers a convenient basis for the discussion that follows.

2. The notion of *fact* (5:786a) is more complex than appears at first sight. A fact of ordinary experience is usually expressed in language and so is somewhat language-dependent,

becoming fully intelligible only within a particular linguistic system. Similarly, a fact expressed in the language of science frequently presupposes a complete conceptual system without which the fact itself is unintelligible. Some would hold that there are no pure facts in science, that every fact is "theory-laden" in the sense that so-called factual statements involve some theoretical construction and therefore can be interpreted only within the context of a particular theory. Much the same can be said about indirect measurements and alleged experimental confirmations of abstruse theories. These considerations should have a sobering influence on the scientist who tends to read too much into his science; yet to insist that there are no facts in science, or that all measurements and experiments are hopelessly imbedded in unverified theory, is to give science over to an ultimate skepticism and to despair of its ever attaining definitive knowledge of the physical universe.

3. Frequently what is alleged as a fact is actually a measurement, and this is capable of more precise analysis. A *measurement* (9:528b) is a process or technique of correlating numbers with things that are not patently numbered in the order of nature [§17.7]; usually what is measured are quantities [§9.5], although appropriate techniques can also be devised for measuring qualities [§9.6]. (1) *Quantitative* measurements presuppose a unit, which may be one that occurs naturally or one fixed by convention; such a unit must be homogeneous with the thing measured, and must be invariant throughout the measuring process. Moreover, a measurement is not merely a physical process but involves also an intellectual operation, a judgment of comparison between the object measured and the measuring unit. (2) *Qualitative* measurements are of two types, extensive and intensive; the first arises from the quantification a quality receives from the extension of the body in which it is present, whereas the second is associated with the degree of intensity of the quality itself (12:4a). The measurement of the extensive aspect of physical qualities, being effectively the same as the measurement of length, area, and volume, has the same requirements as that for quantitative measurement. Measurements of a quali-

ty's intensive aspect are usually more difficult: sometimes this is ascertained from an effect, i.e., the change the quality produces in a body other than that in which it is subjected, called an *instrument*, sometimes from a cause, i.e., from the agent that produces the quality's intensity in the subject. It should be noted that no physical measurement can be made to an infinite degree of accuracy, but this need not preclude its validity, so long as a judgment can be made of the range of magnitudes between which the result attained may be reduplicated.

4. A physical *law* (11:334c) is usually construed as a generalization from facts or from measurements; expressed mathematically, it states a functional relationship between variables, usually few in number. Such a statement presupposes that all other possible variables actually remain constant; again, since a measurement may be graphed as a point indicating the simultaneous values of two variables, a law may be likened to a line drawn through a succession of such points. These considerations pose problems for the philosopher, since it is impossible to know all the variable factors affecting a physical object, and since an infinite number of lines can be drawn through a finite number of points; how, on such bases, is one to make a valid generalization? In answer, some adopt an instrumentalist view of scientific laws, holding that they are neither true nor false but merely symbolic representations that enable their users to predict future events or to contrive experiments. Others, under the attraction of symbolic logic [§65], assign to them a truth value but admit to insuperable difficulties in deciding their truth; therefore they retreat to the level of formal analysis where they can speak of law-like statements rather than laws themselves, and seek ways, such as their ability to warrant counter-factual inference, to distinguish law-like statements from other statements. The view of critical realism (11:335c), on the other hand, admits to laws having a truth and an ontological basis in the natures of physical agents and reagents, which are themselves a principle of *uniformity* (14:396b), and can be recognized as such through the work of man's intellect.

5. Associated with the difficulties of knowing uniformities

in nature as expressed by scientific law is the *problem of induction* (16:217d). The problem is stated by inquiring how, on the basis of a limited number of instances, one can make a universal generalization, particularly when the next instance one examines may disconfirm the generalization and show it not to be true. Those who restrict themselves to the use of empirical methods attempt to avoid the problem by assigning only a probability (and not truth) to any general statement, and then measure that probability in terms of the amount of evidence confirming the given statement. This weakens, of course, the ontological claims that can be made in the name of science. Realists oppose these and other efforts to justify induction [§5.11] on the grounds that they are misguided, since they implicitly seek to reduce all induction to deduction, and that they are, despite their formal elegance, quite out of touch with scientific practice. It is simpler, for them, to maintain that scientists commonly make valid causal inferences to the truth of their laws from the objects they study, because they attain sufficient *a posteriori* knowledge of the natures of these objects to justify such inferences.

6. A *theory* (14:73d) is a coherent set of principles that form a frame of reference for a field of inquiry and from which laws can be deduced. It differs from a law in that a law, apart from logical quantifiers such as the term "all," contains no terms that do not appear in the observation statements on which it is based; a theory, on the other hand, does contain non-logical terms that do not appear in laws or observation statements. For example, a law might be "All copper is a conductor of electricity," where each of the terms except the "all" stands for something that is in some way observable, whereas a theory would be "All conductors contain free electrons," where the "free electrons" designates something that is not observable. The entities named by such non-observational terms are referred to as theoretical entities, and these evoke interesting philosophical questions relating to their ontological status. Some philosophers hold that theoretical entities (such as the two hundred elementary particles discussed in high-energy physics) are as

real as the tables and chairs of ordinary experience, whereas
others regard them as theoretical constructs that serve an instrumental function but have no extramental existence. For an empiricist, theories are obviously much more difficult to verify than
laws; realists, on the other hand, do not preclude the possibility
of arriving at knowledge of the existence and nature of theoretical entities by reasoning from their effects to them as proper
causes.

7. Closely connected with the understanding of theories is
the use of *models and analogies* (16:295d) in science. A model
is an idealized or postulated representation of an unobservable
entity or process, such that the elements of the representation
are analogous to entities that are at least partly understood from
elsewhere [§31.5]. Associated with the model is a theory indicating how the model may be expected to behave and so per-
mitting specific predictions to be made; on the success of these
the warrant of the model mainly depends. Instrumentalists and
realists again disagree on the role and value of models in scientific research. The former see them merely as instruments for
calculation and control, whereas the latter view them as providing a partial (and analogous) insight into the structures of
the real, and thus as enabling the mind to grasp the existence
and natures of entities that transcend the order of phenomena.

## §68. PHYSICAL SCIENCES

1. *Classical mechanics* (9:532d) is the science of the local
motion [§18.3] of material bodies; it was among the first of the
modern sciences to assume definitive form and provides conceptual apparatus that is used by most of the physical sciences.
Among its concepts that are of interest to philosophers are the
following. (1) *Force* (5:1002a) has the general meaning of
a power of action or of overcoming a resistance; it is defined
in Newtonian physics as the product of mass and acceleration,
and thus is operationally linked to the concept of mass. (2) *Mass*
(9:412b) is often used, though improperly, as a synonym for

matter [§16.3] or for a not definitely determined "quantity of matter"; in its scientific meaning it denotes merely the inertia of a body that characterizes its acceleration under the influence of a given force. Newton originally defined it in terms of the density and the volume of the matter contained, but since density is in turn defined using mass, his definition is regarded as circular. Mach offered a more acceptable operational definition that, based on an arbitrary but definite body being taken as the standard unit of mass, permits the mass of any other body to be determined unambiguously by physical operations; this procedure would suggest that mass itself is a relative concept. (3) *Energy* (5:343c) has the modern meaning of the ability to do work; it is a concept with a long history, has taken on many different meanings, and figures in important principles such as that of the conservation of energy and that of mass-energy equivalence [§68.3]. It is a good example of a complex, constructed concept that has no simple reference to the objects of ordinary experience, whose meaning and ontological import can only be discerned through an evaluation of the entire conceptual network of which it is an integral part. Yet to say that this and like concepts are mere conventions with no ontological significance whatever is to rob mechanics of all value as a science of the real. (4) *Gravitation* (6:710d) refers to the motion of bodies as they approach each other under the influence of gravity. In Newtonian mechanics gravity is the force by which all bodies in the universe attract one another and is a function of their mass; it is frequently conceived as a pull, though Newton himself did not endorse this interpretation. According to Einstein gravitation is but a manifestation of the curvature of space-time, itself determined by the distribution of masses or energies in the universe.

2. Newton's *laws of motion* (10:32a) formulate the basic principles of classical mechanics; though extremely useful, their ontological status is the subject of much debate, and illicit philosophical inferences, extending to a rejection of proofs for God's existence [§20], have been drawn from them. Strictly speaking these are not laws in the sense already discussed [§67.4]; a

detailed examination of them shows that they are (1) not *a priori* truths, (2) not evident from experience, (3) principles based on limit concepts, (4) not entirely conventional, and (5) theoretical rather than experimental laws in the sense of inductive generalizations that can be verified within definite limits. (For philosophical implications, see 10:34d-35d.)

3. The *laws of thermodynamics* (14:81b) govern all forms of energy and mass-energy conversion; because of this they are frequently taken as principles of universal validity and a world view is built upon them. This is what underlies various thermodynamic arguments for or against the "thermal death" of the universe, creation in time, free will, and the existence of God. Most of these are illicit philosophical inferences, for the following reasons: (1) the laws are extended far beyond the range for which they have been experimentally verified; (2) very little can be deduced from the laws without the aid of additional assumptions; and (3) the sense attributed to the laws is rarely precise; more particularly, (a) the first law is neither true by definition nor essential for the construction of physical theory, and (b) the concept of entropy in the second law is not uniquely defined, and for every different definition of entropy something different can be said about the validity, range, and interpretation of the second law.

4. *Quantum theory* (12:8a) is a mathematical model of the atomic and subatomic domain that yields correct quantitative predictions for a very extensive list of experimental phenomena. It is particularly of interest to philosophers because of its incorporation of the Heisenberg *uncertainty principle* (14:385d), which is seen to have important implications regarding *determinism* (4:811a) and *indeterminism* (7:430d) in the universe. Some hold that the Heisenberg's uncertainty relations express subjective indeterminacies, i.e., they refer to man's imperfect knowledge of things, not to things themselves, whereas others hold that they express objective indeterminacies, i.e., they refer to something that characterizes matter or reality. The two positions are not mutually exclusive, for it may well be that there is ontological indeterminacy in the universe (lodged not in absolute

chance but in the potency of primary matter [§16.3]) and that this grounds epistemological indeterminacy because of man's subjective limitations in comprehending it. Again, as in the case of thermodynamics, one should be wary of extrapolating interpretations that relate to the sub-structure of matter to the domain of ethical or religious inquiry, e.g., proposing such theories as arguments for the existence of free will or of God's influence in the world. (See also *probability*, 11:815a, and *randomness*, 12: 79b.)

5. *Relativity* (12:224a) is the generic name given to two physical theories created by Albert Einstein, known separately as the special theory of relativity and the general theory of relativity. In the first the laws of physics remain the same for all frames of reference in uniform relative motion, whereas in the second they remain the same for all frames of reference accelerating with respect to one another. Both are highly complex theories developed through the use of non-Euclidean geometries; they have interesting implications with regard to the concepts of causality, simultaneity, length contraction, time dilation, and the curvature of space, and they generate a number of intriguing paradoxes—all of which defy understanding and resolution without a proper physical interpretation of the mathematical formalism in which the theories are expressed.

6. The *structure of matter* (9:478d) is of major interest in *chemistry* (3:535d), but it is also a subject of perennial discussion by philosophers. Modern explanations of the properties of matter in bulk are based on the *atomic theory* (1:1014d) and the view that all chemical elements are made up of atoms, which in a chemical compound are combined into larger complexes called molecules. The composition of aggregates out of elements, it should be noted, is not an alternative to the matter-form composition of substances [§16], known as *hylomorphism* (7:284c), since matter and form are co-constituting substantial principles; as such they are not to be confused with *elements* (5:250a), which enter into the structure of compounds but whose change itself requires a matter-form explanation. No inconsistency need be involved, however, in invoking both a substantial composition

and a structural composition when explaining the properties of bodies. *Elementary particles* (5:251a) are unstable sub-atomic components of elements and on this account are not themselves called elements. They are theoretical entities that pose philosophical problems relating to their extramental existence, their so-called creation and annihilation, and their relation to more ultimate substrates such as energy and primary or proto-matter (see 5:261c-263b).

7. The *universe*, from the viewpoint of its *origin* (14:461a) and its *structure* (14:464c), is studied in astronomy (1:988d), but it is likewise discussed in philosophy of the physical sciences. As to origin there are two competing theories: the first concludes to the existence of a large-scale evolutionary development of the universe as a whole; the second, called the steady-state theory, postulates the continuous creation of matter to compensate for the decrease in density due to the expansion of the universe and to avoid the concept of a general evolutionary change. Observational tests to date generally support the first theory and assign the universe an evolutionary age of the order of $10^{10}$ years. The actual creation [§47.2] of the universe in time cannot be strictly proved or disproved on the basis of either theory. With regard to structure the universe or cosmos is taken to mean the assemblage of galaxies, clusters of galaxies, and intergalactic matter that are within the limit of observational techniques; present-day discoveries through radio astronomy and space exploration (16:422c) are yielding information at too rapid a rate for any simple conclusions to be drawn. The overall configuration of the universe, however, constituted of millions of galaxies that are thought to be receding from each other, continues to be discussed in terms of the curved space-time of general relativity, wherein the universe as a totality is seen as finite but unbounded.

## §69. LIFE SCIENCES

1. *Biology* (2:566b) is a systematic body of knowledge concerned with organisms and their vital processes; it developed as

a science in relative independence from physics and chemistry, being more closely associated with *medicine* (9:581a) in its origins. Although it employs methodological canons similar to those already discussed, it does not have well-articulated laws or unified theories to the same degree as the physical sciences; instead it is organized around various unifying themes or concepts, such as that of *organism* (10:757a), *evolution* (5:685b), or the *molecular* basis of life (see 2:561b). The philosopher of science is interested in a number of questions relating to the logical and epistemological characteristics of the life sciences (8:736b) generally, such as whether there are any distinctively biological concepts and whether the basic principles of biology have the same relation to the discipline as do those of physics. For example, do such concepts as vital organization, heredity, and purposive behavior have a more intimate or direct relationship to ordinary experience than the empirically based but partially stipulated definitions of concepts such as force, mass, and energy [§68.1]? Is prediction as important in biology as it is in physics? Would it be possible to deduce the basic principles of biology from a suitably chosen set of principles from physics and chemistry? There are no simple answers to these questions, perhaps because biological concepts are so distinctive, perhaps because biology itself lacks a sufficiently powerful theory to enable it to specify principles governing basic normal vital processes and to explain systematically all deviations from these principles.

2. The problem of the reduction of life processes to explanations in terms of the inorganic is usually discussed under the rubric *biological mechanism* (9:541a). Just as *mechanism* (9:537d) itself attempts to explain the entire physical world through the principles of mechanics, so biological mechanism broadly attempts to reduce all vital operations to the laws of physics and chemistry. There are various ways of proposing this, however, which may be categorized as follows: (1) *physical* mechanism holds that biological laws may be derived from a set of postulates including the basic laws of physics and chemistry and a small set of additional, compatible postulates; (2) *biological* mechanism in the strict sense is partially defined by its

opposition to *vitalism* (14:724d) in the latter's attempt to intro-
duce non-empirical factors into biology; it recognizes the possibility, however, that some biological laws may elude reduction
to those governing physical or chemical processes; and (3) *philosophical* or Cartesian mechanism is a more or less *a priori* claim
that processes are clearly and distinctly understood only when
they can be conceived mechanically. Most philosophers favor the
weak reductionism of the second type, since it permits the search
for underlying mechanisms in a theoretical way, without ruling
out other ways of understanding vital processes and their principles [§22].

3. Related to the problem of reductionism is that of *biogenesis*
(2:563c), the process by which life [§21.1] has its origin. The
term properly refers to the way in which living things always
arise through the agency of pre-existing organisms; its opposite is
abiogenesis, the generation of living things from inanimate
sources. Present-day abiogenetic theories are better designated by
the term *biopoesis,* which holds that abiogenesis is not an on-
going phenomenon and that only the first living form or forms
arose in the remote past from inorganic matter by spontaneous
generation. Biopoesis has received some experimental support
through the discovery of complex protein molecules and of
viruses, but as a theory it is still highly conjectural. The *virus*
(14:711d) is believed by some to be the smallest "living" form,
but actually it is an obligate intracellular parasite and cannot
reproduce outside a living cell; until someone succeeds in culti-
vating a virus *in vitro,* many scientists will not accept it as the
missing link between the living and the non-living. But from the
viewpoint of hylomorphism [§68.6], it may be noted, biopoesis
is not impossible. One can hold that living forms below the level
of the human pre-exist in the potentiality of primary matter
[§16.3]; this granted, the problem becomes one of identifying
an efficient cause or cosmic agent of sufficient power to educe
such forms from matter [§35.8]. That plants have properties not
found in the inanimate is only to be expected: water has properties different from the hydrogen and oxygen from which it is
constituted, and even a watch has properties not found in its

parts. Thus there seems to be no repugnance to biopoesis on the part of the organism's intrinsic causes; granted a sufficiently powerful and knowledgeable agent, biopoesis could take place in the order of nature.

4. A similar problem is that of *organic evolution* (5:685b). Evolution may be defined as an irreversible process of developmental change in time, which during its course generates novelty, diversity, and higher levels of organization; organic evolution would propose that all known species of plants and animals descended by a natural process of modification from a single or a few organic forms over a period of perhaps two billion years [§99.2]. The problem is complicated for the philosopher by the difficulty of defining natural species [§8.2] and of explaining, from the viewpoint of causality, how the higher can come from the lower. Granted that such species can be defined accurately, the resolution of the latter problem can possibly be found in the complex interplay of both univocal and equivocal agents [§35.8] acting upon organic matter to produce an effect slightly different from the univocal parent. Mutations are caused by many factors outside the univocal agent, such as cosmic rays and chemical changes caused by atmospheric conditions. Again, many parent-progeny endowments remain latent and are induced only by the requirements of adaptation. No single univocal agent is sufficient to explain, say, the origin of the bird from reptile stock, but a unified complex of univocal and equivocal causes, some acting quite *per accidens* over a long period of gradual change, may be sufficient reason for the origin of the new species. This unified convergence of univocal and equivocal causes would also be sufficient to explain the natural origin of life by biopoesis, provided that the dynamic order of causes could be accounted for. Although the development of life thus manifests the presence of some opportunism and randomness, the dynamic order of the process as a whole still requires explanation.

5. It is this *dynamic order* of the organic world—so dependent upon the order of the microcosm on the one hand and upon the order of the megalocosm on the other—that raises for philosophers the question whether or not the ultimate explanation

of evolution demands the existence of a transcendent cause as *designer*. The classical arguments for the existence of God obtain with as much force, if not more, in a dynamic unfolding order as they do in a universe of static order alone. Thus it would appear that organic evolution must be complemented by some form of theism to be complete. This is not to say that God in his intelligent providence and governance [§46.7] of this dynamic order is seen to make a miraculous intrusion upon the natural causes and laws with which he has endowed his creation. In a real sense the laws of nature *are* the operation of his governance. But the dynamic order of nature, especially in the unfolding process of evolution, makes the inference of a sufficient coordinating and governing cause seem a necessity.

6. *Genetics* (6:331b) is the branch of biology that is concerned with *heredity* (6:1056a), i.e., the transmission of traits from parents to offspring; it is the development of this science that has supplied information concerning possible mechanisms whereby the evolution of organic species could be explained. The central concept is that of the *gene* (6:324a), which is analogous to the theoretical entities of modern physics; extensive research has been done on its chemical structure in terms of DNA and other molecules to explain various phenomena of inheritance (6:324c). Apart from its speculative aspect, the philosopher is interested in genetics because of the ethical dimensions of its applied aspect, usually spoken of as *genetic engineering* (16:188c). Eugenicists have frequently thought that genetics would supply society with the means of improving the inborn qualities of the human race (5:627c). Ethicists in the present day question the morality of many of the techniques proposed to do this, e.g., *in vitro* fertilization and cloning; moreover, since genetic experimentation is irreversible, they regard the more grandiose plans of positive eugenics as at ground unethical. If human genetics is to be practiced at all it should be in the direction of therapeutics rather than toward the attainment of questionable social goals.

## §70. TECHNOLOGY

1. *Technology* (13:967c) is closely associated in the minds of many with modern science, although it has had a long history of relative independence from science and its methods. In its modern understanding it is defined as the application of scientific knowledge to practical purposes in a particular field. Technology has been of special concern to sociologists, who are interested in studying its social effects (13:971d): among these may be included the gradual displacement of men by machines, with the consequent lightening of the physical burdens of *work* (14:1015c); the increased ability it has given men to deal effectively with their environment; and the economic effects it has produced in the areas of productivity, employment, and dislocations in the labor force. From this perspective it is seen as having brought obvious and great benefits, as well as having created social and economic problems [§80.5] that are not easily solved.

2. The *philosophy of technology* (16:446a) is a discipline of quite recent invention. The term itself has a wide variety of meanings, including (1) social or ethical critiques of technology, (2) religious critiques, (3) treatments of technology from the specialized perspectives of phenomenology or existentialism aimed at discerning the "pure essence" or the "existential meaning" of technology, (4) metaphysical analyses attempting to situate the phenomenon of technology in a larger speculative context other than the religious or the phenomenological, (5) studies based on the techniques of linguistic analysis focusing on the meaning and uses of the term technology and related expressions, (6) the common-sense "philosophy" of practicing engineers, applied scientists, and science managers, and (7) what some refer to as "comprehensive philosophies of technology," i.e., studies that combine two or more of the above approaches in an attempt to produce a philosophical synthesis of the meaning of technology as a phenomenon distinct, but not necessarily separable, from any other subject of philosophical inquiry. From such studies have emerged two traits that seem

to characterize the technological enterprise: (1) its essential relation to, and dependence upon, modern science; and (2) its involvement of a social group that is identifiable as the carrier of technology, viz, the technical community, which includes a large number of scientists, nearly all engineers and technicians, and research managers in government or industry or specialized research institutes. The term technology, then, can be taken to cover this scientific and technical community, including its inner structure and inner functions, its relationships to other social phenomena, its products, its particular values, and its implicit view of human nature [cf. §66.3]. The expression "philosophy of technology" will then mean a set of generalizations or a systematic treatment, in philosophical language, of one or another or all of the above aspects of this social phenomenon.

3. In their *assessment* of technology and its values most philosophers are pessimistic, seeing it a tool in the hands of the ruling class to enslave the masses, the "myth of the machine" that leads to the "pentagon of power," an unmitigated evil and source of alienation, a concealment of authentic Being, and so on [§§102.6, 103.6]. A few are optimistic, proposing that a technology of behavior [§73.4] can lead to a cultural utopia, or that technology itself can be a transforming force in a totally new philosophy of culture that is appropriate to the contemporary world. The latter group includes the futurists, who attempt to develop some form or other of science-based social planning for the future, which they call "futurology."

# CHAPTER 12.

# PHILOSOPHY OF
# THE BEHAVIORAL SCIENCES

## §71. ANTHROPOLOGY

1. Anthropology is commonly defined as the science of both man and his works and so has two main divisions: the study of man from the viewpoint of his origin and biological development, called physical anthropology, and the study of his works, i.e., his social behavior, beliefs, languages, artifacts, etc., called cultural anthropology. *Physical anthropology* (1:605d) covers a wide range of interests and disciplines, but its major fields of investigation include: (1) the study of primates, the taxonomic order in which man is included at the head of the animal kingdom, and not only living primates but fossil primates as well, to determine levels of organization and order of appearance in an evolutionary sequence; (2) the study of fossil man; (3) the study of race (12:42d) and race differences (12:47d) that may be the result of evolutionary processes; (4) the study of evolution in living human populations, especially in terms of genetic factors; and (5) anthropometry, or the study of measurements as applied to man, not only the physical dimensions of his skull, etc., but data obtained by more sophisticated x-ray techniques and indirect methods of quantification.

2. The central interest in physical anthropology is the problem of *human evolution* (5:676a, 16:213d), sometimes discussed under the term *hominization* (16:211d). From a philosophical perspective this is best understood in the context of organic evolution [§69.4]. The anthropological distinction be-

tween the physical and the cultural, however, reinforces the philosopher's insight that man's nature must be defined in terms of both body and spirit. Man is a rational animal, an animal body informed and energized by a spiritual soul [§29]. His intelligence and free choice distinguish him from other primates, and, indeed, from the entire material universe. Man's capacity for culture, for fashioning a technology, for constructing a language, for judging and reasoning, and for creating sciences, arts, societies, laws, and moral and religious codes must be, at root, spiritual. This spiritual capacity cannot have its origins in primate potentialities or in a purely material substrate. The human spirit must have its origin in the immediate creative act of God [§47]. Yet the continuity of man's bodily development from the lower primates to his present state is as well-documented as any animal phylogeny. To reconcile the two requirements these evidences impose, one may describe the origin of the human species as follows. When the hominid body was so disposed by the natural processes governing the rest of primate development, God created and infused the soul of man, elevating what was formerly a hominid to the stature of a new, distinct, and unique species, *homo sapiens*. Philosophers are not in agreement as to whether, besides this divine act of creation and infusion, a further special and immediate disposition of the hominid body was also necessary. Since, in either case, the act of infusion would itself be a further disposition beyond that provided by hominid development, the origin of the whole of man would result from a special divine creative act. But man's animal origins would just as truly stem from the natural process of biological evolution. Thus man would find his origins in the delicately co-ordinated agencies of primate evolution and direct divine causality.

3. *Cultural anthropology* (1:597d) is the other main branch of anthropology; as its name indicates, its central concept is that of *culture* (4:522c). The term culture is not easily defined, but its main characteristics may be described as follows. Culture consists of patterns, implicit and explicit, of and for behavior acquired and transmitted by symbols, constituting the distinctive achievement of human groups, including their embodiment in

artifacts; the essential core of culture consists of traditional ideas (i.e., historically derived and selected ideas) and especially their attached values; and culture systems may, on the one hand, be considered as products of action, on the other, as conditioning elements of further action. Anthropologists usually analyze culture in terms of its component elements: (1) abstract qualities, such as behavioral and cultural patterns and their arrangements; (2) substantive aspects, or the content of the culture; (3) and the organization of this content into systems and subsystems that show some measure of integration. Topics in the second category that interest philosophers include *ethics* in primitive societies (5:578c), primitive *law* (8:560a), and *religion* in primitive culture (12:246c).

4. The growth of culture and cultural change are discussed by anthropologists in terms of various theories, such as (1) *evolutionism*, which discerns analogies between the expansion of cultures and biological evolution; (2) *historicalism*, which seeks to determine the historical causes of the formation of customs and cultures in terms of environment and neighboring influences; and (3) *diffusionism*, which is impressed by the similarities of cultures and explains these by the transmission, or diffusion, of ideas and techniques from one society to another. Philosophers are interested in *cultural evolution* (5:671d) mainly to show how it differs from biological evolution and to emphasize that the extraordinary diversity of human behavior manifests man's essential distinction from other animals, and so confirms the existence of a distinctive nature behind his activities.

5. The major subdivisions of cultural anthropology include *archeology* (1:747a), which is the science and art of reclamation and interpretation of material traces of man's cultural activities in the past; *ethnology*, which is concerned with comparative studies of culture sequence and process, but not those of the prehistoric past—rather ongoing cultures or those for which written records survive; and *linguistics* [§57.1] in both its descriptive and comparative aspects. Social anthropology is sometimes regarded as a specialty within ethnology; there is no clearly defined relationship or distinction between anthropology and

sociology, but some see sociology as being concerned with large, literate communities, especially those of the Western world, whereas anthropology focuses on small, non-literate groups. There is also a blending of anthropology with psychology to produce a subfield of ethnology concerned with the study of culture and personality. Finally, economic anthropology combines aspects of economics and anthropology to discern the influence of economic systems (5:59c) and notions of property (11:859c) on societies and their culture.

## §72. MODERN PSYCHOLOGY

1. A more extensive and detailed study of the behavior of contemporary man is provided by the modern science of *psychology* (11:966d). This discipline differentiated itself from the older, philosophical psychology in the mid-19th century under the attraction of empirical methods provided by the natural sciences (11:970a). It is usually distinguished from the parent discipline on the basis that (1) it is based on controlled observation and experiment, as opposed to spontaneous and common-sense experience, and where possible makes use of measurement [§67.3]; and (2) it is concerned with observable aspects of behavior that can be tested and predicted, and not with non-observable entities such as mind and the soul and its powers. Yet even the latter concern leads it to seek knowledge of the various capacities and dispositions that give behavior consistency and meaning. Thus contemporary psychologists speak of capacities such as intelligence, learning, imagination, memory, perception, and conceptualization, and investigate dispositions such as motives, traits, interests, attitudes, and temperaments. None of these can be observed or measured directly, and thus their study involves the development of indirect methods and quantitative techniques that require interpretation for their proper understanding.

2. The *methodology* (9:750a) of psychology derives from that of the natural sciences [§67], with appropriate adjustments

made to accommodate the complexity of the phenomena being investigated; obviously in human behavior it is more difficult to isolate relevant factors that influence the outcome of a test or experiment and to obtain an objective description of these in quantitative terms by means of measurement. As a consequence there are some nuances in the methodological terms employed, as for example: (1) *hypothesis* means roughly a tentatively suggested answer to a specific problem; it is framed as a question in so specific a way that it can be tested empirically by an experiment or controlled observation; (2) *subjects* are the persons observed, and here sampling and statistics become important, since many factors such as age, education, and cultural background can influence the outcome; (3) *variable* is a generic term for any relevant factor that plays a role in a test or experiment and has to be brought under control; since the more common technique is to employ measurement, the term variable usually connotes that factors can and do vary in a quantitative sense; (4) *control* is a key concept that is not easily defined, since it assumes that all important factors can be isolated and either kept constant or be made to vary in some knowable fashion; (5) *results* are the summarized observations and nothing more; they usually provide the direct answer to the question formulated in the hypothesis; and (6) *interpretations* are inferences that are drawn from results; these have more the character of generalizations, but on this account they are open to discussion and possible non-acceptance.

3. *Measurement* (9:529d) in psychology means the assigning of numbers to quantitative variations in a distinguishable attribute of behavior, or of behaviorally related objects, with the expectation that something true or predictable may be derived from the mathematical properties of the numbers or from their relationship with other variables. The procedures of such measurement are concerned primarily with the construction of a scale or measuring device, and secondarily with the application of that scale to a particular behavior or object, such as occurs in *psychological testing* (11:958d). A wide variety of tests, questionnaires, and inventories have been developed to measure per-

formances, abilities, and aptitudes. It is important to note, however, that these do not measure the individual as such, but only as part of a group; this limitation derives from the ways in which tests are devised and validated, frequently in terms of a percentile ranking or other statistical procedure. Unlike the laws of physics, the generalizations and predictions that result from these procedures are group generalizations and group predictions, and they make no pretense to being directly applicable to any individual's behavior.

4. *Psychometrics* (11:976a) is the discipline that treats generally of the application of mathematical methods to psychology. Among the topics studied are statistical rationale, scaling methods, test item selection, and factor analysis. The discipline is concerned also with devising mathematical models for understanding and predicting behavior; among these may be mentioned systems analysis, theories of perception and learning, decision making, and information theory (7:511b).

5. *Experimental psychology* (5:754a) is sometimes used as a synonym for modern psychology, but more properly it applies to the branch of that discipline that makes extensive use of experimentation. An *experiment,* in this context, is a contrived situation wherein the investigator purposely brings about the event he wants to observe under conditions he himself can vary. It is essentially an instrument of research, and on this account much time and effort is put into experimental design; when it works its value can hardly be exaggerated. It is not the only method available to the psychologist, however, since verbal reports and introspection can also provide valuable information. It is somewhat unfortunate, moreover, that psychologists tend to study those aspects of behavior that lend themselves more readily to experimentation, to the neglect of others that are possibly more important for understanding the human person.

6. Some types of experimentation, particularly those that may prove dangerous to life or well-being, are better performed on lower animals than on humans, for then a more rigorous degree of control and a wider range of stimuli can be employed. This possibility has given rise to a specialization within the

discipline known as *comparative psychology* (4:87b), which makes comparative studies of the behavior of various forms of animal life; a related specialization is *physiological psychology* (11:340b), which explores the behavior of man and of lower animals as this relates to physiological processes and functions, e.g., neural mechanisms, brain stimulation, and hormonal control.

7. Other branches of psychology that employ special methods or techniques include *differential psychology* (4:865d), which is concerned with special approaches and their interrelationships; *developmental psychology* (4:865d), which investigates behavioral changes over the entire life span, including the subfields of *child psychology* (3:572a) and *adolescent psychology* (1:134a); *dynamic psychology* (4:1130b) and *group dynamics* (6:815b), which study the motivations of behavior generally and in groups, respectively; and *social psychology* (13:335d), which is an interdisciplinary study drawing heavily on anthropology, psychology, and sociology to investigate the experiences and behavior of the individual in society [§76].

## §73. SYSTEMS AND THEORIES OF PSYCHOLOGY

1. Psychology in the U.S. is presently characterized by a trend away from *systems and theories* (11:973d); it is largely preoccupied with the limited types of generalizations already discussed and avoids theoretical formulations that go much beyond the observational data. The view of theories in psychology is thus anti-realist and similar to the instrumentalist position in the natural sciences [§67.6-7]: their role is that of instruments, providing a framework within which data may be organized, aiding in the formulation of questions that can guide experimentation, and suggesting interpretations that might be drawn from the data. Yet various systems and theories have been influential in the formation of psychology as a science, and the attitudes they engendered still persist. In the next several paragraphs a brief outline is given of five major systems that have exerted a major influence in the past, and the following paragraphs

summarize the principal theories that continue to attract attention.

2. *Structuralism* is concerned with the analysis of conscious contents in an attempt to identify the elements of consciousness (4:206d) and the laws by which the elements are related. The proper subject of psychology, in this system, is immediate experience, which is experience itself as distinct from what it is that is experienced. The method of investigation of immediate experience is *introspection* (7:597d) or self-observation by a highly trained observer, and its object is to identify and record the elements of conscious experience. The mental elements are also related to physiological responses, which are measured by the elaborate apparatus of psychophysics (11:980a). The philosophical framework that underlies interpretations of results is one of psychophysical parallelism, which itself proposes to solve the mind-body problem (9:866c). Structuralism has little or no influence in contemporary psychology, although in modified form it continues to be of interest in the science of linguistics (16:434a) and in cultural anthropology [§103.2].

3. *Functionalism* defines psychology as the study of mental activity and emphasizes the behavior of adapting to the environment. Consciousness, the primary concern of structuralism, is replaced by the functionalists with behavior, which is viewed as adaptive and purposive. All sensory stimuli affect behavior and all behavior is initiated by some sort of sensory stimulus. Functionalism does not reject introspection as a means of obtaining data, but it broadens the method considerably, gives greater emphasis to laboratory experimentation, and extends this to the use of animal subjects. The scope of investigation is also broadened beyond that of structuralism to include problems of motivation (10:36a) and learning as well as that of attention. This viewpoint has had a profound influence on the development of American psychology.

4. *Behaviorism* (2:227a) is the most influential and possibly the most controversial of all American systems. It defines psychology as the science of behavior and maintains that behavioral acts can be, and should be, described objectively. Terms such

as consciousness and mental life find no place in behaviorism, for behavior itself is regarded as composed entirely of glandular secretions and muscular movements. One of the basic postulates of behaviorism is that there is a strict causal relationship between stimulus and response: so, given the stimulus, one should be able to predict the response, and given the response, he should be able to identify the antecedent stimulus. Although some behaviorists accept the results of psychological tests and verbal reporting, they place emphasis on impersonal observation and use the conditioned-reflex method as the method of choice. The philosophical foundations of behaviorism may be characterized as either an extreme positivism or a naive and mechanistic materialism; unfortunately one or other of these affects the mind-set of many psychologists and is responsible for their antimetaphysical attitudes in the interpretation of results.

5. *Gestalt psychology* (6:455a) was a revolt against the analysis and elementalism that characterized both structuralism and functionalism. The over-riding principle of Gestalt psychology is that the whole dominates the parts and constitutes the primary reality; in light of this principle Gestaltists have investigated all areas of psychology, but the major focus has been in the study of perception (11:115a). Here the primary concern has been on the relationship between perception and its antecedents, in contrast to the emphasis of the behaviorists, who are more interested in the relationship between the antecedents and the behavioral response. The data of Gestalt psychology are immediate unanalyzed experiences, and the characteristic method is introspection, with little emphasis being placed on past experience or learning. The primary contribution of Gestalt psychology as a system is its accentuating the whole-part attitude, which has largely been supported by subsequent investigations; it is still an active force in psychology.

6. *Psychoanalysis* (11:953a) regards psychology as the study of psychopathology with particular emphasis on neuroses; a central concern is the unconscious motivational forces involved in the behavior of the individual. As a system psychoanalysis involves several assumptions: (1) psychic life is determined;

(2) the unconscious (14:387d) plays a predominant role in the determination of behavior; (3) the most important explanatory concepts are motivational or dynamic; and (4) the history of the individual plays an important role in determining contemporary behavior. Freudian psychoanalysis develops a theoretical structure of the mind as a composite mechanism (9: 660b) with three main functional parts: (1) the *id* (7:333b), the reservoir of inherited instinctual impulses and the seat of the deepest part of the unconscious; (2) the *ego* (5:191d), that part of the id which has been modified by relations with the external world and which represents reason and common sense in contrast to the id, which contains the passions, and (3) the *superego* (13:809a), the internalized representative of authority, prohibitions, values, and ideals. The methods advocated by psychoanalysts are basically methods of psychotherapy (11: 985c); principal use is made of hypnosis, dream analysis, and free association as techniques to explore the unconscious. Other systems of depth psychology (4:782a), in addition to Freudian psychoanalysis, are Adlerian *individual psychology* (7:472a) and Jungian *analytical psychology* (1:473b).

7. Just as the term hypothesis has a somewhat different meaning in the behavioral sciences than it has in the natural sciences, so does the term *theory* [§67.6]. Rather than containing a few coherent principles under which all the laws and observational data of a field of inquiry are embraced (a feature partially shared by the notion of system in psychology), a theory in the behaviorial sciences applies to only relatively delimited areas of empirical investigation. Otherwise, however, the criteria employed to assess the scientific sophistication of a theory are similar to those of the physical sciences, viz: (1) formality, i.e., the extent to which the theory can be formulated as a deductive system and is quantitatively expressible; (2) comprehensiveness, i.e., the degree and extent to which it incorporates existing empirical findings; (3) predictive power, i.e., the ability to predict as yet unobserved phenomena; (4) heuristic power, i.e., the capacity to generate meaningful hypotheses for empirical testing; and (5) sensitivity to empirical evidence, i.e., the de-

gree to which the theory can assimilate new data or research findings.

8. The more important theories in present-day psychology include the following: (1) *theories of learning,* which probably show the greatest sophistication; these are mainly under the influence of behaviorism, where emphasis is placed on stimulus-response (S-R) relationships, reinforcement, etc., or of Gestalt psychology, where pattern organization plays an important role and the results are termed cognitive or field theories; (2) *theories of perception,* where neo-behaviorists seek explanations in terms of S-R relationships, Gestaltists on inherent organizing factors; and (3) *theories of personality,* which aim at a higher degree of integration and comprehensiveness than the first two types, but are not so well developed empirically, with the result that the theories are found to be more speculative, rationally based, and somewhat less rigorously stated; many are under the influence of psychoanalysis and existentialist thought, e.g., *existential psychology* (5:728a).

9. Most of the material sketched above applies primarily to the behavior of normal people, although the meaning of *normality* (10:496b) is itself a problem for philosophers. A considerable amount of investigation is devoted, moreover, to *abnormal psychology* (1:24a), to the study of mental disorders (9:655a), and to other matters pertaining directly to psychiatry (11:945a). Branches of psychology that are more related to psychotherapy include *clinical psychology* (3:956b) and *counseling* (4:380b). These are of less interest for the speculative philosopher, although some therapeutic matters raise ethical problems that require solution, e.g., the moral aspects of psychosurgery (11:985a).

## §74. PHILOSOPHY OF THE BEHAVIORAL SCIENCES

The materials discussed in this chapter suggest an observation regarding the *philosophy of the behavioral sciences* generally. This field of study, somewhat like the philosophy of the social sciences [§75.3], is thought to be under-developed by comparison with the philosophy of the natural sciences [§66]. The reason for this is that the disciplines treated, anthropology and psychology, stay rather close to empirical data and make few if any ontological claims; since their main subject of inquiry is man, they can get along with a common-sense notion and the simple reflective knowledge each person has of his own being. Whatever philosophical points need be made, moreover, are more fully considered in philosophical anthropology [§29.1] or philosophical psychology [§21], and so the empirical part of the inquiry can be conducted as though neutral to philosophical commitment. The major philosophical reflection on behavioral disciplines therefore consists of a study of their methodologies and the special type of knowledge these can be expected to yield.

# CHAPTER 13.

# SOCIAL PHILOSOPHY

## §75. SOCIAL PHILOSOPHY AND SOCIAL SCIENCE

1. *Social philosophy,* along with its companion discipline, political philosophy, studies man as he is a member of society; as practical, it is concerned with ordering human acts to the common good, and so conceived its problems are mainly those of social ethics [§49.5]. Social philosophy is not exclusively moral in its interests, however, for in addition it has the task of investigating the nature of social reality, its components, and the relationships that obtain between them. In this investigation it overlaps to some degree with political philosophy [§81]; for purposes here social philosophy will be understood as concerned with the problems of society in general and of the family in particular, leaving the consideration of the state to political philosophy. The basic supposition on which both disciplines depend is that man is a social being; by nature he is dependent on others at every stage of life, for existence and for the fulfillment of physical, emotional, intellectual, social, and even spiritual needs. Furthermore, peace and order in human society require the conformity of individual members to certain expectations in their interaction with each other, whether individually or collectively. Such conformity is essential if the common good [§54.1] is to be attained in family life, in education, in economic behavior, and in various political communities. In its complete understanding, therefore, social philosophy cannot be merely descriptive or analytical; it must also be prescriptive or normative, indicating how men ought to act so as to achieve their perfection in society. [Note that in the *New Catholic Encyclo-*

*pedia* matters relating to social philosophy are frequently combined with those pertaining to social theology (13:314a) under the comprehensive title of *social thought* (13:341d-361b) so as to permit a distinctively Catholic treatment.]

2. *Social science* (13:338b) is a more recent category of knowledge than social philosophy; it is a term applied to disciplines that make specialized studies of society and social relationships, and whose concerns are descriptive and predictive, not prescriptive or normative. Sometimes the social sciences are conceived broadly enough to include the behavioral sciences as well as history; they would thus encompass anthropology, economics, geography, history, jurisprudence, political science, psychology, and sociology. A more recent tendency has been to constitute the behavioral sciences as a distinct category, and, under the influence of behaviorism [§73.4] and of attempts to explain social phenomena psychologically [§72.7], even to reduce all the social sciences to one form or other of behavioral science. Also, since pragmatism as a philosophy is eminently suited to non-prescriptive disciplines, there is a tendency on the part of social scientists to by-pass the traditional normative concerns of social philosophy and to substitute instead one or other kind of philosophy of value [§62].

3. The philosophy of the social sciences is concerned mainly with the problem of choosing various *models* of science that suit the different disciplines (13:338d-340d, 390b-393d) and with investigating the *methodology* (9:753d) that these impose upon them. Since social science developed as a category of knowledge under the attraction of the physical sciences, there have been repeated attempts to adopt models based on the natural sciences (German, *Naturwissenschaften*) for generating a science of society. In general, mathematical methods of physics are not directly applicable, although development of statistics has permitted the use of quantitative procedures and mathematical models are finding increasing use, especially in economics [§67.7]. The principal natural-science models are the mechanical and the biological: the mechanical model stresses the independence of the individual within society and attempts to describe and predict be-

havior on the basis of various forces and conflicts that develop within a competitive society; the biological model likens society to an organism with its own principles of integration that develops and evolves by adjustment and adaptation. Those who favor a mechanical model generally see the basic laws of social life as invariant with respect to place and time, and so as synchronic; the organicists, on the other hand, usually subscribe to historical relativity and to evolutionary theory and see such laws as changing in time, or as diachronic. The other major alternative is a model based on the cultural sciences (German, *Geisteswissenschaften* or *Kulturwissenschaften*), which focuses on man's freedom and moral responsibility and his consequent ability to transcend nature and mechanical forces. Those who subscribe to this model are not so impressed by the methods of the natural sciences, develop techniques for delving into man's intentions, motivations, and capabilities, and focus less on the prediction than on the understanding (*Verstehen*) of his societal behavior [§99.2]. Regardless of the model they adopt, most social scientists employ methods that are similar to those of the behavioral sciences [§72]. They are interested in propositions that are empirically testable, commonly employ operational or stipulative definitions, formulate hypotheses that can be verified or falsified, and collect and analyze data through experimental techniques, questionnaire design, interview methods, etc. The interpretation of their results focuses either on validity, for those who wish to *understand* the socio-cultural realm, or on reliability and precision, for those who aim to *predict* man's behavior in social contexts.

4. *Sociology* (13:400c) as a special science deals with the structure and functions of social pluralities and systems under the aspect of interaction or interdependence. Following the cultural-science model, social action is viewed as rational, motivated behavior, though affected also by non-rational influences; it cannot be studied in physical terms alone, but account must be taken of the meaning of such action for the actors, and so beliefs, attitudes, goals, and values assume considerable importance. One of its central concepts is that of social order,

or the underlying regularity of human social behavior. Sociology differs from the other social sciences precisely in its concern for such common elements of order and conflict that characterize all forms of social life; thus it is distinct from *economics* (5: 61d), which is concerned with social interaction from the point of view of the production, distribution, and consumption of goods and services. *Social work* (13:361b) has a yet more restricted focus: it may be defined as an organized group of services designed to help people meet their needs or to cope more effectively with their problems in social functioning.

## §76. SOCIETY

1. A *society* (13:386b) is a permanent union of human beings who are united by modes of behavior that are demanded by some common end, value, or interest. It is broader in meaning than a *community* (4:80a), which is a natural form of society in which men are more intimately bound by specified ends and natural forces, and an *association* (1:964d), which is a social system freely organized to satisfy particular needs and interests. Since society itself is not possible unless based upon some common moral and legal understanding with social laws and controls to sustain it, some characteristics of associations and communities are found also in society.

2. Guided by experience, and thus by the findings of the social sciences, the social philosopher regards it as empirically established that man can attain the full development of his nature only in association with others. Human nature [§29] therefore constitutes the *ontological basis* for society; it manifests this through its biological, psychological, and theological tendencies. Biologically, man's nature is ordered to marriage [§78] and the family [§79]. Psychologically, the impulse to be a member of a social group and to be appreciated as such is characteristically human. Teleologically, man seeks happiness and conformity with the natural law [§§51.4, 54.3]; both of these, in turn, urge him to establish an order of social life guarantee-

ing freedom and common utility as conditions for the achievement of a fully human existence. In consequence, viewed ontologically; human nature needs social supplementation for its integration; again, since different potentialities are found in individual humans, human nature is capable of bringing about such
supplementation. Hence man is by nature a social animal.

3. Because man is a composite of body and soul, and hence
a person who is responsible [§53.7] for his own conduct, the
society he forms is, unlike other unities, unified by an intrinsic
principle, the self-binding will of its members. In this specific
sense society is a *unity* resulting from an actualized moral order,
a *unitas ordinis*. Nevertheless society rests also on an extrinsic
formative principle that adds to the note of order one of
organization. The reason for this is not only that the self-
binding will of its members is to some extent defective, but
also that the concrete demands of society's intrinsic ends are not
fully recognizable by all its members, and, furthermore, that
the lasting realization of the social end from one generation
to another can be secured only by organizational means that are
legal or administrative.

4. The function of society is to actualize its inherent end,
the *common good* (4:15a), viz, the conditions that make a
fully human existence possible for all its members [§54.1]. Because the individual depends on others to bring about the end of
society—the principle of solidarity [§80.4]—the individual good
is part of the common good. Again, the individual as a member
of the community has to achieve ends and realize values on his
own responsibility—the principle of subsidiarity [§80.5]—to the
extent that this is possible. But the common good is a reality
over and above the good that individuals can achieve separately;
consequently, in realizing the common good, society emerges as
a *reality* of a special kind. It cannot be defined simply in terms
of the disjunction between substance and accident [§§9, 34];
society is not a substance, but neither is it a mere ontological
accident. Both nature and nurture are important for forming
the fully human existence of the individual as a person, and
to this extent the category of relation [§9.7] is not alone suffi-

cient to describe the being of society. For it would suggest that society is a structure consisting in relations between fully developed persons, whereas man reaches the fullness of his human existence only through social interaction. It is, of course, true that the existence of society depends upon the existence of man who ontologically is a substance [§22.2-3]; but society also forms the person and brings him to the state of maturity, without which he would not be fit to leave his fellow men and live in solitude.

5. Since the ends to be realized through social cooperation are many, society necessarily has a pluralistic *structure*. This pluralism is of two kinds. (1) One is derived *directly* from the social nature of man, in which are rooted not only such vital structures as the family [§79] and the state [§82] but also the territorial as well as the vocational community and the ethnic-cultural group. Because based directly on human nature as such, they are found everywhere in mankind and in its history in one form or another. (2) The other is based *indirectly* on human nature, namely, on common purposes open to man's choice [§50.6]. This kind of pluralism intensifies in proportion to the growth of population and to the development of civilization. It results from the articulation and particularization of both material and mental ends and values, whose pursuit results in an increasing variety of associations and in a growing measure of socialization (13:383b), i.e., closer interdependence among men. In view of both sources of pluralism the structure of society is always historically patterned: fundamentally it is grounded in human nature, but in its concrete aspects it is continually changing.

6. Only a person [§29.6] is capable of having responsibility and of acting accordingly. Yet society as a whole is responsible for actualizing its own ends, and it carries out this responsibility through its various organs. Therefore society is a person; but because its bond of unity consists in a common responsibility it is called a *moral person*, to distinguish it from the physical person of the individual man. It is also called a *juridical person* because it possesses natural rights by reason of its responsibili-

ties and is capable of legally relevant action. Thus person itself is an analogical term. Society may also be called an organism, in the sense that organisms have intrinsic ends; so it is common to speak of the body politic, its members, and its organs. Less properly is society a mechanism, although it can be modeled along mechanical lines as a harmony of self-balancing interests (individualism) or as a unity organized for extrinsic ends by a ruling group (collectivism) [§75.3].

7. There are many *kinds* of society. (1) The first classification is that into the *all-embracing* society, such as the state [§82] or the organized society of nations, and *particular* societies, referred to also as intermediate structures, because they serve as social units between the individual and the all-embracing society through their particular ends, responsibilities, and rights. (2) Another division is that into *necessary* communities, *relatively necessary* communities, and *free associations*. Necessary communities, such as the family and the state, are indispensable to human existence and are based directly on human nature; they also impose indisputable moral obligations. Relatively necessary societies also are based directly on human nature, but they are structures with limited functions such as ethnic groups. Free associations, e.g., the literary club or the stock company, are based on human nature only indirectly; they have their origin in the free choice of their members and are limited to serving man in various spheres of culture [§71.3]. (3) In another sense of free there is the division into a *free* or *open* society and a *totalitarian* or *closed* society. In the first the state fully recognizes human rights, particularly that of free public opinion, and allows *communication* (4:32d) with individuals and associations outside its domain in an unhampered way; in the second such communication is excluded and the government assumes unlimited dominance over the individual. (4) Again, the *juridical* society may be differentiated from the *amicable* society. The first rests upon legal provisions, e.g., a municipality or a business corporation, whereas the second rests upon a good-will agreement on the part of its members, as in a sports club or charitable organization. (5) Yet another

division is that into *perfect* societies and *imperfect* societies; the first afford all the requisites for the full development of human nature, e.g., the state in the natural order and the Church in the supernatural, whereas the second are capable of performing their functions only as members of a perfect society. (6) A related distinction is that between the term society itself when used in a narrower sense to designate *relative* autonomies, as compared to the more *absolute* autonomy of the state. In this sense society is composed of individuals and smaller social units with their own particular ends and responsibilities; the state, on the other hand, has the all-embracing end and effects the basic ordering of social functions in the over-all society.

## §77. AUTHORITY

1. It follows from the fact that common ends are constitutive of society that a power of direction must be vested in some *authority* (1:1111c). To the extent that social ends are ontologically implicit in human nature [§76.2], authority itself is ontologically grounded; otherwise, it is established by the agreement of wills of those who freely unite themselves for the pursuit of a common goal. Authority is *necessary* not only because the realization of common ends by a self-determining group requires coordination, but also because a governing power must determine concrete objectives pertaining to the common good as well as methods to attain them. The mode of exercising authority and the extent of its competence depend very largely on the form of society in which it operates. It is practically confined to a rule of custom in the case of the homogeneous ethnic community living as a national minority, whereas it is comprehensive in the case of a heterogeneous society such as a large territorial state, for this must rely to a great extent on organizational means.

2. Few if any societies can survive for any length of time unless there is a firm and stable principle at work to assure, by unified action, the achievement of their common end. A multi-

plicity of practical judgments is inevitable in every non-the-
oretical situation. It is true that certain situations may generate
a kind of spontaneous unified activity, such as that which takes
place in times of emergency—e.g., an unjust attack or a natural
disaster. Even here, however, society has to fight against treach-
ery and plunder, factors that make unanimity arising only from
collective consent highly improbable. For this reason it is preferable to define authority as a moral power exercising an essential
*function* in society as a cause of *united action.* The basis of
this definition is that the rich plurality of means for achieving
the common good of any society demands the election of one
from among many. The power to make such a choice lies in
authority, which is a moral power residing in the regulator of
the society. The desired unified action that is indispensable for
the attainment of the common end comes from compliance
with rules that bind all the members of the society in question.
Therefore, except in some emergency situations, authority must
exercise a vital function to guarantee consistent unified action.
This necessity for authority in society, however, is not to be
identified with the need for any particular form of government;
the question of authority and that of the exercise of authority
are quite distinct, and the first can be answered with assurance
even though the second may be difficult to decide in particular
situations.

3. The *source* of civil authority (1:1113d) is ultimately
God, not by any specifically divine institution, but by the fact
that God is the author of nature and human nature demands
authority. In this general perspective, submission to authority
is enjoined. The *designation theory* holds that the power that is
proper to authority comes from God but that human beings
designate the ruling person by cultural conventions. This is a
modification of the *divine-right theory,* which holds that power
is from God and that the person in whom it is vested also is
designated by God. The *transmission theory* holds that civil
authority is proper to the civil multitude, that the multitude
not only designates the ruling person but also transmits to him
the authority originally given by God. Both the designation

theory and the transmission theory guard the integrity of the individual while enjoining obedience to authority. The *social contract theory* (13:314a), on the other hand, ascribes the source of authority to the multitude alone, who yield all powers to the state, thereby destroying the freedoms of the individual [§81.4].

## §78. MARRIAGE

1. *Marriage* (9:258a) is a universal social institution that defines a mating relationship for the founding of a family and binds it for the protection and rearing of progeny. As an institution it is a complex of social norms governing the relationships of the mated pair, their kinsmen, their offspring, and their society. It serves the culturally defined needs of the family and other groups based on *kinship* (8:202b), and through them, the needs of the society in general; for marriage enables a society to perpetuate itself both biologically and culturally. Marriage and mating are not synonymous; either can occur without the other. Marriage nevertheless gives form and acceptance to the mating complex in a society and promotes the solidarity of the kinship groups that are involved in the marital matrix. The institutional forms of marriage are highly variable since, like kinship relationships in general, they are socially determined; the forms in any given instance depend on a specific culture, its demands, its proscriptions, and its permissiveness.

2. Four *kinds* of marriage arrangements are commonly recognized: (1) *monogamy*, in which one man and one woman are joined; (2) *polygyny*, in which one man is married to more than one woman; (3) *polyandry*, in which one woman is married to more than one man; and (4) *group marriage*, in which both sexes are represented by more than single parties. Anthropologists once attempted to relate these forms within evolutionary schemes, holding that the origins of marriage could be traced to a condition of primitive promiscuity, after which group marriages developed; little evidence has been adduced to

substantiate such theories. Monogamy has been the one form of marriage universally recognized and permitted, though only a minority of societies have made it obligatory; it is also the most prevalent form, since the expense of plural marriage has been beyond the means of most people in all societies. Polyandry is comparatively rare; where it does occur, usually a husband's brothers, living in the same household, share rights to his wife. Polygyny is by far the more common form of polygamy; it generally occurs because of a surplus of women and for economic reasons, since wives may perform productive labor, share in the tasks of maintaining a large household, and serve as visible evidence of acquired wealth.

3. The principal *motive* for marriage in every society is the desire for legitimate offspring, since marriage is the approved means for the founding of a family. Obviously the mutual comfort sought in the married state includes satisfaction of the sexual needs of the partners, as defined and expected in the society. But the union is entered into with some idea of permanence to ensure the care and enculturation of the young, and their arrival enhances the lives of the partners both psychologically and economically. Ways of doing things and value systems are passed on from parents to children. In the process the needs of communities for the maintenance of value systems are met and family institutions are perpetuated. Property interests especially are often protected and furthered by marital alliances; another strong motive is the need for division of labor in daily routine and for cooperation in specialized tasks. This is seen in the economic sphere, in which the extended family assigns work to its members according to considerations of age, skills, and status; even in the nuclear family a man finds the assistance of his wife and children to be an asset.

4. Within Christian societies it is commonly held that there are two *ends* of marriage, one *primary*, the other *secondary* (9:267d). The primary end is procreation-education, whereas the secondary end is mutual aid and the allaying of concupiscence (4:121d). The reason for the first is that the sex act is generative by its very nature: intercourse, or the process by

which sperm from the male is transferred to the female, is an act that is open toward and positively directed toward the generation of another human being, and so as an act is essentially procreative. The reason for the second is based on the nature of conjugal love—the mutual and reciprocal conditioning, enrichment, fulfillment, perfection, and complementation that flow naturally from a sexually differentiated union; this leads also to the aid spouses give one another in maintaining the household as a place and an instrument for the generation and rearing of their children. Because of the adverse connotations of the adjective "secondary," which for some might mean unimportant, unessential, or merely accessory, it has been proposed that the terms *mediate* and *immediate* be used instead of primary and secondary. In such usage the immediate end of marriage, i.e., the end attained first in time, is that of mutual help and support, at one and the same time corporeal, affective, and spiritual, which is the means of man's personal and social perfection; the mediate end, on the other hand, is the procreation-education of offspring. Thus the immediate end is essentially personal, the mediate end, social. Whichever terminology is used, it should be emphasized that there is no contradiction between the two ends, but rather order, dependency, and mutual implication. The complete sense of the marital act is not love alone, but conjugal love, which breeds new life; it is loving fecundity, or reproductive love. Conjugal love is essentially fertile. The child is not foreign to the personal values in marriage; rather the child is itself a sign of conjugal love, a sign that conjugal love and parental love are inseparable.

5. The two *properties* of marriage are *unity* and *indissolubility*. (9:270b). The natural ends of marriage become impossible of attainment when a monogamous union is displaced by polygyny or polyandry, or when permanence is removed through separation or divorce (4:928a). The primary end of marriage is possible, though difficult to attain, with polygyny, but the secondary end is usually frustrated: complete conjugal love is almost impossible for a wife who has to share her husband with competing rivals, and her children also suffer when

they receive only a share of their father's divided attention, particularly when their mother is degraded in the arrangement. Polyandry frustrates both the primary and secondary ends of marriage: the sexual demands on a woman cohabiting simultaneously with several men usually induces sterility, and the child, not knowing who his father is, usually ends up without a father's love and support. A dissoluble marriage likewise militates against the primary and secondary ends: whenever the bond is severed the children are deprived of either parent or both, and so suffer the irreparable loss of love, security, guidance, protection, attention, and training; moreover, a husband and wife cannot surrender themselves fully to one another when there lurks in the mind of either even the possibility that their union might be broken. Love demands constancy and permanence; the conjugal act is itself a sign and a symbol of a union of total self-surrender.

6. *Contraception* (16:103a) frustrates the primary end of marriage in an attempt to fulfill the secondary end, and on this basis is judged to be contrary to the natural law. *Abortion* (16:28c) introduces a disorder into human nature itself by directly intending the destruction of innocent human life. *Fornication* (5:1029a) is opposed to the very institution of marriage: the unwed are not responsibly related to each other so as to provide a stable family situation in which possible issue of their union can be properly cared for and brought to maturity. Thus injury can result to offspring and also to the community, which is likely to be burdened with their care. *Adultery* (1:151a), like fornication, is a disorientation of sex (13:147d) from its natural end, and it adds the further malice of injustice to the married partner who is wronged by the adulterous act.

## §79. THE FAMILY

1. The *family* (5:825d) may be broadly defined as a primary social group or nuclear unit based on a procreative partnership of the sexes and normally constituted by the community

of parents and children. The meaning of the term is sometimes extended to include the entire group of persons living in one house or under one head, i.e., the household. In common usage the term may also denote all the persons sharing a common line of descent, e.g., the Wallaces. In its proper sense the family is a natural society, an institution of nature, in the sense that some form of community between parents and children is required by human nature and consequently arises spontaneously wherever men exist. The mutually complementary heterosexual nature of men and women, as well as the relatively helpless condition of human infants at birth, involves fundamental needs that can adequately be satisfied only in the family. As a matter of fact, although the major functions fulfilled by the family are separable from one another and might conceivably be carried out by separate institutions, they are not separated in any known social system. Thus, with the exception of religion [§60.1], the family is the only social institution that is found formally developed in all societies.

2. Wherever the family exists, it combines two basic *functions*. It regulates sexual behavior for purposes of reproduction, and it provides for the integral development or socialization of offspring. Although in some family systems the functions fulfilled by the family may be so extensive and inclusive that the family constitutes the primary social instrument for such activities as education, protection, production, worship, recreation, and social control, it is only the two basic functions mentioned above, providing as they do for man's essential sexual, reproductive, educational, and economic needs, that invest the family with a many-sided utility rendering its universality inevitable. Hence the two basic functions must always be fulfilled, whereas others may be dropped or added according to the shifting demands of the total social system. As a primary unit of society, the family affects and is affected by all relevant changes in its social environment. When societies increase in density, complexity, and technology, the accompanying division of labor and specialization leads to a clearer articulation or delimitation of various institutional objectives, with the result that the non-essential

functions of the traditional family are gradually taken over by other institutions and the character of even its essential function tends to be modified.

3. Because form and functioning of existing family systems are subject to change, it is preferable to emphasize basic family *objectives* rather than specific, culturally conditioned means. In sum, only the stable family, i.e., the family founded on a permanent, exclusive, indissoluble union, adequately provides for the fitting development and expression of mature creative love. And only the community of life and love thus established can fully supply the nurturing domestic environment within which the child can be reared to assume full adult status in society. Thus the family holds a place of crucial significance in the development and destiny of man, for it socializes him as a child and determines the basic framework of relationships within which he fulfills himself as an adult.

4. The *child* (3:569b), the link between generations, receives his orientation toward group behavior in the family. As he learns what is expected of him he begins to fill subordinate social roles, and during adolescence he prepares for adult life; throughout these periods he learns the necessity of obedience (10:602a). Emancipation from parental control occurs when the adolescent leaves home, e.g., when he contracts a valid marriage, reaches his majority, or enters the armed forces. One who is financially self-supporting but remains at home is under parental control; a physically or mentally incapacitated child who remains at home may never be emancipated. Concomitant with the duties of obedience and respect for his parents, the child has basic rights [§56.5]. Most essential is his right to life. He also has a right to spiritual direction and to instruction in religion, so as to develop a sense of God, a sense of direction, a sense of responsibility, and a sense of mission in life. Every child also has a right to opportunities to develop physically, mentally, morally, and socially; to love and understand under the care of parents; and to education. A handicapped child has a right to special treatment, education, and care. Every child has a right to protection against neglect, cruelty, exploitation, and discrimi-

nation in every form. In most countries parents have a legal
right to custody and control of their child; they also have the
corresponding duty to support the child: to provide him with
food, clothing, shelter, education, religious instruction, medical
care, and any other necessity. Parenthood also carries with it
the right to discipline a child and to delegate this authority to
someone else. (For a fuller development, see 11:356a-358b).

## §80. SOCIAL JUSTICE

1. *Social justice* (13:318c) is the virtue that ordains all
human acts toward the common good. It is a special virtue,
specified and distinguished from other virtues, but it is also a
general virtue because, ordered to it under a certain aspect,
are all acts of other virtues and not only the acts of justice
[§56.1] in the particular sense of the term. Social justice is
equivalent in meaning to general or legal justice [§56.3], being
a modern expression for these traditional terms that are easily
misunderstood in the present day. It is of the essence of social
justice to demand from each individual all that is necessary for
the common good. But just as in the living organism it is
impossible to provide for the good of the whole unless each
single part and each individual member is given what it needs
for the exercise of its proper functions, so it is impossible to
care for the social organism and the good of society as a unit
unless each single part and each individual member is supplied
with all that is necessary for the exercise of his social functions.
The following paragraphs spell out some of the implications of
this statement (see 13:354b-361a).

2. Because man is a *person* [§29], (1) in all his relationships within society, in all institutions and in all environments,
he can never be considered as a *chattel* or as a mere instrument.
(2) The *work* of human beings cannot be placed on the same
level as the forces of nature, and so cannot be assigned a
monetary value as can merchandise; it is a free and conscious

human activity, an expression of the personality of the worker, and as such is always noble even when expressed in modest forms and in economic activity. (3) Work is an obligation, not only because the members of the human race can perfect themselves through work, but also because it enables them to enjoy a decent standard of living (13:640c), meet their family responsibilities, and fulfill their social obligations. But if work is an obligation it is also a right, for every duty presupposes a corresponding right in human society, and thus man has the *right to work* (12:498c). Work itself thus becomes the natural source from which man draws his livelihood. (4) It follows that the remuneration of work cannot be left to the changing laws of the market, nor can *wages* (14:763a) be fixed by an arbitrary decision of those occupying high places in the ecoomic order or by those invested with civil authority.

3. With regard to man's possessions, (1) private ownership, even of productive goods, is a natural right, a right that belongs to man by virtue of his dignity as a person and not because of any concession by public authority. This right to *private property* (11:849c) is man's because he is spiritual, intelligent, and free and responsible for his own livelihood and destiny; each man is responsible for the support and government of the family he decides to form and is bound to contribute personally to the common good. (2) Private ownership serves an individual function, since the individual is prior to society, and property is itself a defense and guarantee of the fundamental expression of human liberty. (3) In the familial order, private ownership is considered an element of stability, serenity, and efficiency in the pursuit of the ends proper to the family unit. (4) Private ownership has a social function also, since the goods man owns can serve the entire family of mankind, providing for the needy and for the accomplishment of noble works without compromising the owner's way of life or his economic and social position. (5) Not only individuals and their respective families but other organized groups, intermediate associations, and public agencies can also lawfully own private property, even productive prop-

erty; and they can be owners insofar as it is necessary for the effective attainment of their specific goals and the common good.

4. In the matter of the common good [§§54.1, 76.4] and man's social obligations, (1) individuals as well as intermediate groups and social enterprises are obliged to contribute to the interest of the common good, and they do contribute when they pursue their own special interests in true harmony and without damage to others. (2) The public authority is especially obliged to guarantee the common good, for the latter is the reason for the existence of this authority and the goal toward which it must work. It must do so, however, by recognizing, respecting, and promoting the basic rights of the individual as integral to the common good. (3) Man being by nature social, human beings live normal lives when they mutually assist each other; again, each one succeeds in perfecting himself when with the same activity he contributes to the perfection of others [§76.2]. It follows that force cannot be accepted as the supreme criterion in the control of human relations, as in the liberal doctrine of free competition, the communist doctrine of class warfare, or the doctrine of group pressure or economic or political superiority. Social relations must be governed by men working together and mutually collaborating in truth, justice, love, and freedom. All of this may be summed up as the *principle of solidarity*.

5. Since individuals, families, intermediate groups, and public authority are the units present and working in society, some criterion must be used to decide the sphere of action proper to each group so as to assure the attainment of social justice. Such a criterion is the *principle of subsidiarity* (13:762a). According to this principle intermediate associations and public authority do not claim to do those things that individuals and families are able to accomplish unaided, nor does public authority claim to do those things that intermediate associations can and in fact do accomplish. The basic justification of the principle is that human beings create or maintain a society not for the purpose of being absorbed by it, but in order to reach goals that

otherwise they would not be able to reach, goals that they foster and pursue as means of affirming their own personality. (For a more detailed discussion of economic problems, see *economics and ethics,* 5:82b, *economic justice,* 5:50c, *natural law in economics,* 10:266d, and *poverty,* 11:642b.)

# CHAPTER 14.

# POLITICAL PHILOSOPHY

## §81. POLITICAL PHILOSOPHY
## AND POLITICAL SCIENCE

1. *Political philosophy* (11:510d) or politics is the part of philosophy that deals with political society, its nature and its end, which is the highest human common good. It is distinguished from political science in the modern sense of that discipline [§81.5] by its concern with the first general principles of all practical activity, to which any circumstantial and detailed study must ultimately be referred. Because it remains at a general level it generates greater certitude [§40.3] than do the detailed disciplines; for example, one can say with confidence that whenever many persons are constituted in such a way that a community results, a ruler-subject relationship will manifest itself, but it is much more difficult to say with regard to this community precisely what this ruler-subject relationship will be. Political philosophy is a practical rather than a speculative discipline [§13.6], for its aim is to perfect man in accordance with his nature through the process of self-government; in this respect it is like ethics [§49.1], and its perfection requires the development of political virtues, especially political prudence. The common good to which it is directed transcends that of the family; indeed, the diversity of trades and activities that comes from a union of families marks the beginning of the political community. The first objective of this community is to make possible a full sufficiency of material goods, and after this to make possible the perfection of human life in the virtues and the arts. Thus the state is not ordered to mere activity of life,

but to activity of life according to the highest virtues; its end is the common good of its members, i.e., the good of the virtues, both speculative and moral, and of the arts [§51.4]. Because it aims at the highest human good, political philosophy is said to be architectonic with respect to all other practical disciplines: they have quite specific ends in their direction of human doing or making, whereas political philosophy directs and coordinates all activities to produce the perfect human society wherein man can alone find earthly happiness.

2. In its *classical* conception (11:525b) the state [§82] is the most complex and perfect society, and is the end and integration of the other societies of family and village; so its form and composition are owed to many different elements—wealth, freedom, equality, and virtue. The forms of government are distinguished basically in terms of the character and secondarily in terms of the number of the ruling class. Since the virtue proper to rulers, political prudence, does not, unlike art, determine the end of action, government [§83] is bounded by jurisdiction, namely, the order of rights that follow from the nature of man and the true end of human life. These rights are either substantive or procedural: by the first is meant all that is implied in living and living well; by the second is implied the various acts that are indispensable for the making of choices by free men, viz, deliberation, counsel, and judgment. They permit three main forms of good government—good because they respect the nature of a free man and tend toward the common good. In *monarchy* (9:1020b) and *aristocracy* (1:798d) the one most virtuous man or a few most virtuous men exercise power, and in moderate *democracy* (4:745b) the many, on the principle of equality, rule for the common good. The first two forms rightly consider that freedom, equality, and wealth are merely the material cause and not the final cause of political life; they take virtue to be this final cause. The democratic form, on the other hand, is open to the danger of making freedom and equality the final cause of political life to the point of ostracizing the virtuous, thus tending to its natural perversion, extreme democracy or mob rule. This perverted democracy, like

the perversions of monarchy (tyranny) and of aristocracy (oligarchy), is improperly political. All good forms of government, however, have their defects and disadvantages, and in choosing the best form men are effectively avoiding the worst.

3. The *medieval* development (11:526d), apart from addressing the complex interrelationships of Church and state (3:726c), contributed new ideas on the role of law and leadership in government. The political community, again, is one of self-governing men. Since law as a measure and rule must be homogenous with what it measures, the homogeneity of human law with the community whose acts it rules is found initially in the derivation of the first human law, the constitution, from the community of free men. At the same time, because the individual good is impossible without the common good of all, this good is an end that requires the establishment of some form of government. Two elements of constitutional government thus emerge: the first is the element of consent, based on man's moral freedom; the second is the principle of necessity of rule to which consent is given. There is, finally, a third element of *constitutionalism* (4:249d), possibility, which corresponds to man's physical freedom. The problem of the best constitution is that of combining the elements of consent and possibility with the perfection of the governing principle. One way of doing this is through the *mixed monarchy,* combining elements of democratic, middle-class government with the effective leadership provided by royal rule. Being based on consent and possibility, middle-class government gives a foundation for stability and policy-making changes, whereas the actual exercise of power is entrusted to the ruler, the one best-qualified man who, because limited by the people, is conceived as their representative.

4. *Modern* theories of political life (11:529a) depart rather drastically from these classical and medieval teachings. The principal revolution consisted in severing political philosophy from its ties with ethics and the moral order and in making it a pure art of ruling and of securing power [§95.5]. Usually it conceives government as arising through some form of *social contract* (13:314a), based on the sanctity of private property

and the rights of its more skillful acquirers [§77.3]. The state comes into being when men in the condition of "nature" become aware that the peaceful pursuit by each of his private good spells the common good, the latter understood to be merely the collectivity of private interests. The state arises when this knowledge is made practical by rules of mutual security. The constitution that results is usually that of an executive who is subordinated to a legislative assembly in which representation is based on numbers and wealth; this effectively subordinates government to an economic power that supplies direction to society from extra-political processes and institutions. Thus politics is cut off from its traditional role of perfecting man in accordance with his nature, and there is no longer concern with the individual as such. From this, by easy steps, arise the philosophies of political *liberalism* (8:701c) and *utilitarianism* (14:503c), and the reacting doctrines of *conservatism* (4:214d) and *totalitarianism* (14:210b) that characterize the modern era.

5. *Political science* (11:516b) is related to political philosophy in much the same way as social science is related to social philosophy [§75]. As an academic discipline it is practically synonymous with politics or government, some universities preferring one term, others another. Yet there is no precise or accepted definition of either politics or political science. Some consider politics as a process or activity not limited to formal government alone, but involving the theory and practice of managing all forms of group activity. As a science in the sense of the social sciences, political science is thought to be empirical and concerned exclusively with facts and postulated relationships between them; thus it is not concerned with values and is perforce non-normative. Much of its concern is with descriptive treatments of Amercan local and national governments and with discussions of public law, political theory, and international relations. Recent emphases have been on the role of ideologies in government, on public administration, on the study of political parties and elections, and on public opinion. Its *methodology* is similar to that of the behavioral and social sciences; it uses statistical and mathematical methods, experiments with various

kinds of model building, and develops distinctive procedures for quantifying political experience, such as polls and public opinion surveys.

## §82. THE STATE

1. The *state* (13:644c) may be defined as the independent and sovereign political community. The term is derived from the Roman-law concept of *status rei Romae* and replaces the older and original terms, the Greek *polis* and the Latin *res publica* or *civitas*. The state has elements of both community and association, and is included in the most comprehensive and highest society [§76.1], mankind, which has its proper common good, its specific international law, and its historically variable form of government. As a body politic the state has its own supreme internal order of positive law [§54.2], ordered to a distinct common good that is the ultimate authority within its own order, binding a people who inhabit a defined territory. Although each state claims *sovereignty* (13:487b) and independence from other societies of the same order, states are interdependent and bound to recognize the community of nations and its public international law, and of course the natural law [§54.3], which is ultimately the foundation of the state and the critical norm for all man-made positive law [§84.4]. States are thus the primary subjects of public international law, regardless of their internal constitutions, whether unitary or federal, republican or monarchic, national or multi-national.

2. Three basic *elements* of the state are commonly distinguished: (1) a distinct territory with more or less strictly determined boundaries; (2) a multitude of people already individualized by language, tribal customs, religion, or other cultural forms of living together, and (3) a positive constitutional and legal order that determines, legitimizes, and limits the one political authority and the basic relations between ruler and ruled and between its citizens—the bond of law (*vinculum iuris*). Some would add to the first element the wealth of the

nation, i.e., its raw materials, soil fertility, climate, and all economically relevant abilities and skills of the inhabitants. The state is commonly viewed as a perfect society because it possesses and controls all the means necessary for the realization of its specific end. More than any other temporal community, the state, as its name implies, tends toward perpetuity and survival into an indefinite future.

3. The state, as the perfect society [§76.7], includes other societies but is not to be identified with them. During bellicose occupation or complete subjugation of a belligerent nation, society continues to exist under the protection of international law while the state is inoperative and even destroyed. For war is directed against the state and its armed forces, not against society and its institutions, the peaceful life of its families and the private life of its private citizens, and their properties and rights under civil law. The real distinction between *state* and *society*, and between public and civil law, is essential for the free state as well as the free society. Although the line of separation between the two is not rigid and defined once for all, but fluid, shifting the line radically in favor of society results in anarchy (1:476c), and shifting it radically in favor of the state results in totalitarianism.

4. State and *nation* (10:219a) are not necessarily co-terminous. Historically the first nation-states developed from the struggle against the universalism of Christendom, the Church universal, and later as secularized democratic sovereignties resulting from or inspired by the French Revolution. As a product of such historical forces the nation is a stable community of persons and families who have developed a common culture [§71.3], e.g., a common language, literature, customs, and often a common religion, as well as a distinct feeling of belonging together and of being different from neighboring communities, a common awareness of a historical destiny, and a consensus of accepted value preferences often but not necessarily based on ethno-biological factors. The nation-state is not the only legitimate political form of an independent state; some would even regard it as an inferior form because of its tendency to promote

doctrinaire, quasi-religious *nationalism* (10:240c) with its many attendant dangers.

5. The individual historical state, though independent and perfect in the sense described, was never totally self-sufficient and wholly enclosed or isolated. It was and is a definite part of the highest and most comprehensive community, *mankind* itself. This community of nations is not a mere formless collection of individuals but is based upon their common nature, their common Creator, and their common law, i.e., the natural law of the community of nations, states, and cultures. (This community is the true complement of the Church universal, the perfect supernatural society, established for the salvation of all nations and cultures.) As such a community, mankind has its own *international law* (5:576d) that is based on natural law; in its positive form this is customary law and treaty law, either bilateral or multilateral. Such law is, of course, imperfect law, since as a law of coordinate (as opposed to subordinate) bodies it lacks a formal and continuous legislative authority, an enforcing executive authority, and a supreme judicial authority having final and comprehensive jurisdiction [§83.4]. The defense and the enforcement of rights issuing from the law is left to the decisions of the different states. The individual state has the right of war and peace (*ius belli ac pacis*).

6. In consequence, the doctrine of the *just war* (14:795b-807a) developed by necessity. According to this doctrine war can be just only under the following conditions: (1) there must be a grave injury or a grave violation of rights by a state, continued in spite of diplomatic representations made to it; (2) only states can legitimately wage war; (3) the war must be conducted for a limited end and by legitimate means; and (4) the foreseeable evil consequences of the war must not be greater than the actual injury inflicted. If these conditions are fulfilled, a just war is a defense of the legal order as well as an instrument for the protection of the rights of the state, even if it is technically the aggressor. Excluded are wars of annihilation, wanton conquest, and aggrandizement; ideological war; and, under the modern technology of arms, aggressive preventive war. Although

the doctrine is clear, in most wars each opposing power is usually subjectively convinced of the justice of its cause. Moreover, international life is the natural field of power politics, which often leads even unintentionally to situations in which war seems inevitable. Internally, whether in a federal or a unitary state, most conflicts are peaceably settled except for those that become irrepressible and lead to civil war.

## §83. GOVERNMENT

1. The concept of *government* (6:650d) is closely allied to that of the state, since it designates the concrete system through which the objectives of the state are attained. As one of the elements that constitute the state [§82.2], government may be viewed as the machinery through which the state operates. More specifically, it consists of the combined organisms and mechanisms, such as the legislature, the courts, the executive branch, the bureaucracy, and the political parties (11:506c) that shape and implement public policy. While government is an apparatus, it is also a process through which the people of the state seek to meet the common problems that inevitably arise in the course of social living. Since the problems that face man in the course of history change and since government is a social invention of man designed to meet his needs, no government can be unchanging in form or frozen in its functions over a lengthy period of time.

2. *Power* may be defined generally as the capacity to make and enforce decisions, rules, and regulations affecting the behavior of individuals and groups. It exists in many forms, but under the special aspect of being coercive and able to use force, it is exercised in modern times only by government in the name of the state. Such coercive power is regarded as the necessary condition for minimal order. Individual interests no less than those of corporate bodies within the state must bow to the legitimate broader ends of the state, preferably through conviction but if necessary through coercion. Yet there are limits to this

exercise of coercive power, and these are usually spelled out by some kind of constitution, written or unwritten, that forms the basis for government and specifies the structures and conditions of governing. Thus, practically speaking, the selection and the acceptance of contractual limitations by the people is what legitimates power. To invest the political power with authority [§77], i.e., to make it legitimate by meeting the expectations of the governed concerning the wielding of authority, is the central goal of all government and politics.

3. Nevertheless, the difference between the theory of limited power and the practice of unlimited power has led man historically to seek ways and means of restraining the misuse of power. The medieval extortion of the Magna Carta from the king by the nobles of England, the rise of legislative assemblies, the institutionalizing of judicial review, and the rise of the modern political party system are all inventions of man aimed at a proper channeling and use of power. The most workable system is one of institutionalized *checks and balances*, wherein the misuse of power is made difficult by cutting it up and assigning it to different departments of government, each of which is concerned about protecting its own interests and resisting encroachment by the others. The theory behind this is that, where there is no concentration of power, there can be no major abuses.

4. The conventional *separation of powers* theory in modern government holds that there are three distinct kinds of governmental power: legislative, executive, and judicial. (1) The legislative is concerned with the passage of laws or general rules of conduct to supplement existing custom or other unwritten law, such as common law. (2) Executive power consists in the execution of laws and the administration of public programs. (3) Judicial power consists in interpreting laws and deciding in cases of dispute what discrete acts are permitted or required or prohibited in execution of the law. The three-power system undoubtedly offers protection against potentially tyrannical government, but criticisms have been voiced against its ability to meet social needs and to assure military preparedness in times

of rapid change. In practice it can prove unwieldly and ineffi-
cient, and attempts to delegate quasi-legislative and quasi-judi-
cial powers to administrative agencies so as to meet pressing
needs result in the creation of expensive bureaucracies.

5. There are many *forms* of government that have evolved
since classical Greece. The following are some classifications
that show the range of contrasting governmental forms. (1)
Parliamentary form vs. presidential form: in the first the executive is theoretically the creature of the legislative, though in
practice the executive is master because of party discipline;
in the second the president is independent of the legislative,
and judicial review is provided to assure separation of powers.
(2) Unitary form vs. federated form: the first has a central
source of authority and local governments are merely its creatures; the second distributes powers and functions through two
or more semi-independent levels of government in the same
state. (3) One-party system vs. a two-party or multi-party structure: the one-party system corrupts the formal structure of the
government easily and can be a disguise for a dictatorship;
two-party systems have been found to promote stability more
than multi-party systems. (4) Anarchism vs. totalitarianism: the
first considers coercive power in government as an undiluted
evil; the second puts everything under governmental regulation
and uses coercion when necessary. As it turns out, all forms of
government line up somewhere between these last two extremes.
This being so it is not difficult to understand why philosophers
continue to debate whether government itself is only a necessary
evil or a positive help in reaching the good life.

6. In the present world the most pervasive form of totalitarian government is international *communism* (4:46c). The
word communism when used by itself may designate a politico-
social doctrine, a socio-economic system of production, or a
political movement and its methods of control. When qualified
as international or world communism, however, it does not
refer so much to a general theoretical principle as it does to the
power organization that, though spread over the whole world,
originally had its center in Moscow and its highest common

authority in Lenin (8:632a). This power organization is held together by its own peculiar ideology and by a mode of discipline that it demands of all its members. The ideology is that of dialectical and historical materialism (9:444d; 13:488b), and its key principle is that the determining factor in each human society is not spiritual (and therefore not religion, philosophy, politics, or law) but rather material, viz, economic production [§98.3]. In this it is allied to the movement known as *socialism* (13:368c), which may be defined as the attempt to reconstruct society on the basis of the common ownership of the means of production. Such reconstruction was undertaken in reaction to individualism (7:474b) and capitalism (3:81c), on the thesis that these movements lead to the exploitation of the proletariat by the owners of the means of production; this in turn induces class conflict, which should be intensified, because it results inevitably in revolution wherein the proletariat seizes power and expropriates the expropriators. In effect, both socialism and communism make collectivity supreme at the expense of the individual, whom they deprive of his natural rights [§56.5]. By fostering and intensifying social conflict, moreover, they make solidarity and subsidiarity [§80.4-5] impossible, and so are powerless to create institutions that preserve man's dignity and his rights in society as a whole [§103.6-7].


## §84. PHILOSOPHY OF LAW

1. The *philosophy of law* (8:556b) studies the nature of law [§54], with particular reference to the origin and ends of civil law and the principles that should govern its formulation. The discipline may be elaborated historically in light of the teachings of various schools, or it may be elaborated systematically in the context provided by a particular school such as Thomism. A related discipline is *jurisprudence* (8:63d) in its more theoretical aspects. As understood by lawyers this term denotes a working knowledge of a particular system of law, and refers particularly to the exercise of private and public

decision-making functions and scholarly critiques of the resulting actions. The same term can also be used, however, to denote philosophical studies that principally concern the general
nature of law, legal institutions, and legal processes in the application of law, and in this sense it is practically equivalent to
the philosophy of law.

2. There are two main schools of jurisprudence, whose
members may be referred to as positivist jurisprudents and natural law jurisprudents respectively. The position of legal *positivism* (11:623d), whatever else it may include, may be described as minimally involving the assertion that in defining the
nature of law of a political society the proper object is to separate the law as it is from the law as it ought to be, or to
separate law from morality. The position of the *natural law*
school (10:262d), on the other hand, is just the opposite:
it maintains that law cannot be separated from morality, and
that the main task of the jurist is to construct and maintain
a body of law, a *corpus iuris,* that adequately implements the
natural law. This is so because the fundamental principles of
the natural law, universal and immutable as the human nature
from which they derive, require rational application to the constantly changing political, social, economic, and technological
conditions of dynamic civil society. The details of such application constantly change along with the circumstances of human
existence in a particular society, and so there can be no unquestioning complacency in the *status quo.* Proper law-making
therefore demands a reasoned acceptance of the good and a rejection of the bad in all that is new, and advocates a critical
search for the better. It insists, furthermore, that effort toward
the improvement of the *corpus iuris* be made in the light of the
origin, dignity, and destiny of man [§29] and in the knowledge of the origin, nature, and purpose of the state [§82].

3. The relationship between natural law and civil law, on
this understanding, is the basic *problem* of jurisprudence. It is
a particularly difficult and delicate problem in a society such as
that of pluralistic America, where large groups of citizens
sincerely differ, theologically and philosophically, about the

morality of many activities and institutions and about the proper public policy of the state concerning them. The following is but an outline of a solution to this problem consistent with the principles of social and political philosophy already presented.

4. It is necessary, first of all, to distinguish between a principle of the *natural law* [§54.6] and a rule of the *civil* law. The former is universal and immutable, the latter is not. A principle of natural law can be known by man, because he can know his nature and essential relationships; but a principle of the natural law cannot be made, changed, or destroyed by man because he cannot make, change, or destroy his essential nature. Conversely a rule of the civil law must be made and can be amended or repealed by man's legislative or judicial process. Thus a rule of the civil law lacks the universality and immutability of a principle of the natural law. This is the precise reason why rules of civil law, as they are enacted, amended, and formulated from time to time and from circumstance to circumstance, should always be consonant with the principles of natural law. It is why the natural law constitutes the general *norm* to measure the justice or injustice of civil law.

5. Among the changeable and changing *rules of civil law* are: the rule of consideration in contracts, the rule of hearsay in evidence, the rule of recording in property, the rule of witnesses in wills, the rule of strict liability in torts, and hundreds of others, from the rules governing statutes of limitations to traffic rules and minor procedural regulations. As rules they have a certain generality, but they are subject to exceptions, and they require change, gradual or drastic, as time, circumstances, and wisdom demand. They are practical and subsidiary means whereby the civil law, more or less efficiently, applies the principles of natural law to human beings living in the constantly changing economic and political conditions of modern society. (For more details, see *natural law in economics,* 10:266d, and *natural law in political thought,* 10:268d).

6. Three factors have contributed to the *confusion* and *misunderstanding* concerning the impact of natural law upon

civil law. (1) The misuse of natural law terminology in support of laissez-faire rugged individualism, seen in turn of the century judicial decisions that piously exalted property and contractual rights to the detriment of other basic human rights and the genuine needs of the common good [§76.4]. (2) The lack of familiarity of members of the legal profession with the writings of natural law philosophers and reliance upon secondary, unscholarly sources of information. (3) An unfortunate propensity, on the part of natural law enthusiasts, to claim too much for their philosophy. The naive proposition "All we have to do to solve our practical problems is to apply natural law" is similar to the false panacea "All we have to do is to apply the Constitution."

7. The natural law itself is inadequate to solve the complex problems of a dynamic human society. It requires implementation by civil law; and such implementation involves not merely argumentation and research, but validation even by trial and error. But the *goal* of law-making and of government itself simply cannot be attained without an on-going search for the best civil laws to enact for the personal and the common good.

# PART THREE

# HISTORY OF PHILOSOPHY

*The aim in this third part is to present a general sketch of the problems of the historiography of philosophy, together with an overview of the main developments in ancient, medieval, modern, and contemporary periods. References continue to be made to the* New Catholic Encyclopedia, *where the reader can find full details of the lives, thought, and works of individual philosophers as well as the movements to which they belonged or gave rise. Indication is also given when a philosopher's writings are contained in the* Great Books of the Western World (Chicago: Encyclopedia Britannica, 1952), *abbreviated GBWW together with the volume number. The student should attempt to read in its entirety at least one work of a major philosopher in each of the four periods, and the GBWW is convenient for this purpose. (The names of major philosophers are given in capital letters, e.g.,* IMMANUEL KANT; *each has influenced the development of philosophy in a significant way, even though the treatment here may require that his contribution be reported in only a sentence or two.) Should it prove impractical to read an entire work, reference to the* Syntopicon (GBWW 2-3) *will indicate important passages from all philosophers relating to the fifty* Great Ideas, *which include philosophy, God, man, being, cause, etc., and all of which have some bearing on the history of philosophy. A careful reading and analysis of such works and passages is an integral part of the philosopher's formation.*

# CHAPTER 15.

# HISTORY OF PHILOSOPHY

## §85. PHILOSOPHY AND HISTORY

1. The history of philosophy (11:299d) is a special branch of the history of culture [§71.3] whose object is the critical study of the formation and development of philosophy from its beginnings to the present. Being a composite discipline it can be defined only in terms of the notions of philosophy and history on which it obviously depends. The term *philosophy*, as has been seen [§1.2], was generally identified with science or *scientia* from antiquity to early modern times; this identification would make the history of philosophy the same as the history of scientific thought. More recently, however, science came to be separated from philosophy and the two have been set in mutual opposition as though constituting distinct fields of knowledge [§1.10]. This division has been aggravated by the fact that practically every modern philosopher has proposed a different and distinctive notion of philosophy in accordance with his basic view of reality. Such understandings of philosophy have had diversifying influences on the concept of the history of philosophy. For this reason it is convenient here to retain the classical notion of philosophy, regarding it as synonymous with science and attributing to the history of philosophy a scope broad enough to encompass the formation and development of all systematic knowledge. This scope need not prevent such a history, once provided with a breadth and diversity of materials, from being subdivided into particular histories of each of the branches into which this knowledge has subsequently come to be divided.

2. The term *history* is similarly capable of different under-standings, the more important being (1) the ontological reality of the past, and (2) man's knowledge or science of that reality [§59.1]. (1) In the *ontological* sense historical being is included within the general concept of being, though the two are not convertible: all real things have duration, yet not all of them have a history. God, for example, as the absolute and immutable Being, has an eternal duration but not a history; all contingent and changeable beings, on the other hand,—and these include minerals, plants, animals, and man—have a history. Being his-toried is, in fact, a property of man, not as regards his nature, which is unchangeable, but as an accidental modality of his actions (both individual and collective) insofar as they take place in time. In this sense man's historical reality is the result of past actions that are not completely past, since some of their virtuality remains to continue actuation into the future. (2) In its *scientific* sense history consists of the critical study and explanation of past facts considered in their chronological suc-cession by investigating their mutual relations, their antecedents and consequents, and their influences and reactions. This in-volves a search for their meaning and interpretation, so that the facts are presented within a total or partial view of the whole. History so understood can be truly scientific even though the facts of the past are particular and thus lacking in univer-sality; this is possible because, once past, such facts acquire a type of necessity in the sense that whatever has been done cannot not have been done.

3. Philosophy is historical and has a history, since it is a product of man's intellectual activity elaborated in the course of time [§19.4]. To understand this it is convenient to make a distinction between philosophy or *scientia* achieved (*in facto esse*) and the same discipline in the process of becoming or of formation (*in fieri*). Since the goal of philosophy is true and certain knowledge, philosophical knowledge once achieved is unchangeable and timeless and to this extent stands outside of history. In the process of becoming, however, philosophy must be identified with the temporal flux of its formation and with

the stages at which man's mind arrives in its pursuit of the truth [§39]. Obviously the *history of philosophy* is concerned with philosophy, but not in the sense of knowledge achieved (which in the ideal case would be completely systematic), rather in the sense of knowledge being acquired. For this reason the historian of philosophy focuses more upon the vicissitudes encountered during philosophy's temporal development than upon its content in itself. On this understanding, being historied is not a property of philosophy as true and certain knowledge, but rather as a type of knowledge that develops and comes more perfectly into being throughout time. Once achieved, philosophy is not concerned with what men have said but with what the truth is about the matters they consider. The history of philosophy, on the other hand, is concerned with ascertaining the truth of what men have said in their efforts to come to the possession of the truth they seek both individually and collectively.

4. Reality (12:117c) is one, and the problems it poses are the same at all times and for all men. Truth is also one [§32.4], since it is convertible with being and must ultimately consist in the adequation of human concepts with things as they are in themselves. On this account it would seem that there should be only one *philosophy* and only one system of thought that is exactly representative of reality. As a matter of fact, however, there is a plurality of *philosophies* and a multitude of diverse and even contradictory philosophical systems [§1.11]. There are many reasons for such diversity, both subjective and objective. Among the subjective may be enumerated (1) the basic limitation of man's knowing faculties with respect to their proper objects, and even more with respect to transcendent objects [§§25.4, 41:1]; (2) the nature of man's intellect [§§2, 25], which is rational and discursive; (3) man's inability to perceive the essences of things intuitively; (4) the influence of environmental and of social and political circumstances peculiar to each stage of history; and (5) the influence of philosophers upon each other. Frequently philosophy develops not by a direct study of reality itself but by discourse on the opinions

of others; thus one system gives rise to another, sometimes by way of reaction, sometimes by way of reconciliation and elaboration. Objective causes of philosophical pluralism include (1) the complexity of the world of being and the intrinsic difficulty of the problems it presents to the human mind, and (2) the need for special techniques and conceptual tools that are not easily acquired by man when faced with the problems of daily living. Yet there are also factors that promote philosophical unity, such as the commonality of being and the identity of human nature. The history of philosophy thus evidences a type of progress, obviously not rectilinear but nonetheless exhibiting overall advances, even though marked by fluctuations, oscillations, and occasional regressions.

## §86. PHILOSOPHICAL SYSTEMS

1. From the diversity of positions adopted by philosophers a variety of *philosophical systems* have evolved throughout history. Some of these are known by the names of their founders, others by geographical or temporal designations, and these will be treated in subsequent sections. There are yet other systems that have a more lasting character, representing as they do basic options that are open to man's intellect when confronted with the perennial problems of philosophy. These can be conveniently enumerated under the themes of being, truth, knowledge, God, and ethics.

2. As regards the basic problem of *being*, the more important systems are the following. *Realism* (12:110b) holds that beings really exist and that man's faculties are able to know them. *Idealism* (7:340c) distrusts the veracity of the senses and so breaks the contact they provide with external reality, elaborating itself systematically upon combinations of ideas; *logicism* (8:966c) is akin to idealism to the extent that it confuses ontological being with logical being and attempts to solve philosophical problems with logical concepts alone. According to *monism* (9:1061c) reality consists of one being or principle, either

finite or infinite, of which all other beings are simply emana-
tions or modalities that do not alter its essential unity. *Dualism*
(4:1073b), on the other hand, invokes two opposed and heterogeneous principles as explanations of being, e.g., good and evil,
matter and form, potency and act, mind ,and body, or noumena
and phenomena. *Materialism* (9:441d) regards matter as the
only reality; *spiritualism* (13:590c), as opposed to this, holds
for the existence and primacy of a reality that is distinct from,
and not derived from, matter or corporeal being.

  3. Systems concerned with the problem of truth may be
classified as positive or negative. Among the positive are included realism again, eclecticism, and dogmatism. According
to *realism* there is such a thing as truth: it is one, identical,
absolute, unchangeable, and all minds can attain it in a complete or partial way. *Eclecticism* (5:40c) maintains that each
philosophy succeeds in attaining only a portion of the truth;
purged of their errors and properly selected, these portions can
be coordinated into a single system. *Dogmatism* (4:956d) locks
itself within systems expressed in absolute formulas of supposed
universal value. Among negative positions the principal are
skepticism, relativism, and solipsism. *Skepticism* (13:275d)
maintains a position of doubt, asserting either that truth does
not exist or that it cannot be discovered by the human mind.
*Relativism* (12:220d) sees truth as at best partial and changeable, depending on the way the knowing subject perceives it
and varying according to the circumstances of place and time.
*Solipsism* (13:420b) is more restrictive still: it holds that a
person can know only himself and that there are no grounds
for acknowledging the existence or the truth of anything apart
from self.

  4. As regards the problem of *knowledge* many theories or
systematic explanations have evolved throughout the course of
history (18:234a). *Subjectivism* (13:757d) has features in
common with both solipsism and idealism; it emphasizes the
role played by the self or mind (as the knowing subject) in
interpreting experience. Its antonym, *objectivism*, is less frequently used in philosophical discourse; it would stress the

apartness of the thing known, i.e., the object, from the one who knows it. *Sensism* (13:94b) makes sense perception the primary cognitive process and holds that whatever is intelligible must be also sensible. It is related to *phenomenalism* (11:256b), which would attribute existence only to appearances or to sense data precisely as experienced. A more general system is *empiricism* (5:325a), which insists that knowledge begins with the senses or with sense experience; an extreme form would limit all knowledge to that provided by sensation and so deny epistemic validity to ideas, whereas a less radical form would insist that experience be the final test for the validity of ideas or that any knowledge transcending the data of experience can be at best probable. *Rationalism* (12:90a) is usually opposed to empiricism; it would exaggerate reason's independence from the senses in the knowing process. It is related to idealism and to *transcendentalism* (14:236b), which claims to find a foundation for absolute truths immanent in the human mind or soul. The term *intellectualism* (7:561d) has a somewhat different connotation: it designates a philosophical system in which intellect or conceptualization is accorded primacy, not over the senses however, but over the will or affectivity, and thus it is opposed to *voluntarism* (14:745c). In similar opposition to rationalism and intellectualism is *irrationalism* (7:658b), which distrusts reason and relies for its certitudes on feelings, emotions, instincts, intuition, will, desires, and experience. Systems of knowledge that evolved out of disputes over the problem of universals [§7.3] include *nominalism* (10:483a; 16:318d), which attributes existence to individuals alone and refuses to admit a common nature inherent in similar individual things as the basis for their resemblance, and *conceptualism* (4:108d), which holds that terms can designate universal concepts, but that concepts as such signify nothing actually, potentially, or virtually universal outside the mind. Both are opposed to *realism* (12:110b) in its absolute and moderate forms.

5. Concerning the problem of *God* the basic systematic positions are atheism, agnosticism, and theism. *Atheism* (1:1000b) explicitly denies the existence of God; it has assumed

various forms throughout history, such as those of *secular humanism* (7:226c), *scientism* (12:1225b), and *naturalism* (10: 271d). *Agnosticism* (1:205c) does not deny God's existence but rather professes ignorance about this; its claim is that God is humanly unknowable and so it is not incompatible with belief in his existence, provided one does not attempt to prove it. *Theism* (14:9d), on the other hand, maintains that God is rationally knowable and that his existence can be proved; most theists are monotheistic in their commitments, but they usually do not deny the possibility of divine revelation as a source of knowledge about God. Although etymologically similar to theism, *deism* (4:721d) repudiates revelation as a source of divine knowledge and generally regards God as totally outside the material universe, not as immanent within it, as theists tend to maintain. Some theists argue that there is an eternal, infinite, and intelligent God but that he is not a creator and does not exercise providence over the world; others see him as free, creator, and provident ruler of all creation. *Ontologism* (10: 701d) is most sanguine in its claims about knowledge of God: it affirms that the idea of being, which is immediately and intuitively present to the human intellect, is God himself. *Pantheism* (10:947d) holds that there exists only one being, the universal principle of all things, and that the world is identical with this principle; a variation is *panentheism* (10:943d), which views all things as being in God without exhausting the infinity of the divine nature. A partial pantheism would identify God with the soul of the world (14:1027b) or with some other principle such as cosmic energy or primary matter. *Emanationism* (5:291d) is a form of pantheism according to which all things emanate or flow forth from God as from a primal source or principle. It is different from *exemplarism* (5:712c), which sees God as providing a divine exemplar in terms of which all of being can best be understood.

6. With regard to the problems of *ethics* there are many systems that variously construe the goal of human action or the source from which ethical conduct should derive its norms or principles. According to *eudaemonism* (5:621c) man's ulti-

mate good consists in happiness or in some state or condition
of general well-being or welfare; thus it provides a teleological
explanation from which rules of morality can be derived. *Hedonism* (6:983d) locates man's good in pleasure, either his own
or that of others. *Egoism* (5:193d) urges that each man should
seek his own pleasure or good and ignore that of others, except
when this would be to his disadvantage, whereas *altruism*
(1:355b) locates the good in the well-being of others and would
make the quest for the happiness of one's fellow man the basic
moral value. *Utilitarianism* (14:503c) is a generalized form of
hedonism: it holds that human pleasure is the only thing good
in itself and pain the only thing evil in itself, and it judges the
rightness of an action on its contribution to human welfare,
which it attempts to maximize. *Deontologism* (4:777d) is an
ethics of duty based on man's intuition of moral principles;
akin to it is *ethical formalism* (5:570a), which holds that
moral value is determined by formal rather than by material
considerations, i.e., by the agent's attitudes and intentions rather
than by what is done and its consequences. *Situational ethics*
(13:268b) opposes any universal principles or laws as determinants of morality and would decide the rightness of an action
on the basis of concrete individual situations and how these
appeal to one's conscience.

## §87. HISTORIOGRAPHY OF PHILOSOPHY

1. The *methodology* employed in the history of philosophy
is essentially that of historical investigation (9:743a). Unlike
some speculative disciplines history is not concerned with possible, abstract, and universal essences, but with concrete facts and
with particular and real events; it does not prescribe how
matters should have occurred but it investigates and reports how
and why they did occur. Its method embraces two basic functions, namely, the heuristic and the hermeneutical. (1) The
heuristic function aims to investigate the facts and to reconstruct these as they actually happened. This is done by studying

the writings of philosophers, using direct and indirect sources and auxiliary sciences, and reconstructing the thought they convey as accurately as possible. Beyond this the historian of philosophy may classify thinkers and their systems, locate them in their proper coordinates of place and time, and take account of explicit relations of dependence and interaction among them. (2) The hermeneutical function [§57.4] goes beyond the statement of facts to their explanation and interpretation. This involves a search for the reasons behind the facts, how some may perhaps serve to explain others, and how their interactions are to be interpreted. It may seek broad generalizations but must do so cautiously, refraining from imposing a priori schemata on the facts and from having recourse to non-historical elements.

2. The *division* of the history of philosophy is effected in various ways and according to different criteria, none of which is completely satisfactory. Perhaps the best is that based on chronology or periodization because it takes account of the temporal succession of the facts; it would be ideal if philosophy truly developed in a straight and ascending line of homogeneous progress, which of course it has not. Again, there are frequent gaps of centuries over which one system may have influenced another, such as Aristotelianism (4th century B.C.) in its impact on high scholasticism (13th century A.D.). The widely used division of philosophy into ancient, medieval, modern, and contemporary (see chs. 16-19, *infra*) is based upon Western history, but it does not fit well the development of Oriental cultures or the actual growth of philosophy itself. Another criterion is geography or ethnology, and according to this philosophy may be divided into Chinese philosophy (3:608a), Indian philosophy (7:458b), Greek philosophy (6:733b), Arabian philosophy (1:722d), Spanish philosophy (13:548d), American philosophy (1:438b), Latin American philosophy (8:483a), Jewish philosophy (7:977a), and so on; alternately, one may speak of recent philosophical thought in the U.S., the United Kingdom, France, Germany, etc. (16:341a-348d). Philosophy itself transcends nation and race, however, and to this extent such divisions are likewise defective. Yet other criteria are the enu-

meration of problem areas, such as philosophies of nature, of being, of knowledge, etc.; or of various disciplines, such as the history of logic (8:958a), the history of psychology (11:970a), and the history of ethics (5:573c); or of various systematic approaches, as already noted [§86]; or of various schools, such as Platonism (11:433d), Aristotelianism (1:799c), Neoplatonism (10:334a), Thomism (14:126d), Scotism (12:1226a), Cartesianism (3:157b), Kantianism (8:127d), and Hegelianism (6:990a).

3. The history of philosophy has its own history, which may be referred to as the *metahistory* of philosophy (11:303a). Among the Greeks a certain prominence was given to the anecdotal and to expounding the opinions of various sects (doxography), and among the Schoolmen there was much exposition and criticism of philosophical views on a broad range of problems, but neither of these groups intended to produce true histories of philosophy. Much the same could be said for Renaissance rediscoveries of the lives and teachings of ancient philosophers, the eclectic manuals and questionnaires of the 16th and 17th centuries, and the compilations of various encyclopedists (5:333a-335d) up to the end of the 18th century. It was during the 19th century that the scientific study of history in all its branches was inaugurated: this was based on a critical and objective investigation of facts and documents, and from this period date the great general histories of philosophy, complemented by vast numbers of monographic studies on individuals and schools. The result has been a moving revelation of the process involved in the formation and development of philosophy, one of the great achievements of the human mind, itself spanning centuries and utilizing the contributions of many peoples.

# CHAPTER 16.

# ANCIENT PHILOSOPHY

## §88. EARLY THOUGHT

1. By *ancient philosophy* (11:303b) is meant primarily ancient Western philosophy from its beginnings among the Greeks on the Ionian coast of Asia Minor to its last manifestation in Neoplatonism. As used here the expression also includes those forms of Chinese and Indian thought that contain elements of philosophical reasoning under a moralistic or religious exterior.

2. The desire to know, begotten by wonder at the marvels of nature, led men to philosophize: they did so when they began to penetrate into the deeper nature of things and to seek by reason the most basic causes of what they knew by experience. The philosophy they produced, at least among the Greeks, stood in marked contrast to credulous acceptance of the theogonies and mythological cosmologies, the timeworn traditions of the race embodied in the poets Homer (GBWW 4) and Hesiod (6:736c,742c). These ancient teachers of Greece often spoke the truth, but they used the language of belief and not that of proof. Greek philosophy (6:733b) emerged as a conscious reaction to such dogmatism, when men took experience rather than tradition as the starting point of their thought.

3. Only with the Greeks did ancient philosophy reach consciousness of its nature as a rational investigation of things. In contrast, the philosophical thought of the East remained hidden in religious beliefs or in the traditions of national culture. The great master of *Chinese philosophy* (3:608a), Küng or Confucius (4:156a), was content to transmit and comment on the

teachings of the ancients without inventing anything new in his ethical reform. Lao-Tzu (8:379c) was perhaps more metaphysical in his Way, known as Taoism (13:935d), yet even this was primarily a mystical-philosophical exposition of the principles that should govern one's moral life. Much more rational was the *Indian philosophy* (7:458b) of the Brahmans (2:747c), since the Upanishads (14:473c) formulate a speculative system that is essentially metaphysical. But it was elaborated by the priestly caste primarily as a wisdom of salvation, a quest for union with a higher being, and as such it was endowed with the attributes of a religion. Like Brahmanism, of which it is a corruption, Buddhism (2:847c) proposed an anthropocentric philosophy of self-salvation. The Persian dualism of Zoroaster (14:1133d) was a mixture of religion, mythology, and reason in a non-philosophical form.

4. If the Greek quest for philosophical wisdom showed a marked reaction to myth and uncritical tradition, it did not thereby represent a break with the general culture of the race. The Greek regard for the individual and his personal freedom and for the ideals of *paideia* (see 10:862d), i.e., the shaping and educating of man to his true form, was constantly reflected in the philosophers. Of equal and even greater importance, perhaps, was the Greek feeling for the whole, an architectonic sense that looked for the bond that integrates individuals and events into a greater unity: the *harmonia,* the "golden chains" that bind all things together. In the *pre-Socratic* period the main preoccupation was the search for the one source, the *phusis* or nature, whence come the scattered particulars of everyday experience. The "physicists" of Ionia, in the 7th and 6th centuries B.C., all held to one principle from which things evolve: Thales, water; Anaximander, the boundless or unlimited; and Anaximenes, air. More recondite was the thought of Pythagoras (11:1055b) and his followers, who studied the *phusis* in terms of number; yet this too was a search for the harmony and inner unity of the cosmos.

5. Two later thinkers, Heraclitus and Parmenides, inaugurated a more metaphysical turn by attempting to penetrate be-

hind the world of ceaseless change to discover that which truly
is. Heraclitus (6:1046b) was primarily a teacher of moral wisdom
who discerned behind the physical world and human life an all-
abiding, all-ruling law or *logos* as the principle of unity amidst
universal change and opposition. The world process interested
Heraclitus chiefly as an illustration of this law, that men might
learn from the order of the cosmos to order their own lives.
In contrast, Parmenides (10:1027a) wrote an epic poem con-
centrating on the reality, the "that which is" of the physical
world, in opposition to current illusions on the nature of the
universe. He raised the problem of *being*, arguing that *logos* or
reason proves that the existent cannot be what one's senses reveal to him, something manifold and in motion; rather it must
be something whole and indivisible, motionless and perfect.
Hence Zeno of Elea (14:1117c), his follower, sought to prove
that "there is no many."

6. The last of the naturalists, Empedocles (5:323c), Anaxagoras (1:483a), and Democritus (4:751c), generally retained
Parmenides's position that being alone is and yet sought to explain obvious motion and change. Each in his way, these thinkers
posited basic unchanging *elements* whose combination would
give rise to the things of experience: Empedocles adopted four
basic elements; Anaxagoras, an infinite number of principles;
and Democritus and the school of Abdera, unchanging *atoms*
(1:1020d).

## §89. CLASSICAL GREEK PERIOD

1. None of these early philosophers, save Anaxagoras and
those of Abdera, lived on the mainland of Greece, much less in
Athens. The scene shifted with the coming of the classical
period of Greek philosophy, even as philosophy itself passed
from concentration on the world of nature to more metaphysical
interests. In this change the Sophists (13:437c) provided the
transition, since they focused attention on man and the city-
state; unfortunately they often emphasized rhetoric and elo-

quence at the expense of truth. In reaction to their ideal of speaking well, Socrates (13:407c) professed a new *sophia*, the wisdom of thinking well, a wisdom of the inner man who lived what he thought: the true philosopher. In this he set the pattern for Plato and Aristotle, who as true Socratics and lovers of wisdom sought to penetrate reality and human life to their ultimates.

2. For PLATO (11:430b, GBWW 7) the philosopher is the man liberated by right *paideia* from slavery to the senses, whose life is formed and guided by knowledge of true being, found only in the Forms or Ideas. He pursues true virtue and wisdom, and so his conduct is not based on his own opinions but is modeled on the transcendent Forms of the virtues, e.g., of justice and temperance. Thus does the rational part of his soul achieve mastery over the less noble elements within him. True knowledge, he soon realizes, is not found in sense experience, but in the stable and fixed beings of things beyond transient phenomena, the world of Forms or Ideas; ultimately he must come to the best and highest of the Ideas, the Good itself. Philosophy, for Plato, does not give final answers to even the deepest questions, but it spurs the philosopher ever upward to a more perfect vision of the absolute.

3. ARISTOTLE (1:809a, GBWW 8-9), long known as "the Philosopher" personified, was more scientific and logical than Plato in his pursuit of knowledge. Yet, as a Socratic, he did not separate philosophy from life; moreover, as a disciple of Plato, he also was convinced that philosophical knowledge is not concerned with the particular sensible, but with the essences of things and their ultimate causes and principles. Against Plato, however, he refused to have recourse to a separate world of Forms to answer the problem of being. Rather he saw forms within things as explaining the being attributed to them. Moreover, since the form of a sensible being is itself subject to potency and to change, one must posit the existence of supra-sensible beings that are actual and imperishable, the heavenly bodies; beyond them, again, is a perfect principle whose very entity is pure act. The god of Aristotle is the first unmoved mover of the

heavenly spheres, the final cause that produces motion by being desired; such a god's inner life is thought thinking itself, and otherwise he is quite unrelated to the world of nature, which he did not produce and does not govern. The form in living things and in man is called a soul, but Aristotle is not clear that man's soul or mind survives his body. Thus his ethics and politics are earth-bound and centered on the perfection of the individual within the city-state. Despite such limitations, however, the doctrine of Aristotle represents the peak of Greek thought. As the history of Aristotelianism (1:799c) reveals, all succeeding philosophers, Greek, Arabian, Christian, and modern, stand in some debt to him.

## §90. POST-ARISTOTELIAN DEVELOPMENTS

1. Greek philosophy after Aristotle reflected, and to some extent caused, a change in Greek political outlook. With the conquests of Alexander the Great (1:295b) human thought burst the confines of the city-state and saw men as members of a world commonwealth. So the Cynics (4:563b) proclaimed themselves cosmopolitans, citizens of the world rather than of a particular city-state. Influenced by them, Zeno of Citium, the founder of Stoicism (13:717b), also Cleanthes and later Chrysippus elaborated a physics whose monistic materialism made of the world a harmonious whole activated by a principle called god, fire, mind, fate, or logos. The ethical ideal of Stoic thought was life in agreement with nature in a passionless and calm detachment from all self-love and worldly interests. Less appealing because more individualistic, Epicureanism (5:466c) resembled Stoicism as an ethics based on a monistic physics. Its goal, as formulated by Epicurus (5:468b), was pleasure, less in the hedonist sense of the Cyrenaics (4:570b) than in that of peace of mind and freedom from pain. To rid men of fear of the gods and of death Epicurus adopted a form of atomism wherein the gods have nothing to do with the world or with men and death brings dissolution of soul as well as of body.

The skepticism (13:275d) that marked other Greek thinkers of this period was itself intended to be a step toward happiness.

2. Further witness to the spread of Hellenistic culture are to be found in the *Jewish philosophy* (7:977a) of Philo Judaeus (11:287c) and in the smattering of *Roman philosophy* that appeared in the republic and empire. Jewish tradition was marked by a distrust of reason and philosophy, so Philo appears as an exception; he sought to develop his religious belief by elements taken from Plato and the Stoics. After him there was little or no speculative thought among the Jews until Avicebron (1:1130b), whose *Fons vitae* is manifestly Neoplatonic in inspiration, and Moses Maimonides (9:79d), whose *Guide for the Perplexed* is preeminently Aristotelian. Among the Romans, philosophy was hardly more than a reflection of Greek thought tempered and shaped by the Roman spirit. Stoicism, as expounded by Seneca (13:80a), Epictetus (5:466b, GBWW 12), and Marcus Aurelius (9:195d, GBWW 12) had a special appeal for its rugged moral tone, as a help in forming the good citizen. Epicureanism was popularized by Lucretius (8:1061a), whose didactic poem *On the Nature of Things* (GBWW 12), developed atomism as a comprehensive materialistic philosophy.

3. The last great philosophical movement of pagan antiquity was a revival of Platonism (11:433d) reaching its climax in what is now known as *Neoplatonism* (10:334a). In many instances this movement was marked by a deeply religious coloring as philosophy came to be used as a medium for union with the divine. Middle Platonism (11:434d), as expounded by Plutarch (GBWW 14), Celsus (3:382b), and others, accented the transcendence of God, multiplied intermediaries between God and the world, contrasted to an extreme the dualism of matter and spirit, and laid great emphasis on revelation, mysticism, and ecstasy. These characteristics carried over into the teachings of PLOTINUS (11:433b, GBWW 17), the first of the Neoplatonists. At the same time Plotinus drew from Plato, Aristotle, and the Stoics to construct a synthesis that was the last stand of intellectual paganism against the growing appeal of Christianity. His map of the intelligible world, derived from an analysis of

human knowledge, was designed to point the way to union with the One, the first principle of all. The school of Plotinus thrived in such disciples as Porphyry (11:593c) and Proclus (11:825b); through them it deeply influenced patristic culture. The direct descendants, however, of Plato, Aristotle, and Plotinus were the proponents of Arabian philosophy (1:722d).

4. Ancient philosophy came to a kind of official end in 529, when Justinian (8:96a) banished the philosophers from Athens and confiscated their schools. By that time, however, it had left its mark on Christian thinkers and had produced the new movement of Christian philosophy.

# CHAPTER 17.

# MEDIEVAL PHILOSOPHY

## §91. PATRISTIC PHILOSOPHY

1. Christianity is not a philosophy but a revealed religion, a means of salvation. Yet because it answers many questions asked by philosophy, dialogue and even conflict between these two forms of knowledge was almost inevitable from the beginning of the Christian era—whether in the early centuries, the period of patristic culture, or later, in the Middle Ages, in what has come to be called scholasticism. Under *medieval philosophy*, then, we shall consider both periods, that of *patristic philosophy* (10:1103c), to examine the philosophical teachings utilized by the Church Fathers, and that of *scholastic philosophy*, to see the distinctive Christian philosophies elaborated in the Schools.

2. The first dialogue between Christianity and philosophy, held by St. Paul in the Areopagus of Athens, was an apparent failure, for the wisdom of Christ was ridiculed by the philosophers as foolishness. In succeeding centuries many philosophers continued to regard Christianity as a specious doctrine of little or no value, and, on their part, many Christians felt that philosophy was the invention of the devil and the source of errors and heresies such as those of Gnosticism (6:523b). Yet rhetoricians and philosophers who had been converted to Christianity were not inclined to abandon entirely the wisdom they had acquired by rational methods, but proposed to put it to use in the service of Christ. An early instance of this new attitude is found in the Greek apologists (1:677d) of the 2d and 3d centuries, who employed the techniques of rhetoric, law, and phi-

losophy to defend their new-found faith. In so doing they came
to see, as did Justin Martyr (8:94b) and Clement of Alexandria
(3:943a), that whatever truth is found in the philosophers is
but a fragmentary sharing in divine wisdom; moreover, in the
providence of God, as Clement and Eusebius of Caesarea (5:
633c) held, Greek philosophy is intended to be a preparation
for the gospel and a pedagogue to Christ. For Clement it also
had value for defending the faith and presenting it in such
fashion as to win a hearing; properly used, it perfected the Christian, helped him to understand what he believed and to grow
in virtue, and made him a true Gnostic, a learned and holy man.

3. Once secular learning had thus been brought into the
service of Christ, the way was open for a greater collaboration
of philosophy and Christianity. Origen (10:767c), who had
studied under Clement in the school of Alexandria, felt the need
to know philosophy and to use it in the explanation and defense
of Christian dogma. Often at fault because he went too far in
his speculations, and the center of a long controversy after his
death (10:771c), Origen nonetheless paved the way for others
who followed his ideals in more orthodox form. Even his adversaries, such as Methodius of Olympus (9:742a), an admirer of
Plato, owed him more than they admitted. A deeper problem
that arose in the 4th century was that of either absorbing or of
being absorbed by the culture of Hellenism (3:653a). More
than one heresy, e.g., Arianism (1:791b) and Apollinarism
(1:665d), was closely connected with Greek philosophy; more
than one churchman, as was said of Synesius of Cyrene (13:
884d), was more Platonist than Christian. Yet others, such as
Epiphanius of Constantia (5:478d), were deadly enemies of
all classical culture and Greek philosophy.

4. A happy balance is to be found in three great thinkers of
Cappadocia who share a common love and admiration for Origen: Gregory of Nazianzus (6:791a), who gave attention to
man's knowledge of God in a series of sermons admired by
Augustine; Basil the Great (2:143b), who synthesized the cosmological knowledge of his day and in a famous letter to his
nephews showed how Christians could profitably use the classics;

and Gregory of Nyssa (6:794a), the best philosopher of the three, who continued his brother Basil's work with a study of man, *De hominis opificio*, and another on death and the Resurrection in manifest imitation of Plato's *Phaedo*. Gregory's influence is apparent in the work of Nemesius of Emesa (10:317b) entitled *On the Nature of Man*. In the early 6th century the writings of the enigmatic Pseudo-Dionysius (11:943a) the Areopagite made their appearance in Syria, presenting a curious blending of Christian teaching and Neoplatonic thought. The unknown author apparently sought to convert the Neoplatonists and turn them into Christian philosophers; instead, his works, along with the scholia of John of Scythopolis (7:1074c) and Maximus the Confessor (9:514d), had greater influence among Christians of both East and West. The last of the *Greek Fathers* to enter the scene, John Damascene (7:1047d), summarized Greek patristic thought in his *Exposition of the Orthodox Faith* and made ample use of Dionysius's doctrines.

5. Among the *Latin Fathers* before Augustine one can trace no set pattern. Minucius Felix (9:883a) composed his *Octavius* in imitation of Cicero with some dependence on Seneca. Tertullian (13: 1019b) relied on Soranus the Stoic to explain the nature of the soul and thus fell into materialism. Marius Victorinus (9:231a) remained a Neoplatonist even after his conversion, since he used that philosophy to help explain the Trinity. Without his help St. Augustine (1:1041b, GBWW 18) would hardly have achieved a concept of the spiritual, so deeply had he fallen into Manichean materialism. When he came to the Church it was not to abandon whatever good he had found in philosophy but to vindicate its use for the Christian. Whatever truth the philosophers had discovered must be taken away from them by the Christian and built into the structure of a deeper wisdom. Philosophy for him was thus not an independent discipline but a part of his search for God, and every one of its branches was made to contribute to that search.

6. After Augustine, in the period marked by the migration of nations, there was little philosophical thought beyond that of Boethius and Cassiodorus. Preeminently the mediator be-

tween ancient culture and the Middle Ages, Boethius (2:631c)
left his mark on logic, the problem of universals, liberal arts,
and theology; while Cassiodorus (3:184a), author of a *De anima*,
introduced learning and intellectual culture into monastic life.
Isidore of Seville (7:674a) and the Venerable Bede (2:217a)
deserve mention as encyclopedists. In addition Bede marks a
transition to the Middle Ages (9:812a), since from his monastic
tradition came those who would achieve a rebirth of learning
in the Carolingian renaissance (3:141d).

### §92. SCHOLASTICISM AND ITS PRELUDE

1. The spirit and tradition of patristic philosophy was not
abandoned in the revival of learning under Charlemagne. Alcuin
(1:279a) and his pupil Rabanus Maurus (12:37b) continued
the ideal of Augustine, making philosophy and secular knowledge the handmaids of faith. At the same time the court of
Charles the Bald witnessed a philosophical controversy on the
nature of the soul carried on by Ratramnus of Corbie (12:93d)
and Hincmar of Rheims (6:1122b), and was intrigued if not
scandalized by the bold thinking and writing of John Scotus
Erigena (7:1072c). Possessed of some knowledge of Greek and
widely read in Pseudo-Dionysius, Maximus, and Gregory of
Nyssa, as well as in Ambrose (1:372c) and Augustine, Erigena
undertook a daring and powerful synthesis of philosophy and
theology in his *De divisione naturae* to show how the multiplicity of things proceeds from the oneness of God and is in
turn brought back to him. Even here, however, philosophy was
a meditation on Holy Scripture and the faith, not the exercise
of reason for its own sake.

2. Only after Erigena, and partly under his influence, did
Western thinkers make any real distinction between philosophy
and revealed doctrine, to the extent that they began to cultivate
logic for its own sake. *Dialectics* in particular attracted fresh
interest in the 11th and 12th centuries, and often intruded itself
in areas where it had no place (4:846a). Yet it is here that one

finds the real beginnings of the movement known as *scholasticism* (12:1153c), which reached its high point in the 13th century. Often indeed this early scholasticism, as in Peter Abelard (1:15d), thought it could answer such metaphysical questions as the nature of universals by the doctrine and method proper to logic, or explain the mysteries of the faith by pure dialectics. At the same time, the sound use of reasoning in Lanfranc of Bec (8:361c) and Anselm of Canterbury (1:581a) opened the way to a wholesome flowering of doctrine in the 12th century. From the school directed by Anselm's pupil, Anselm of Laon (1:584a), came theologians who by the middle of the century had done much to systematize theology in numerous *Sentences* and *Summae* (13:94d), often in imitation and rivalry of Peter Abelard's theological synthesis. The same tendency to summarize theology marked the work of the Parisian School of Saint-Victor, under masters Hugh of Saint-Victor (7:194a) and Richard of Saint-Victor (12:483a), who at the same time were much interested in philosophy and in mysticism. The most complete and most influential of such books of *Sentences was* that of Peter Lombard (11:221c), composed at Paris in the 1150s. Cistercian writers, influenced by Bernard of Clairvaux (2:335c), produced many treatises on the soul as prefaces to spiritual doctrines, seen in the works of Isaac of Stella (7:663b), Alcher of Clairvaux (1:270d), and William of Saint-Thierry (14:938b); Alan of Lille (1:239d) was also important for his methodology and the scope of his theological productivity.

3. Though Paris was gradually becoming the intellectual center of the West, in the early 12th century it was rivaled as a center of philosophy and unsurpassed as a seat of classical humanism by the School of Chartres. The last and greatest of the pre-university cathedral schools of Europe, under Bernard of Chartres (2:335b), Gilbert de la Porrée (6:478b), and others, it became known for its feeling for antiquity, its Platonism, and its growing interest in science. Its most representative thinker was perhaps John of Salisbury (7:1071c), who also mirrored the learning of Paris and was a witness to the growing importance of its schools.

4. Those schools, organized about 1200 as the guild or "university of the masters and scholars of Paris" (10:1012a), prepared the way for the flowering of scholasticism proper in the 13th century. Yet without the influx of new literature and ideas, through the *translations* of hitherto unknown works of Aristotle and of the Arabian and Jewish philosophers and scientists (14:248d), the intellectual horizon of the West would never have been broadened beyond the narrow limits of earlier centuries. With the rise of Islam (7:676c) there had been an extensive development and spread of ideas within Aristotelianism (1:802a), which had been harmonized with Neoplatonism and placed alternately in the service of, and in confrontation with, Moslem belief. The principal writers this movement produced were Alkindi (8:183c), Alfarabi (1:308c), Avicenna (1:1131a), and Averroës (1:1125d). Some scholastics, such as William of Auvergne (14:921b), made use of Avicenna, but Averroës became increasingly influential as a guide to the thought of Aristotle, with consequences that soon gave rise to a crisis at Paris [§93.3].

## §93.  HIGH SCHOLASTICISM

1. Although it is difficult to locate philosophical movements chronologically and geographically, mid-13th century Paris is generally regarded as the focal point of the movement known as high scholasticism (12:1155b). The Englishman Roger Bacon (12:522a) was a product of the University of Paris, where he lectured in arts longer than any other master. His preference, however, was for mathematics and its methods, which he traced to the Oxford master, Robert Grosseteste (12:530d), who taught the Franciscans (6:38d) and was one of the most original and versatile minds of the century. At Paris the foremost Franciscans to use philosophy in the service of theology included Alexander of Hales (1:296b), John of La Rochelle (7:1057d), and Bonaventure (2:658b). These thinkers used the new learning sparingly in their attempts to sift truth from error and were more

proficient in the older traditions of *Augustinianism* (1:1063c).
Some of the characteristics of their thought are the following:
(1) an emphasis on the primacy of faith when discussing the
relationships between faith and reason (5:807d); (2) focusing
on the soul and God as the principal objects of philosophical
inquiry; (3) developing the doctrine of divine illumination
(7:366d) as a theory of knowledge; (4) employing the notion
of seminal reasons (13:68d) to explain some creaturely activity;
(5) according a primacy of the will and of affective powers over
the intellectual; (6) teaching a universal hylomorphism extending even to spiritual substances; (7) holding for a plurality of
forms (5:1024c) in created composites; and (8) maintaining
the impossibility of creation *ab aeterno.*

2. A marked contrast to the Franciscans is found in the
thought of Dominicans (4:974b) such as Albert the Great and
Thomas Aquinas. Among the scholastics Albert (1:254d) was
the first to appreciate the importance of the newly imported
Greek-Arabic learning for science and philosophy, and set himself to making encyclopedic summaries for his students which
earned for him the title "the Great" in his own lifetime. He had
many followers among German Dominicans, including Theo-
doric of Freiberg (14:22d), Ulric of Strassburg (14:379d), and
Meister Eckhart (5:38d), but his work bore principal fruit in
the monumental syntheses elaborated by his pupil THOMAS
AQUINAS (14:102a, GBWW 19-20). Although respectful of
Augustine, Aquinas rejected many of the traditional teachings of
Augustinianism, e.g., the theory of illumination in knowledge,
the plurality of forms, seminal reasons, and the notion of soul
as a complete substance (for which he substituted the concept
of form). Called the "Angelic Doctor"—for the honorary titles of
other scholastics, see 4:935c—he brought Aristotelian natural
philosophy and metaphysics into the heart of theology and developed a unique synthesis known as *Thomism* (14:126d) that
put pagan knowledge at the service of faith. Some of the characteristic Thomistic theses include the following: (1) the pure
potentiality of primary matter and its first actualization by substantial form; (2) individuation by determined matter, *materia*

*signata;* (3) a rejection of spiritual matter; (4) man's rational soul as the unique substantial form of his body, endowed with spiritual powers or faculties that are really distinct from it; (5) an abstractive theory of knowledge originating with the senses but capable of attaining universals; (6) the human mind's ability to reason to the existence of God and some of his attributes from the visible things of the world; (7) God's nature as Pure Act and *Ipsum Esse Subsistens,* unlike that of creatures composed of essence and existence as really distinct principles; and (8) the concept of being as analogically, and not univocally, predictable of God, substances, and accidents.

3. Aquinas's knowledge of Aristotle and Averroës put him in good position to oppose the *Latin Averroism* (1:1127c) that developed into a strong movement at Paris after 1255. Masters such as Siger of Brabant (13:204d) and Boethius of Sweden (2:633b) sought a philosophy free from theological control and were accused of holding a theory of double truth (4:1022a), i.e., teaching that a proposition may be true according to reason and false according to faith, by Bishop Tempier (13:992c) of Paris, who condemned their doctrines in 1270 and 1277. Among other theses defended by the Averroists were the following: (1) the world and all its species are eternal, and thus there was no first man; (2) God and celestial causes act on the world with necessity, and contingency is found only in the sublunary world owing to the presence of matter there; (3) there is only one possible intellect for the entire human race (7:557a)—as opposed to Avicennism, which holds for one agent intellect for all men; and (4) as a consequence, human reason cannot demonstrate man's personal immortality.

4. The condemnation of 1277 was sweeping and included incidentally some of the distinctive teachings of Aquinas; this circumstance led William de la Mare (14:928c) to draw up a *correctorium* of passages in Thomas's writings so as to preserve orthodox Franciscan teaching. Early Thomists such as Richard Knapwell (12:480c), Thomas Sutton (14:123b), and John of Paris (7:1064b) replied with a series of *correctoria* (4:349c) of their own, and bitter controversies thereupon broke out between

Franciscans and Dominicans. In other quarters the scholastic world continued to be divided over the distinction between essence and existence (5:548c), the unicity or the plurality of forms, illumination, the soul and its powers, and the like, well into the 14th century. Masters who figured prominently in these disputes included Giles of Rome (6:484d), Henry of Ghent (6:1035d), Godfrey of Fontaines (6:577d), Peter Thomae (11:229b), and Walter of Chatton (14:788a). In the midst of this intellectual turmoil JOHN DUNS SCOTUS (4:1102a) sought to create a new synthesis; in a critical yet positive spirit he undertook to examine anew the limits of reason contrasted to faith, the problem of knowledge generally, the object of metaphysics, and the doctrine of being, giving greater emphasis to divine freedom and to metaphysical proofs for God's existence. The main theses of the *Scotism* (12:1226a) that emerged from this effort include the following: (1) the univocity of the metaphysical concept of being, the proper object of the human intellect; (2) God and creatures as two modes of univocal being, infinite and finite respectively; (3) metaphysics as the first and foremost study for man, preceding that of the special sciences; (4) the supremacy of God's freedom and love, and the primacy of the will in man; (5) the actual formal distinction *a parte rei* between the soul and its powers; (6) the plurality of forms or *formalitates*; (7) "thisness" or *haecceitas* as the principle of individuation; (8) a denial of the pure potentiality of primary matter; and (9) a denial of the real distinction between essence and existence.

## §94. LATE SCHOLASTICISM

1. The last of the great scholastics was WILLIAM OF OCKHAM (14:932a), who epitomized the spirit of criticism that pervaded the early 14th century. His contemporaries called the position he developed the modern way (*via moderna*) in contrast to the old way (*via antiqua*) of Aquinas and Scotus, and this exerted a pronounced influence, along with Thomism and Scot-

ism, in the later development of scholasticism. _Ockamism_ (10: 630c) is itself a variety of nominalism (10:483a, 16:318d) that espouses the following doctrines: (1) concepts are universal in a purely functional sense and do not refer to a common nature possessed by things individually; (2) reality itself is a collection of absolute singulars, the distinguishable units of which are substances and qualities; (3) motion does not exist as an entity really distinct from the moving body; (4) God can will anything that does not involve a contradiction, and even natures are radically contingent upon the divine will; (5) it is always possible to have one singular without another, and God can produce any effect without its proper cause; (6) man intuitively grasps the individual thing sensibly affecting him here and now; (7) all other knowledge is abstract and non-necessary, and even the conclusions of philosophy and science are at best highly probable, including those that profess to demonstrate the existence of transcendent realities such as God or the human soul.

2. Under the influence of Ockham, scholastic thought after 1350 moved away from the metaphysics developed so persistently in the 13th century and began to examine new questions. One evidence of this change was the 14th-century interest in the philosophy of language and in the development of logics of terms and suppositions, patterned on the earlier writings of Peter of Spain (7:1013b) and William of Sherwood (14:939b). At Oxford the beginnings of a mathematical physics of space and motion were made by Thomas Bradwardine (14:116a) and others at Merton College, including John of Dumbleton (7: 1050), Richard of Swyneshed (12:484a), and William of Heytesbury (14:925c), who also devoted themselves to a study of logical antinomies known as _insolubilia_. At Paris John Buridan (7:1037d), Albert of Saxony (1:259c), and Nicholas Oresme (10:454b) anticipated, by their teachings on impetus (7:400b), gravitation (6:710d), and the universe, many later discoveries in physics and astronomy; their doctrines, while developed in an Aristotelian framework, marked a clear departure from the physics of classical antiquity (12:1200c). More extreme versions of the Ockhamist position were worked out by John of Mire-

court (7:1061) and Nicholas of Autrecourt (10:447c), who moved increasingly toward skepticism.

3. While new ideas occupied the professors of the arts faculties, the theologians tended to crystallize into schools. Thomism, which had become the official doctrine of the Dominicans, was championed by Harvey Nedellec (6:939b), John of Naples (7:1062c), John Capreolus (3:91c), and later by Tommaso de Vio Cajetan (2:1053b). Among the defenders and developers of Scotism should be mentioned Antonius Andreas (1:647d), Francis of Meyronnes (6:32c), Hugh of Newcastle (7:192d), and William of Alnwick (14:920b). Within the Augustinian Order (1:1071c) the doctrines of Giles of Rome were made official even within his lifetime; these were developed by James of Viterbo (7:813a) and Augustine of Ancona (1:1058a), among others.

4. With this, Paris unfortunately became a city of conflict and confusion. Religious-minded scholars revolted against it, while the growing number of humanists sought to restore the classical concept of the liberal arts and return to a pre-scholastic type of culture. In Germany, the vitriolic attacks of Martin Luther (8:1085d) on the schoolmen and on philosophy, and the ravages of the Reformation (12:180d), destroyed whatever scholasticism existed in that country. Only in Spain did the movement show new life with the rise of middle scholasticism. (12:1158b).

# CHAPTER 18.

# MODERN PHILOSOPHY

## §95. RENAISSANCE PHILOSOPHY

1. The time span of *modern philosophy* (11:310a) reaches from about 1400 to 1900, although there is no sharp division setting it off from either its medieval roots or its contemporary fruits. The whole development includes three main phases: the Renaissance transition (1400-1600); the classical modern methods and systematic explanations, of which the two most important are empiricism and rationalism (1600-1800); and the 19th-century attempts at philosophical reconstruction. Each period made a distinctive contribution to the process, and yet modern philosophy itself developed certain broad characteristics: (1) it grew in the context of modern cultural and national factors; (2) it used vernacular languages increasingly and developed a technical philosophical vocabulary in each linguistic area; (3) it was heavily influenced by the methods, concepts, and problems evolved in the physical and then the biological sciences; (4) it gradually dissociated itself from theological frameworks, although religious interests continued to have a definite bearing on philosophical inquiries; and (5) the growth of historical awareness led to its special interest in genetic questions and human historicity.

2. Somewhat typical of *Renaissance philosophy* (12:370a) is the work of Nicholas of Cusa (10:449a), which embodied the early Renaissance disenchantment with the medieval systems, its epistemological uneasiness, and its special concern to rethink man's relations with God and the world. Although religious faith held firm his conviction in God's reality and creative power, he shifted the inquiry about God from a causal basis

to a symbolical use of concepts similar to the mathematical way of dealing with infinite figures. Thus Nicholas heralded the appeal of philosophical methodology to the procedures of mathematics and physics, as well as the modern dialectical correlation between God and a world regarded as his expressive image and the locus for constant social reforms.

3. A form of Christian humanism was developed by the Florentine Platonists (11:437c) Marsilio Ficino (5:907c) and Pico della Mirandola (11:347b), who strongly defended man's freedom, personal immortality, and ordination to God against the attacks of the Aristotelians at Padua, themselves still under the influence of Averroës. Aristotelianism continued to flourish in Northern Italy and Germany (1:805b), though without the distinctively Christian interpretations of man, nature, and the prime mover that had formerly characterized it; the strongest work was done in logical methodology and natural philosophy, and its most important figures were Pietro Pomponazzi (11: 546a), Agostino Nifo (10:465a), and Jacopo Zabarella (14: 1101b).

4. Renaissance Stoicism (13:720d) and skepticism (13: 276d) arose from a continued dissatisfaction with all current accounts of human knowledge and conduct. Justus Lipsius (8:784a) urged that Platonism was too cabalistic; that pure Aristotelianism ran counter to faith in a personal, free, transcendent God and beatitude; and that a sounder view was obtainable from Stoic logic, physics, and ethics. The most radical challenge, however, came from the reformulation of Greek skepticism by Montaigne (9:1072a, GBWW 25) and Pierre Charron (3:512d). They produced a crisis by regarding man's knowing powers as unreliable, by pointing out the large mixture of fantasy and wish in human speculations, and by pitting one philosophical school against another. Right down to Pierre Bayle (2:182a) the skeptical attitude remained strong, thus providing a spur for the great systematic thinkers of the 17th century.

5. Three other facets of the Renaissance mind are captured in the thought of Niccolò Machiavelli (9:31c, GBWW 23), Giordano Bruno (2:839d), and the philosophers of nature.

Machiavelli placed brackets around the social precepts of Christianity and took the attitude of the inquiring scientist toward the realities of political life; his stark findings on the drive toward power and the political management of men pointed up the need for a relevant and yet morally disciplined political philosophy [§81.4]. Bruno's pantheism expressed a passionate desire to comprehend and unite oneself with total cosmic reality, but it was hampered by taking the substance-and-mode relationship as regulative for explaining the relation between God and the world. Although Bernardino Telesio (13:981d) and Tommaso Campanella (2:1110c) took a qualitative and quasi-magical approach to nature, they testified to the need to understand it better and to reorder social life in new ways.

6. The counterpoint to all these movements was the steady current of Renaissance scholasticism, which took on a new life as "second scholasticism" or "middle scholasticism" and continued to achieve new forms (12:1158b). This was the period of the great commentaries on St. Thomas, the new developments in the law of nations and colonial moral problems, and eventually the shift to the teaching manual as the main instrument of tradition. Among the Dominicans, who exerted an influence at Paris and Salamanca as well as in Northern Italy, the more famous were Francisco de Vitoria (14:727a), Domingo de Soto (13:445a), Melchior Cano (3:28d), Domingo Bañez (2:48a), Ferrariensis (5:893d), and John of St. Thomas (7:1070d). Franciscans of note included Maurice O'Fihely (10:658c) and Antonio Trombetta (14:314), and Carmelite professors known as the Complutenses (4:94d) and the Salmanticenses (12:987d) produced important manuals of philosophy and theology respectively.

7. It was during this period also that the Jesuits (7:898b) came into existence, and contributed an unusual number of thinkers and writers for the renewal of Catholic thought. Among the more noteworthy from the viewpoint of philosophy were Francisco de Toledo (14:187d), Gabriel Vazquez (14:581d), and Peter da Fonseca (5:995b), the latter being the moving spirit behind the Cursus philosophicus edited by the Jesuits at Coimbra

(3:983a), long regarded as an official textbook for philosophy in the Schools. Of considerable importance for their work in speculative theology, which also incorporated distinctive philosophical positions, were Francisco Suarez (13:751a) and Luis de Molina (9:1010c), whose systems of thought are known as Suarezianism (13:754b) and Molinism (9:1011b) respectively. The latter was opposed to Banezianism (2:48a) in the prolonged disputes between the Jesuits and the Dominicans over divine grace and man's freedom [§47.7] known as the *Congregatio de Auxiliis* (4:168d). Among the significant theses of Suarezianism are the following: (1) the concept of being is analogous as applied to God and creatures; (2) the actual essence of a creature is not really distinct from its existence; (3) primary matter is pure potency in the order of form, but it has its own act of existence and God can preserve it in existence without form; (4) the primary formal effect of quantity is to give substance aptitudinal extension, not actual extension; (5) predicamental relations are not really distinct from their foundations; and (6) any creature can, by reason of an active obediential potency, be instrumentally elevated by God to exercise any efficient causality on another creature.

## §96. MECHANICAL PHILOSOPHY AND EMPIRICISM

1. The impetus for the great 17th-century systems came largely from the effort of the *mechanical philosophers* and Descartes to counter-balance skepticism with a positive theory of nature and man. A modest role was played by Francis Bacon (2:9d, GBWW 30), even though he did not appreciate the primary lead of mathematics in the study of nature. He gave a new rhetoric to the age by codifying the criticism of scholastic philosophy of nature, by directing attention to the moving efficient causes, and by raising doubts about whether philosophy can say anything about God and the spiritual principle in man. But it was Galileo Galilei (6:250b, GBWW 28) who regarded nature as a divinely grounded system of mathematical intelli-

gibles and who bifurcated the primary qualities in nature and the secondary qualities in the perceiver. And although Sir Isaac Newton (10:424c, GBWW 34) was less confident about the ontological import of mathematical rules, he worked out their explanatory functions with unsurpassed thoroughness.

2. But how does man fare in the mechanically ordered universe? Divergent responses were given to this leading question by Thomas Hobbes (7:42c, GBWW 23) and RENE DESCARTES (4:784c, GBWW 31). The Englishman's importance lay as much in his presuppositions as in his particular doctrines, for he developed the always attractive procedure of generalizing the dominant scientific outlook and, at least in principle, confining the philosophical analysis of man to what is attainable through this generalized method. He postulated a "state of nature" from which man emerges as he builds his political and social world, bartering his freedom through a "social contract" that provides security but otherwise forfeits any objective order of values to be recognized and implemented. Descartes agreed that man can fare well enough in the mechanically constituted universe, but only on the condition that the mechanical conception of nature be integrated with an adequate theory of method, of knowing, and of being. So he sought to combine mechanism with a reflective metaphysics of the self and God in so firmly grounded and closely knit a system that skepticism would be eliminated and the Christian faith would be liberated from an outmoded philosophy of nature. His starting point was a methodical doubt that led him to assert the clear and distinct idea as the criterion of truth, and to invoke God's existence so as to extend the universality of this criterion beyond his starting principle, *cogito ergo sum* ("I think, therefore I am"). From man's clear and distinct ideas of soul and body he further deduced a dualism of mind and matter, regarding both as substances, but never satisfactorily explaining how they can and do unite.

3. Historians of philosophy rightly caution against making a rigid contrast between Continental rationalism and British empiricism. The two groups share many problems and presuppositions, each striving in its own way to blend reason and expe-

rience, to combine the life of reflective mind with the scientific
view of nature. Yet the *empiricists* were much less confident
about metaphysical principles and the dependence of moral
judgment upon a metaphysical account of the God-man relationship, though each worked out his system in his own way. The
important thing about JOHN LOCKE (8:950c, GBWW 35) is
that he tempered all claims made for the human understanding
with a caution born from his training as a physician and his
observation of the non-mathematical methods of Robert Boyle
(2:742b) and others. He rejected all innate ideas and insisted
that the sources of knowledge are experiential, viz, sensation and
reflection; from sensation the mind derives ideas, while from
reflection it becomes aware of such internal operations as thinking, willing, and desiring. For Locke man knows ideas, not things,
and this conception led him into a subjectivism from which he
never escaped. Yet he remained committed to realism, attempted
a proof for the existence of God, saw divine law as the ultimate
norm of moral activity, and argued against Hobbes's totalitarian
notion of the state. George Berkeley (2:326d, GBWW 35) re-
acted against Locke's theory of knowledge, developing a type of
immaterialism that permitted a reflective personal grasp of the
relationships between God and the participant but limited minds
of men. His central thesis was that the whole being of a sensible
thing consists in its being perceived (*esse est percipi*), with the
result that the primary qualities of bodies (extension and motion)
are as mind-dependent as the secondary. By contrast, DAVID
HUME (7:232a, GBWW 35) was strongly attracted to skepticism, which he attempted to overcome by applying the methods
of Newtonian science to the study of human nature. Starting
with the empiricist principle that man's knowledge of things lies
solely in his impressions of sense, Hume denied reality to any
kind of substance, material or immaterial. He also rejected the
traditional concept of causality, replacing it by the phenomenalist
notions of constant conjunction and temporal succession, and thus
rendering it useless for proofs of the existence of God.

## §97. RATIONALISM AND OTHER MOVEMENTS

1. During the second half of the 17th century Cartesianism (3:157b) was plagued by the breakdown of the unity of man, by the recurrence of skeptical doubts over the relation between empirical reality and clear and distinct ideas, and by the eventual substitution of Newtonian for Cartesian physics. The great rationalists—Spinoza, Malebranche, and Leibniz—found it necessary to begin all over again with fresh principles of metaphysical speculation adapted to life's moral ends. BENEDICT SPINOZA (13: 565d, GBWW 31) laid stress on the reforming functions of the theory of method, which had to bring the finite human intelligence to the point of regarding man as a composite modal modification and dynamic expression of the unique and powerful divine substance. The other side of the debate between monistic naturalism and pluralistic theism was taken by Nicholas Malebranche (9:110c) and G. W. LEIBNIZ (8:620a), who defended the reality of many finite substances and volitional centers as being related to the personal God. Leibniz accepted the doctrine of innate ideas, distinguished between the factual truth of contingent matters and the real truth of essences, and invoked the principle of sufficient reason to assure the validity of human judgments. The central concept of his metaphysics was the monad, a substantial but psychical entity that can reflect the entire universe without external stimulus; in his view the human soul is such a monad, and God is the monad of monads, the substance that makes all other substances possible. All three thinkers agreed, however, that man can attain to metaphysical principles of certitude, that the crux of systematic explanation lies in the theory of human unity, and that the entire speculative effort deeply affects the moral reordering of human life and the search for happiness.

2. The minor philosophical movements in the 17th and 18th centuries constituted an influential cultural background for the main endeavors. Among the lesser British thinkers must be counted the Cambridge Platonists (2:1102a) with their rational theology, and the Scottish School of Common Sense (12: 1246b), which tried to break out of the skeptical impasse and

the Humean restriction of knowledge to perceptual objects and associative beliefs. The Enlightenment (5:435a) and the philosophy it engendered (5:439c) embraced a broad spectrum of positions, ranging from the minimal rational theism of Voltaire (14:743c) to the naturalistic atheism of Holbach (7:48b) and Diderot (4:860c), and on to the plan of Jean Jacques Rousseau (12: 690a, GBWW 38) for educating man through the moral sentiments.

3. The great genius of IMMANUEL KANT (8:123b, GBWW 42) was to transcend these Enlightenment divisions and renew the main philosophical task of integrating experience and reason. Unconvinced by metaphysics in the dogmatic form proposed by Christian Wolff (14: 985b), Kant worked out a method of philosophical criticism (4:463c) for inspecting the structure of human judgments and the a priori principles involved in the major spheres of human activity. His critique of knowledge, which sought to cultivate reason "by the secure path of science," was aimed at bridging the gap between rationalism and empiricism; it proposed a type of Copernican revolution wherein objects were made to conform to our knowledge, rather than the reverse, as in the traditional account. This led him to a doctrine of synthetic a priori judgments, as a consequence of which man can know only appearances (phenomena) and not things-in-themselves (noumena); from this dualism Newtonian physics emerged as the prototype of all human science, and metaphysics was reduced to a "transcendental illusion." Kant's critique of morality focused on man's awareness of a sense of duty, the famous categorical imperative (3:240c), which for him became the fundamental law of pure practical reason. Lacking a metaphysics, Kant could only be agnostic with regard to rational proofs for God's existence; yet he saw religion as essential for regulating human behavior, and so confined it to the field of morals, where it became identified with the recognition of all duties as divine commands. To justify this possibility he had to propose immortality, freedom, and God's existence as postulates of pure reason, accepted not through insight or rational conviction, but only on the basis of pure practical faith.

## § 98. PHILOSOPHICAL RECONSTRUCTION

1. The synthesis of freedom and nature proposed by Kantianism (8:127d) was too precarious to last, since it rested upon a dualism of self and appearances that provoked the search for a closer kind of unity in human experience. Philosophical *romanticism* (12:639d) flourished in Germany upon the demand for a principle of synthesis drawn from the inner life of the self and an imaginative view of nature. The drive of men such as Franz von Baader (2:1a) and K. W. F. von Schlegel (12: 1135c) was to expand the scope of vital intuition and to give greater play to the wisdom of the imagination and the passions, as aids in mastering the sharp contrasts in life. On the theological side F. D. E. Schleiermacher (12:1136b) emphasized man's basic feeling of dependence upon a superior power as furnishing the very springs of religious belief.

2. The German *idealists* were then confronted with the need to join Kant's methodic control over concepts with the romantics' feel for the unity and divinity of life. J. G. Fichte (5:906c) made the fruitful suggestion that all phases of reality and thought respond to a common pattern of positional thesis, counterpositional antithesis, and resolving synthesis, and that they do so respond because this threefold pattern is the graven law of the absolute ego and its activity (1:40c). F. W. J. Schelling (12: 1125a) tested this hypothesis from two sides, starting first from nature in order to reach spirit, and then proceeding in reverse from spirit to nature. But it required the surpassing mind of G. W. F. Hegel (6:986c, GBWW 46) to work out the dialectical development of spirit in all modes of experience. In the idealism (7:340c) he elaborated, known as Hegelianism (6: 990a), every opposition is interpreted as expressing the tragic life of spirit. The creative travail of spirit shapes the logical sphere, the domain of nature, and especially the human world of psychic life and morality, history and art, religion and philosophy, as the encompassing system of knowledge. Starting with the opposition between subject and predicate, which is resolved in the otherness of spirit knowing itself, Hegel saw absolute, dialectical

unity to consist ultimately in the act of mind or spirit. The dialectical law in process was simply this: each achieved degree of consciousness advances through self-contradiction to a higher degree that resolves the contradiction; so the highest contradiction of consciousness, the duality of subject and object, is finally resolved in Absolute Mind. For Hegel this spiritualization of the Absolute perfects itself in the collective history of man, for history itself is but the process by which Absolute Spirit unfolds. This idea has application in political thought, where the state is seen as a manifestation of the Absolute and thus as absolutist and authoritarian. The Absolute Spirit also manifests itself in other ways: (1) as art, in the objective form of sensuous manifestation; (2) as religion, in the subjective form of representation; and (3) as philosophy, in the absolute form of pure thought wherein the opposition of objectivity and subjectivity is ultimately resolved.

3. Hegel's awesome synthesis seemed to be suffocating, however, to Soren Kierkegaard (8:174b) as a religious critic and to Ludwig Feuerbach (5:904d) and Karl Marx (9:333c, GBWW 50) as naturalistic critics. They all agreed upon the need to deflate the theory of absolute spirit by referring it back to the human existent and agent, but there was a new parting of the ways over how best to describe the existence and agency of man. Kierkegaard located these perfections primarily in the free individual, taken in his search for happiness, his moral responsibility, and his religious faith in the transcendent personal God (5:730d). The other aspect of the human situation was explored by Feuerbach and Marx, for whom man is not fully real except in his social relations with other men and the natural world. Marx and Friedrich Engels (5:351a, GBWW 50) laid special stress upon the activity of work, the historical law of class struggle, and the vision of a classless society—the main tenets of Marxism (9:334d) or dialectical and historical materialism (9:441d) as embodied in the system of world communism [§83.6].

4. Two varieties of *positivism* (11:621b) were advanced by Auguste Comte (4:100b) and John Stuart Mill (9:849c, GBWW 43). Comte aimed at joining the search for the unity

of knowledge with the social aspirations aroused by the French Revolution (6:186b); hence his objective synthesis ordered all the positive sciences, whereas his subjective synthesis placed these sciences at the disposal of man's moral aims and the positivist religion. Mill was soberly critical of this latter phase, since he was prolonging the empiricist analysis of knowledge and the calculus of social happiness known as utilitarianism (14:503c). Hence he allied positivism with his logic of science and his defense of human liberty in the democratic society.

5. Throughout the 19th century there was a strong attraction toward the philosophy of life (8:745d). Its early version was advanced by Arthur Schopenhauer (12:1176d), who taught the universal presence of a relentless will to live. He sought surcease from this drive partly in aesthetic contemplation and partly in ascetic denial of self. After the works on evolution by Charles Darwin (4:649c, GBWW 49) had appeared, the philosophy of life became expressly evolutionary; indeed it may be regarded as a type of evolutionism (5:694b) akin to hylozoism (7:285d) and panpsychism (10:946c). Whether it should merely echo biology or become a general cosmology and new morality was a disturbing question for FRIEDRICH NIETZSCHE (10: 643b). In answer, and by way of reaction against historicism and traditional metaphysics, Nietzsche analyzed the ideas of God and of absolute Truth as nothing by man's projection into an illusory "beyond"; to counteract these he proclaimed the "death of God" and preached the new gospel of biological and social Darwinism. In it the will-to-power would give rise to the Superman (*Uebermensch*), and the slave morality of Christianity would be superseded by a "master morality, beyond good and evil." An eternal cycle of becoming would, in effect, be the revelation of a cosmological law functioning without a divine lawgiver; in such a context, the certainty of the "eternal return" could justify a joyous affirmation of all existence, signalizing a final victory over nihilism.

6. Minor currents during the first part of the 19th century included traditionalism (14:228d) and ontologism [§86.5], which based certitude on social transmission and a concept of being respectively. In the latter part there was a revival of Kant's

thought in the movement known as Neo-Kantianism (10:
323b) and a spread of idealism beyond Germany in Neo-Hegel-
ianism (6:992b) and its associated schools, which pertain more
to the domain of contemporary philosophy.

# CHAPTER 19.

# CONTEMPORARY PHILOSOPHY

## §99. LIFE, IDEA, AND SPIRIT

1. There is a narrower and a broader meaning for the expression *contemporary philosophy* (11:312c). In the narrower and highly fluid sense, it signifies those problems and positions that are at the center of interest and discussion in a specific situation at present. In a broader way contemporary philosophy includes the major currents active in the 20th century and relevant for its continued inquiries. The latter is the working historical meaning, being comprehensive enough to include the significant prolongations of previous philosophies as well as the basically new approaches developed in the 20th century. There are some special difficulties in studying contemporary philosophy: (1) the sifting process has not gone long enough to distinguish clearly between the weight of argument and cultural influences; (2) the perspective is not fully attained for setting off the major from the minor, but temporarily impressive, contributions; and (3) not all the systematic consequences have been worked out sufficiently to measure a philosophy in the round. However, the main lines of the 20th-century development can be charted and the most prominent landmarks indicated.

2. In various *life philosophies* (8:745d) the theme of life was prolonged: especially (1) in the direction of man's interior activities by HENRI BERGSON (2:323d), and (2) in the direction of cultural unities by Wilhelm Dilthey (4:869c). (1) In order to countervene the positivistic reduction of life processes to physical laws [§69.2], Bergson cited the difference between the physicalist meaning of time as discrete movements along a spatial line

and the reductive human meaning of time as interior duration. This opened up a metaphysical view of evolution as a striving toward freedom, and of human social life as a tension between the closed system of morality and religion and the open attitude best exhibited by the Christian mystics. Thereafter, Pierre Teilhard de Chardin (13:977a) gave a theistic and personalistic interpretation of the evolutionary character of life: its surge is at once from God and toward God, the latter in function of man's ability to concentrate the streams of life in order to advance, in community form, to the Omega Point, the divine spiritual goal of the entire universe. (2) What impressed Dilthey too was that human life finds its expression not solely in the individual's spiritual striving but also in the various modes of cultural activity. In a given historical period these cultural modes of artistic, scientific, religious, and political life unite in a pattern, sometimes called the tone or spirit or characteristic outlook of the age. Dilthey made two methodological findings: the cultural pattern in history discloses itself better to the procedure of sympathetic understanding [§75.3] than to either the positivist sort of physical-causal explanation or the Hegelian dialectic of absolute spirit; and the great differences between one cultural outlook and another can be studied in terms of a common set of humane categories. The method of sympathetic understanding and categorical analysis of the expressive cultural forms was applied to the areas of language, myth, and science by Ernst Cassirer (3:184d); it was further related to the individual existent's free interpretation of his destiny by José Ortega y Gasset (10:788b).

3. During the first part of the 20th century *idealism* flourished in Europe (7:342b) and in the U.S. Among the British idealists Bernard Bosanquet wrote persuasively about the ideal and absolute factor in art and the tension in practical life between absolute standards and particular situations. The most powerful mind was F. H. Bradley (2:744b), who used the principle that the absolute is the totality of experience to argue for the ultimate internality of all relations, the constant breakdown of perceptual objects and empirical facts in the field of

appearance, and the reality of the one undivided life of the absolute. Nevertheless, he denied any direct knowledge of the absolute reality as the union of all differences, and stressed the relative nature of the particular theoretical and practical standards that men do determine in experience.

4. As representative of American idealism (7:344b), Josiah Royce (12:693d) strove to accommodate evolutionary science and modern logic within idealist thought by exploring the dynamic, intentional relationship between an idea and its fulfilling meaning. He compared the bond between finite individuals and the absolute self to that between the living components in an interpreting system and the whole system or community of interpretation itself. On the moot question of preserving the reality of the human selves, Royce was criticized by such representatives of *personalism* (11:172b) as G. H. Howison and E. S. Brightman (2:802c). The personal idealism of the latter emphasized the distinction between the personal God and finite persons, although it added that the divine nature itself contains both infinite and finite aspects to account for the presence of evil.

5. The leading Italian idealists were Benedetto Croce (4:468a) and Giovanni Gentile (6:337b). Croce identified philosophy with history, because the former is a reflection upon the very process of spirit that internally constitutes the latter. He also revived the systematic claims of idealism by following the course of spirit through the theoretical realms of aesthetic and logical expression and the practical realms of economic and moral activity. Act was the key to reality for Gentile, who worked out a theory of *actualism* (1:108a) extending from logic to education.

6. The expression *philosophy of the spirit* (13:572a) is used to designate a loose association between several French and Italian thinkers who examined the life of the spirit apart from the Hegelian framework, in order to preserve unequivocally the integrity of the human person and his religious relation to the personal God. Maurice Blondel (2:617d) accepted from the philosophy of life a stress upon striving interior action, and

from the idealists a respect for the interrelatedness of all domains of thought and reality. In his own synthesis, the philosophical inquiry remained open to the intiative of divine revelation. This inductive spiritual notion of Christian philosophy exerted an appeal in Italy upon M. F. Sciacca. But the renewed need to consider the fundamental philosophical issues in knowledge, metaphysics, and the growing theory of values was felt strongly by Louis Lavelle (8:540b) and René Le Senne (8:675c). They exhibited the resources of the spiritualist position in penetrating downward into human experience at the levels of perception, ontological participation, and moral activity.

## §100. AMERICAN PHILOSOPHY

1. *American philosophy* (1:438b) came of age with the impact of evolutionary thought, the interest it aroused in scientific method, and the questions left unanswered by the idealistic interpretation of evolution, science, and morality. Charles Sanders Peirce (11:52d) emphasized the role of the idea of consequences in determining a particular scientific concept. He also examined the scientific attitude of unrestricted fallibilism, as well as the abductive method whereby the scientific mind develops fruitful new hypotheses. Against the anti-metaphysical bias of positivism he proposed a theory of the categories and a description of reality in terms of chance, continuity, and love. *Pragmatism* (11:633a) as a theory of meaning and truth was popularized by William James (7:815b, GBWW 53). He argued that a pluralistic and melioristic universe, complete with a developing God, is not only more stimulating to man's moral fiber but also closer to the truth about being. The test of practice remained ambiguous in his hands, however, because of the difficulty of distinguishing between the satisfaction and the validation of ideas. The concepts of pragmatism were nonetheless applied to good effect in logic and epistemology by C. I. Lewis (16:341d) and in social philosophy by Sidney Hook (16:342a).

2. *Naturalism* (10:271d) arose as a way of meeting James's

difficulty with satisfaction and validation of ideas without returning to the idealistic absolute. The version proposed by George Santayana (12:1068b) rested on the dictum that everything ideal has a real basis in the natural material world, and everything real has an ideal mode of fulfillment in the order of imagination. Santayana viewed the human spirit as a constant act of transition from matter to imagination and back again, and reduced religion to a refined filtering of aspirations by the play of imagination. Even so, the verdict of JOHN DEWEY (4:835a) was that Santayana flirted so perilously with transcendence that he ended with a broken-backed dualism. Dewey's own naturalism aimed at being anti-dualistic in respect to the soul-body and God-world distinctions, and yet anti-reductionist in respect to the evolutionary levels of experience. He identified the knowable real with the totality of nature that can be investigated by the scientific method. This placed considerable weight upon the logic of scientific inquiry, which Dewey patterned after the biological relation of organism to environment and which he applied to man's artistic, social, and moral experience. Later Ernest Nagel (16:342b) developed naturalism into a philosophy of science, John Herman Randall, Jr. (16:342) into a philosophy of history and of religion, and Stephen Pepper (16:342c) into a philosophy of value.

3. Since his main philosophical work was done in the U.S., ALFRED NORTH WHITEHEAD (14:896b) belongs in American philosophy. He mounted a sustained attack upon the empiricist bifurcation of nature into causal factors and those that appear in the mind, as well as upon the empiricist disruption of causal relations in experience. His own *process philosophy* (16:363d), also known as the philosophy of organism, is a speculative theory combining cosmological and metaphysical features: in it events or actual occasions are the primary actualities, and things or enduring substances are simply sequences or societies of these occasions, each repeating the society's common defining characteristic. Each occasion is self-creative: usually causes are conceived as active agents producing passive effects, but for Whitehead effects actively produce themselves by the way they appro-

priate their causes. The model for such causation is perception in the Kantian sense, wherein the mind spontaneously organizes its sensations into a single intelligible experience; prehension is the more general term, abstracting as it does from consciousness and so signifying any "taking account" of another. An occasion is then the unification of its prehensions, for an effect is the outcome of its causes: the way B prehends A is the way A causally influences B. Thus physical causality and mental experiencing are unified to overcome Cartesian dualism. Moreover, since an occasion produces itself, its causes need not be productive agents; it is enough that they be prehendable objects, which includes future possibilities, values, and ideals in addition to past actualities. Since no occasion can integrate all the conflicting tendencies of its inherited past, each must have an ideal of what it should become to function as a principle of selectivity in appropriation of the past. This ideal, known as the subjective aim, both affects and is affected by the influence of the past, and this reciprocal interaction constitutes the occasion's freedom. Ultimately all individual ideals must be derived from an actuality that is not a temporal occasion, namely, God. God's power is the worship he inspires through the ideals he provides each occasion; God creates by the way in which he persuades each creature to create itself.

4. Another version of process thought with applications to theology (16:365c) is that of Charles Hartshorne (16:343a), the foremost American commentator on Whitehead. Hartshorne's conclusions are similar to Whitehead's, but his characteristic mode of argument differs: he sets up a series of polar opposites, and then asks which is the more inclusive, which can best account for its opposite. So he argues: (1) panpsychism is defensible because mind can account for matter, but not matter for mind; (2) freedom can account for whatever causal determinism there is, but determinism can account for freedom only by explaining it away; and (3) becoming includes being as an abstract aspect of itself, whereas being cannot include becoming without thereby changing. Hartshorne's philosophy of God is known as panentheism (10:943d); according to this God has an

abstract essence as well as a concrete actuality, though only the former can be grasped by the ontological argument. God's omniscience is abstractly absolute as utterly free from error and ignorance, but it is concretely relative to what in fact there is to know. God's abstract essence is eternal and necessary, but his concrete actuality is temporal and contingent upon his own on-going decisions and upon his experience of an emerging world. God knows all there is to know, the actual as actual and the possible as possible; but, under pain of contradiction, future possibles cannot be known by him as if they were already present actualities.

5. *American realism* (12:113a) is another philosophical movement that arose in the U.S. in reaction to the idealism of Royce and that has continued to evolve into various forms. Its main thesis is that things are independent of man's experience of them: "critical realists" differ from "new realists" in that the latter affirm that things are perceived immediately, whereas the former deny this. Roy Wood Sellars (12:113d) and F. J. E. Woodbridge (12:114d) have attempted to work out the details of critical realist positions; John Wild (16:343b) was an able proponent of realism in his early writings and then turned to phenomenology as a tool for realistic inquiry. The ablest and most vocal proponent of a realist metaphysics in the U. S. is Paul Weiss (16:342d), who developed his own ontology after studying Peirce and Whitehead and has applied it in all areas of systematic philosophy.

## §101. LOGIC AND ANALYSIS

1. As originally propounded in the Vienna Circle (12:1214a) consisting of Moritz Schlick, Rudolf Carnap, and Otto Neurath, *logical positivism* (8:964c) had the threefold task of analyzing the basic kinds of propositions that give knowledge, of determining a criterion of verification for these basic types, and of achieving the unification of the sciences. The first task resolved itself into a rigid distinction between the analytic a

priori propositions found in logic and mathematics and the synthetic or empirical propositions expressing sense data. The second step was to reduce all cognitive meaning to what can be verified through a formal test or a purely empirical test. And the third step was to use the language of physics as the basis of unification of the sciences, regarding every proposition that resisted such reduction as being metaphysical, in the pejorative sense of having neither formal nor empirical cognitive meaning. Although this plan was simplicity itself, it ran into trouble when A. J. Ayer (16:344b) popularized it in England. The sharp contrast between the analytic and the empirical was attacked, the principle of verification [§67.1] was weakened to several modes of verifiability in principle, and the physical language was discovered to contain unexpected contributions of mind (13:66a). As a consequence most logical positivists have moved on to broader conceptions of empiricism and in the process have been incorporated into the "philosophy of science" movement (12:1216a, 1212c).

2. The British school of analysis or of *analytical philosophy* (1:470b) built upon the pioneer work of G. E. Moore (9:1105c) and Bertrand Russell (12:729d, 16:344a). What counted most in Moore's refutation of idealism was his method of moving from metaphysical justification to clarification of what is already known. His positive analysis of perceptual and moral problems took a piecemeal approach, fastened upon ordinary modes of discourse, and ferreted out the logical kinds of questions and reasons involved in common-sense talk. Russell's collaboration with Whitehead not only resulted in modern symbolic logic [§65] but also suggested ways of overcoming misleading expressions. His theory of types and descriptions led Russell to distinguish between the apparent and the real logical form of a proposition, to construct ideal languages out of known entities, and thus to devise a metaphysically neutral method of handling traditional puzzles.

3. Ludwig Wittgenstein (14:983c, 16:344b), the leading analyst, regarded philosophy as an activity of elucidation rather than as a theory. He proposed to dissolve rather than solve meta-

physical theories about the world, by showing that they arose from a misunderstanding of the structure and limits of language or from an attempt to express that which cannot be expressed in language but only shown by contrast with what is sayable. As he further developed such *linguistic analysis* (8:773b) Wittgenstein concentrated on the rules for particular language games and the particular meanings determined by such uses. John Wisdom (16:345b) and the Cambridge school took a therapeutic approach to metaphysical conflicts, whereas at Oxford Gilbert Ryle (16:344c), John Austin (16:344d), and Peter Strawson (16:345a) stressed plural usages, category mistakes, good reasons, and descriptive metaphysics.

4. Linguistic philosophy has made important contributions (1) to the philosophy of religion (16:349a, 383a) and (2) to the development of an analytical ethics (16:160b). (1) The early verificationist position rejected religious discussions as useless and out of date: Anthony Flew and Kai Nielsen continue to use "falsification" arguments against traditional interpretations of God-talk, though they remain open to dialogue with theists, who attack them on the basis that theological claims need not follow the logical patterns of empirical science, as though God were a scientific hypothesis. Recent Wittgensteinians such as D. Z. Phillips and W. D. Hudson are sharply opposed to verificationism and maintain that it is impossible to criticize religious language absolutely; since they defend the meaningfulness of the latter, however, and at the same time deny the possibility of relevant rational criticism, they have been characterized as embracing a type of fideism. Those who are concerned explicitly with religious language, such as Ian Ramsey and John Hick, make less stringent claims than those of traditional natural theology, but they argue that the theistic interpretation of life can be as well founded as literary and historical interpretations can be in their own fields, or again, that one can have intelligent grounds for personal commitment to a religious position without having evidence and arguments that finally exclude every alternative. (2) As a result of their work in ethics contemporary analysts commonly distinguish between descriptive ethics, which

investigates moral phenomena empirically as do the social and behavioral sciences, and normative ethics, which attempts to provide guides or norms, in the form of either moral principles or ideals, that can function both as a foundation of moral justification and as a goal for the achievement of moral excellence or goodness. Both of these, in turn, are differentiated from meta-ethics or ethical theory, which deals principally with two related problems: the meaning of ethical terms and the nature of justification. Recent work in metaethics builds on earlier efforts in support of deontological intuitionism, emotivism, ethical naturalism, universal prescriptivism, and good reasons approaches (16: 161a-164c); it is concerned principally with the role of reason in moral discourse, with studies of the meaning and use of moral concepts, and with the problems of defining morality and its object (16:164d-169d).

## §102. PHENOMENOLOGY AND EXISTENTIALISM

1. EDMUND HUSSERL (7:272c) took the first step toward founding phenomenology with his critique of psychologism (11: 962b), i.e., the attempt of J. S. Mill and others to reduce logical meanings to psychic occurrences and their conditions. Husserl distinguished between the act of judging as a psychic phenomenon and the judgmental content or structure of meaning itself. After also criticizing naturalism and historicism (7:5a) for failing to distinguish between the content and the validity of thought, Husserl sought to make philosophy a rigorous science. He put brackets around the natural attitude of unquestioning techniques for examining the essential structure of things (acts and objects), and traced meanings back to the transcendental ego and its constitution of self and world.

2. Max Scheler (12:1123c) and Maurice Merleau-Ponty (9:687a) developed phenomenology in the moral-religious and the psychological spheres respectively. Scheler found a corrective for ethical formalism in the careful study of actual states of soul and attitudes. He used the theory of intentionality to examine

the religious believer's ordination to God, as well as his self-realization through prayer and love of neighbor. His research was distracted, however, by an evolutionary pantheism in which God and man evolve together with life. Such speculations were foreign to Merleau-Ponty, who made phenomenology speak the language of perception again, in order to locate reality in the mutual relation between man and the world. He used the theme of the living body and man's relation to his life world [102.4] as a means of regulating the sciences and of vindicating the act of human interpretation of visible reality.

3. *Phenomenology* (11:256d), like analysis, is more a method of philosophizing than it is a philosophy in itself. As its etymology indicates, it aims merely to set forth or articulate what shows itself. One of its key ideas derives from Franz Brentano (2:785d), namely, intentionality (7:564a), according to which all consciousness is intentional, i.e., has an intrinsic reference to an object that is not a real element of experience; in other words, consciousness is always consciousness of something beyond it, something presented to it but not contained in it. This assures the objectivity (10:608b) of the contents of consciousness and permits a delineation and classification of the fundamental types of intentional objects and, correspondingly, the intentional acts of the subject presenting them. To permit this the phenomena must be described as they really give themselves, free from any cultural, philosophical, or ontological bias: Husserl attempts to achieve such neutrality by a series of reductions. There is, first, the philosophical *epoché*, or bracketing, the setting aside of all presuppositions about reality, the world, man, the distinctions of primary and secondary qualities, the exterior and interior worlds, etc. The eidetic reduction focuses one's attention on the essential structures of what appears, so that one is dealing, not with an empirical description or that of subsistent Platonic Forms, but with the sense or meaning of what appears. The phenomenological reduction crowns this process by bracketing the reality of the phenomena (whether physical or psychical) that one implicitly accepts as existing. To do this is not to deny or ignore their reality, but rather to focus on precisely what in

their appearance or mode of appearance gives them the index of the real. (It is at this point that commentators diverge on interpretations of Husserl: some see him as embracing a type of realism, whereas others see him as an idealist, for he appears to contend that the intentional acts and objects of consciousness exist absolutely, whereas physical objects exist only for consciousness, being nothing more than the system of their concordant appearances.)

4. Other characteristic elements of Husserl's phenomenology are: (1) the distinction between empty and filled meaning-intentions; (2) the affirmation that every object of awareness (perceptual, conceptual, etc.) is given a horizon or field of objects or meanings that contributes to its significance; (3) the fundamental composition of conscious experience consisting of the intentional object, or noema, and the act of intending, or noesis; (4) some transcendental elements, such as the assertion that every dimension of conscious experience fits into the schema "ego-cogito-cogitatum"; (5) other elements that have realist connotations and are not so easy to subsume under transcendental idealism, such as the notions of history and the alter ego, of a time both constituted and constituting, of passive constitution and the genesis of meaning, and, perhaps most importantly, of the world as the passive pre-given ground of all intentional objects. The latter is called the *Lebenswelt*, the encompassing world of man's daily life, whose primordial structures tend to be lost sight of under the "clothing of ideas," basically the ideas and attitudes of the physical sciences. These sciences are themselves in crisis because they are forgetful of their own concrete origins; to overcome this crisis what is needed is a reduction that recovers (or rather uncovers) the primordial levels of the experience of living-in-the-world.

5. The movement known as *existentialism* (5:730d) developed as a form of existential phenomenology (II:259b), although it had its remote origins in the writings of Kierkegaard [§98.3]. The existentialists made their own return to the existent reality of man, partly to liberate him from being a modalized phase of the idealistic absolute, partly to recover the sense of freedom

and moral decision, and partly to gain orientation for the study of being. But each of them made a distinctive development and came eventually to resist classification along with the others. On this account it is difficult to characterize existentialism as a whole, but the following are some of its dominant themes: (1) an absorbing interest in human existence or human living, focusing on the moral existence of the individual; (2) a concern with the individual as a conscious self and a responsible agent, a subject ("thou") rather than an object ("it"), and thus with the themes of consciousness and freedom; (3) a focusing on man in his concreteness and individuality, thus as cut off from his fellowmen, and so leading to a deep concern with alienation, abandonment, anguish, dread, fear and trembling; (4) a fascination with the non-rational element in existence, viz, absurdity (1:60a); and (5) in general, a rejection of God, in whose absence death becomes an absolute, either an absurd stupidity or a ludicrous monstrosity, that negates human existence itself—with a consequent emphasis on negativity, negation, emptiness, the nothingness of non-being (10:487d).

6. For MARTIN HEIDEGGER (5:733c), existential phenomenology led him more positively from Dasein or things-that-are to being, from technology to the pre-Socratic grasp of nature, and from the long Kantian and Aristotelian traditions to the act of thinking in which being can perhaps be enshrined. His analyses of being in the world, being alone with others, and being related to instruments and to integral things, are clues to the metaphysics of being for which he sought. For Jean Paul Sartre (5:734c), on the other hand, both the social and religious projects of man are unavoidable and yet doomed to frustration. Sartre bases this conclusion on a sharply dualistic theory of matter and consciousness in man, reminiscent of the idealistic thesis and antithesis taken in isolation from any unifying principle. Gabriel Marcel (5:736b) and Karl Jaspers (5:73b) maintain a threefold kinship: (1) they are highly critical of the depersonalizing effect of technological civilization; (2) they regard the free human existent as being related to transcendence as well as to the world; and (3) they recognize the limiting effect of

life situations upon the project of reaching God. Marcel works out a theory of recollection and participation in being whereby the human searcher is united to God, whereas Jaspers remains fundamentally ambiguous about this relationship.

7. Some interesting applications of existentialism have been made in theology (5:729d) by Rudolf Bultmann (11:889d) and Paul Tillich (11:890d, 16:454b). Bultmann works from the Heideggerian notion of anxiety—which results from possibility, facticity, and fallen-ness—to the necessity for man to embrace a "believing existence" so as to obtain a grip on his own situation. To do this one must demythologize the Scriptures, i.e., penetrate beneath the myths through which thought was conveyed in a pre-scientific age, and so elucidate the meaning of his personal existence. For Tillich the fragility of human existence evokes in man the question of God as the absolute "ground of being." Although God's being is "univocal," everything else one can say about God is symbolic; yet the symbolic or mythical character of religious language does not prevent it from standing for man's ultimate concern, since symbols have the power of opening out upon levels of being beyond themselves.

## §103. RECENT FRENCH AND GERMAN PHILOSOPHY

1. In the years after World War II *French philosophy* (16: 345c) has been concerned more and more with the problems of man, with the result that particular attention has been paid to epistemology and to the human sciences, especially anthropology and psychology, and questions relating to the nature of reflection and of existence have been treated with care and from a variety of viewpoints. Philosophers have been less interested in philosophical systems and more concerned with concrete and lived experience; their dialectic has played continually between interiority and exteriority, between what is thought and what is actually lived. As in the recent past, the challenge of Marxism has continued to divide French philosophers, and many important

thinkers are still taken up with existentialist and phenomenological themes. Within the past decade, however, existentialism has declined somewhat, Nietzsche has replaced Hegel as the inspiration of the younger generation, structuralism has made substantial gains through the philosophical examination of linguistics and anthropology, and, as in England, the problem of language has more and more commanded philosophical attention and reflection.

2. An anthropologist and sociologist by training, Claude Lévi-Strauss (16:345) has mapped out social anthropology as a science that investigates the logical structures underlying social phenomena. Such phenomena are for him basically symbolic expressions of the human mind, but frequently they are only implicit, unconscious structures that have to be released from the symbolic forms in which they are imbedded and where they function as systems of communication. Lévi-Strauss's most important work lies in his analysis of myth [§60.2]: in his view, myths arise from problems to be solved, just as science does, and they differ from science not so much in their logic as in the kinds of things to which they are applied. He diverges from Sigmund Freud (6:196c, GBWW 54) in maintaining that they do not reveal man's unconscious, instinctual nature, but rather a first rational attempt, albeit at the unconscious level, to construct a wisdom of nature and culture, while remaining in the domain of sensible images available to primitive peoples.

3. Paul Ricoeur (16:346d) studied under Marcel but he is also indebted to Husserl and other phenomenologists. Whereas Merleau-Ponty has been concerned with the problem of perception, however, Ricoeur has turned to questions relating to human will and freedom; in contrast to Heidegger, he is explicitly concerned with questions of method, a trait that leaves him more open to objectivist philosophies than other phenomenologists. Ricoeur's philosophy has evolved through two main stages, the first of which is a structural phenomenology wherein the "structures" of the will are studied for their fundamental possibilities in the light of rational philosophy, without taking account of symbol or myth and the evil and suffering that man experi-

ences in concrete reality. Its second phase may be termed a hermeneutic phenomenology, which studies the "fault" and guilt that escape structural analysis and seeks an understanding of them in the languages of symbols and myths. Ricoeur's thought is of great interest to religious thinkers because of the new insights it gives to the problem of evil through an analysis of its symbolic expressions.

4. *German philosophy* (16:347a) in recent years has shown a concern with the traditional themes of irrationalism, idealism, romanticism, and vitalism; these received the most attention in the first half of the 20th century and continue to be of significance, particularly with the renewed interest in Nietzsche. Similarly, Hegel's dialectics has continued to fascinate the German mind, especially in its application to the revolutionary dimension of social problems, which has been furthered in the post-war years by the work of the Frankfurt School [§103.6]. Perhaps the most important development in German philosophy, however, has occurred in the area where the British and French have also been working, namely, the philosophy of language. German thinkers, somewhat dissatisfied with the physical sciences and with the technology they have produced, have addressed themselves more and more to the *Geisteswissenschaften*, the sciences of man. The analysis and interpretation of language seems to them particularly suited for understanding the singular and paradoxical problems of human existence. As with the French, there has been a concern with the stucture of knowledge, with its role in the sociology of knowledge (8:232c), with the hermeneutical problems it presents, and with the ontology it implies.

5. The name given to the philosophy of Hans Georg Gadamer (16:347b) is hermeneutics, a reminder that Hermes served in Greek mythology as a mediator between the gods and men and so aptly can characterize the science of interpretation [§57. 4]. Gadamer's hermeneutics is less indebted, however, to the psychological individualism of Schleiermacher, Dilthey, and Emilio Betti than it is to Heidegger and Bultmann, the first for the phenomenology of existence uncovered in the study of being and time, and the second for the existential interpretations given

to passages in the Scriptures. Heidegger's contribution arose out of his critical studies of the notions of subjectivity (13:758d) and historicity, which he came to see did not place limits on human understanding or actually compromise objectivity. Rather understanding, for him, is a primordial characteristic of the being of human life itself; it implies no detached self-possession of existence but is molded by history and so is limited only by the facticity of its being. Gadamer has taken up this theme and shown how the thinker actually stands in history, in a manifold complex of tradition, and must acknowledge his historical presuppositions before turning to individual things and their so-called objective analysis. Prior understanding therefore sets a definable horizon for affirmations as answers to questions, which horizon must be provisionally acknowledged and then submitted to criticism in the further process of understanding. An adequate understanding of what has been appropriated from the past, in Gadamer's view, can only result from interpretations that have been translated into one's own language.

6. Dialectical materialism [§83.6] and Marxism [§98.3] early made strong appeal in Germany, but the task of rethinking these movements in contemporary contexts has fallen to a group of thinkers collectively known as the *Frankfurt School* (16:347d); under the leadership of Max Horkheimer the school counted among its members Horkheimer's disciple, Adorno, and a student of Heidegger, Marcuse. Theodor Adorno (16:348a) studied Hegel but did not accept his thesis that the real remains fragmentary and transitory to the extent that it is not also rational— a thesis that led Hegel to adopt a progressivist dialectic wherein the real and the rational ultimately result in a single totality. Whereas Hegel had maintained that only the whole is true, Adorno took the opposite position, arguing that the whole is the non-true. Thus he excludes any identity between the rational and the real, between the concept and the thing conceived; the whole, for him, is always opposed to the particular, being not only its negation but its very non-truth. Adorno's negative dialectic reminds subjective thought that it must not only deny the object opposed to it but that it must even deny itself, so that

its real freedom consists in its ability to affirm even that it is not free. Like Adorno, Herbert Marcuse (16:348b) has been concerned with Hegel, and also with Freud, but the advanced industrial society is the main focus of his philosophical reflection. Technology, as Marcuse learned from Heidegger, furnishes the means whereby the world can be looked on as a tool, and although it was not born of human needs it is nonetheless called upon to satisfy them. Its justification, therefore, depends on how successful it is in filling, rather than subverting, man's legitimate expectations. Yet, Marcuse argues, technology has become the principal means of oppression in an advanced industrial society: whereas in earlier societies there had been a dualism of thought and of being, in technological society man is so absorbed and manipulated by the system that he becomes, in effect, one dimensional. The world of technology is thus given over more and more to material comforts, but in the process it perpetuates misery, violence, and destruction. Some of the negations that have disappeared from industrial society must therefore be reinstated, for these are necessary to call attention to true human needs.

7. German phenomenology and existentialism have generally lacked the atheistic overtones found in French thought and so have had considerable appeal for religious thinkers, with Heidegger usually being favored by Catholic theologians and Jaspers by Protestant. Catholic writers, of whom the Italian-born Romano Guardini (16:198b) is typical, have therefore developed phenomenological, ontological, and existential themes in ways similar to the authors already discussed. Their work has served mainly as a corrective to that of the Frankfurt School, for instead of proposing a negative philosophy that concentrates on anguish, violence, and death, they stress rather the positive, i.e., the good to be found in man and the joy resulting from his elevation to the supernatural state. Again, rather than give way to a radical subjectivism in human action and morality, they have consistently maintained the objectivity of values that is implied in God's promise to man of a merited eternal salvation.

## §104. THOMISM: EXISTENTI
## AND TRANSCENDENTAL

1. In the wake of the papal recommendations after Leo XIII's *Aeterni Patris* (1:165d), there was a renewal within scholasticism (12:1165c) that is sometimes referred to as neo-scholasticism or neo-Thomism (10:337b). The historical labors of Maurice De Wulf (4:836b) and of Martin Grabmann (6: 657b), in particular, restored knowledge of the medieval philosophies and focused attention on the works of Aquinas as containing answers to pressing contemporary problems. As a consequence Thomism underwent extensive development in the 20th century and was placed in dialogue with most other contemporary movements; it is the most extensively developed systematic philosophy in the present day, and possibly has the greatest number of adherents. The two most important developments have been that resulting from the confrontation with existentialist thought, seen in the writings of Maritain and Gilson, and that resulting from the confrontation with Kantianism and other forms of idealism, seen in the writings of a group of philosophers and theologians known as Transcendental Thomists.

2. JACQUES MARITAIN (14:135d, 16:275d) was influenced by Bergson but became interested in the thought of Aquinas after being converted to Catholicism; a penetrating thinker and clear writer, he brought the thought of St. Thomas into the marketplace of the modern world. His deepest and most lasting achievements have been in the area of epistemology, in elucidating the different degrees of knowledge and of their interrelationships, and, more generally, in his pursuit of the various dimensions of an integral, Christian humanism. His contributions to social and political philosophy, and to constructive critiques of modern culture and art, have also been substantial. In his theoretical philosophy he has stressed the authentic existentialism of Aquinas, maintaining the primacy of existence in a realist philosophy of being, and seeing this as providing the basis also for an understanding of knowledge and of love.

3. ETIENNE GILSON (14:137d) also studied under Bergson;

his early work was on Descartes, but this led him to a study of medieval philosophy and to Thomism in particular. One of his central theses is that the philosophy of the Middle Ages in general is a Christian philosophy; by this he means a philosophy that, while keeping the orders of faith and reason distinct, nevertheless considers Christian revelation as an indispensable auxiliary to reason. In Thomas he found a metaphysics of existence [§42] that conceives God as the very act of being (*Ipsum Esse*) and creatures as beings centered on the act of existing (*esse*). His disciples have elaborated his thought as an existential metaphysics (5:726), which they see as a corrective to the essentialism that has insinuated itself into various Renaissance and rationalist versions of Thomistic thought.

4. The roots of *Transcendental Thomism* (16:449d) can be traced to the writings of Désiré Mercier (9:671a) and Maurice Blondel, and to the efforts of two Jesuits, Pierre Rousselot (12:692a) and Joseph Maréchal (9:198b), to rehabilitate critical philosophy in light of the teachings of Aquinas. Kant's transcendental philosophy was to be a search for the unknown presuppositions underlying all knowledge, for its a priori conditions, but this led him to question the realist foundations of thought and the receptive character of knowledge, and ultimately to a rejection of metaphysics. Maréchal countered this rejection by first distinguishing the representational from the existential character of knowledge, and then locating the latter in the judgment as the intellect's activity not of receiving its object but of "structuring" it from sense data. Knowledge was thus for him a dynamism of projecting conceptual contents onto the domain of the real through the judgmental act; the grounds for this was an innate tending of the intellect toward intuition of the Absolute. In a later formulation he proposed the act of judgment as an affirmation of absolute reality, at least implicit and necessary in all intellection, which objectifies the form or concept and so grasps it as being. In other words, beyond the finite determinations of the representation, the intellect is made aware of a further intelligibility precisely by its own tending, in a dynamism unleashed by the concept itself, toward something infinite

and absolute—actually the infinite act of existing that is God. In this way the intellect "constitutes" its object, as belonging, in a finite and participatory way, to the realm of the real. So intentionality as such, i.e., formally as cognitive and representative, necessarily bespeaks the real order.

5. Maréchal's innovative Thomism received new insights from further dialogues with phenomenology and Heidegger by two German Jesuits, Karl Rahner and Emerich Coreth, and with science and the philosophy of history by a Canadian Jesuit, Bernard Lonergan. From these have emerged a new metaphysics in which the being investigated is that which occurs in consciousness; they see such being as more phenomenal in kind and closely assimilated to meaning and knowledge. Thus Coreth writes of an immediate unity of being and knowing in the very act of knowing, and Lonergan looks upon being as whatever is to be known by intelligent grasp and reasonable affirmation, progressing from the structures of consciousness as sensation, concept, and judgment to the structures of extra-mental being as matter, form, and existence. In this way the being of consciousness is extrapolated to the being of the cosmos. For Rahner an analysis of the performance of the human spirit discloses at its very core an innate drive to being as absolute and really existing; this is the very nature of man as "spirit in the world" or finite transcendence. On this basis the judgment asserts the real beingness of the finite object, represented in the concept, and is a situating of it on the spectrum of real analogical being. In affirmation intelligence or spirit does not discover being but rather "performs" being, a performance Rahner locates in the activity of the *intellectus agens*. The underlying finality, however, is non-cognitive and is conative or even volitional: for Rahner human spirit as such is desire or striving, whereas for Lonergan being is the objective of the unrestricted desire to know.

6. Rahner explains the implications of this theory of knowledge by recourse to his notion of the *Vorgriff*, i.e., an anticipation by the soul of being which, while conscious, is preconceptual, nonobjective, and unthematic; all a posteriori knowledge is an objectification and thematization of this. Somewhat differently,

Lonergan allows that man can think about being before knowing
it, in the sense that he can grasp the notions of being before its
concepts are realized in objective and explicit knowledge; as he
puts it, prior to every content being is the notion of the to-be-
known through that content. The being in question through all
this is unlimited, unconditioned, ultimate-absolute being as the
unrestricted horizon of the pure desire to know, not, however,
*the* Absolute Being whom the believer can come to recognize
(in faith) as its ground. This is not ontologism [§86.5] because
the being objectified in the affirmation is not God but finite being
as it points to the divine.

7. At the heart of this type of developmental Thomism lies
the *transcendental method*: first, attention is directed not to
objects to be known but to the intentional acts of subjects in
their very knowing; second, what is sought thereby in a reductive
analysis are the a priori conditions for the very possibility of
knowing finite objects in any objective way. The starting point
of the method is the question: man is ceaselessly driven to question everything except the very fact of his questioning. But this
heuristic character of consciousness is inexplicable unless one
admits some sort of a priori awareness of what it is that the
question seeks. As Coreth explains it, one cannot ask "What is
it?" without betraying some sort of non-objective prehension of
the range of being; being, not merely "for us" but "in itself," is
the horizon of the question. From a more detailed epistemology
that owes something to John Henry Newman (10:412a) Lonergan offers his own explanation: reacting against views of understanding (14:389b) that reduce it to mere concept formation,
he sees it rather as an intuition (7:598d) more properly called
insight (7:545c); this allows for a "higher viewpoint" on which
basic concepts, as subsequent objectivations of insights, undergo
constant revision. It also brings into play Lonergan's original
theory of judgment in which the tentative truth value of concepts is verified by assuring that the judgments involving such
representations are "virtually unconditioned," i.e., the intellect
judges reflectively that the conditions for the verification of the
affirmation have been reasonably met. The resultant intelligibility

is not one of rational necessity but rather that of an "emergent probability." Differing from Coreth, however, Lonergan delimits metaphysics to the objective pole of the horizon of being, denying its extension to the subjective pole, namely, the method of performing, which has to be sought in a transcendental doctrine of methods.

8. Transcendental Thomism provides a knowledge of God (16:194a) in the tradition of Catholic theism, and by an act of intelligence, but one rooted in love. Due to its orientation to the beatific vision, the intellect in this life is able to "perform" being, which is to say that every performance of being is at least an implicit and anonymous attaining to God. In this perspective Rahner maintains that every human consciousness grasps the reality of God in an unthematic, preconceptual way as Absolute Mystery. The authentication of this in reflection is not probative but ostensive: the believer does not strictly demonstrate God's existence but interprets ordinary experience, common to himself and non-believers, as grace and thematizes them accordingly. But only in love, as man's response to God's prior loving of him, does man come to this non-objective awareness of the Absolute Mystery; so love of God, as the deepest factor of knowledge, is both its condition and its cause. Alternatively, Lonergan reasons that man's capacity to know reality demands as its condition the infinite identity of being and knowing, who is God. If consciousness has an unrestricted horizon that is absolute being, this demands reasonably acknowledging *the* Absolute Being as an unrestricted act of understanding. Such an acknowledgment rests upon the virtually unconditioned judgment that unless God exists reality is not fully intelligible. Again, the insight whence the argument proceeds is rooted in love or in what Lonergan calls conversion, i.e., it results from an intellectual conversion to a higher viewpoint explained by "horizon shifts" arising from prior religious and moral conversions.

9. A viable alternative to these recent Thomisms, both existential and transcendental, has been worked out by the Flemish Dominicans, Dominic De Petter and Edward Schillebeeckx. Their theory of "implicit intuition" conceives knowledge as a

dynamism also, but one entirely objective in kind and not sub-jective in the sense of that inspired by Maréchal. It derives not from an unrestricted desire to know but from strictly cognitive elements. Here knowledge is basically a non-conceptual aware-ness of reality, although it is inseparable from concepts; the latter, while not grasping the real by themselves, do refer to reality and so possess truth value, by supplying the objective determina-tion within which alone the intuition can occur as something implicit. In this theory a dynamism of the knowing subject gives way to a dynamism of the contents of knowledge.

# General Index

The numbers indicated are page numbers. For a systematic arrangement of topics see the analytical table of contents, pp. xiii-xx. Names of philosophical movements are included here: those of individual philosophers are not, but they may be located easily in the chapters on the history of philosophy, pp. 277-332, where they are treated in approximate chronological order. Compound expressions are listed by substantive; thus, for "natural law," see law, natural

absolute, 306, 310, 328
abstraction, 25, 38, 71, 89, 192
accident, 88, 97, 98; predicable, 27
act, 49, 94-96, 124; elicited and imperated, 152; human, 79, 151-156, 163; incomplete, 49, 55; indifferent, 163, 165; pure, 134, 135, 139, 143, 156, 280, 292; voluntary, 160
action, 30, 51, 56; immanent and transient, 60
aesthetics, 182
agent, 101, 104; see cause, efficient
analogy, 88-90, 125, 131, 132, 208; of attribution, 89, 90, 126; of proportionality, 89, 90, 125, 132
analysis, 107, 315-318; linguistic, 180
anthropology, 219-222, 323; philosophical, 11, 80
appetite, 74-76; right, 172
Aristotelianism, 281, 290, 298
art, 45, 181; liberal, 40, 188
atheism, 272, 304

atomism, 279, 282
Augustinianism, 291
authority, 238-240, 248
axiology, 188
axiom, 34, 198

beauty, 92, 183
becoming, 42, 50, 51, 314
behavior, 222, 226, 227
being, 49, 50, 73, 86-90, 110, 270, 279, 280, 293, 314, 321; common, 121, 123; finite, 94; historical, 268; mobile, 41; principles of, 93-96; properties of, 91; subsistent, 124-127; see esse; existence
body, 61, 80, 81
brain, 67, 73

Cartesianism, 301, 303
categories, 28-30, 88
causality, 93, 100-106, 302, 314; divine, 139-143;
cause, 35, 48, 49; efficient, 55, 101, 104, 140, 142; exemplary, 105; final, 44, 101, 105,

140; first, 55, 127, 131, 140, 142, 156, 157; formal, 44, 101-103; instrumental, 72, 104; material, 44, 101, 103
certitude, 3, 118
chance, 47
change, 42, 43, 49
choice, 78, 154
circumstance, 163, 164
communism, 260, 306
compulsion, 47, 161
concept, 14, 25, 69, 113; formal and objective, 14, 65, 71-73
conceptualism, 25, 272
condition, 73, 101
conscience, 130, 169; right, 170
consciousness, 69, 83, 111, 226, 319-321, 329
continuum, 51, 54, 196
contract, social, 240, 253, 301
contradiction, 139, 306; principle of, 34, 93
cooperation, 166
correspondence, 116, 194, 195
cosmology, 41
creation, 140, 141, 212, 291
criteriology, 109
culture, 220

death, 145, 287
definition, 16, 33, 38; formal and material, 50, 61
demonstration, 22, 35-37; a posteriori, 36, 49, 126; a priori, 36; propter quid, 36, 133; quia, 36
dialectic(s), 35, 203, 288, 305, 306, 324, 325
difference, 27; individual, 83
disposition, 29, 152
distinction, 31; kinds of, 31-33
division, 16
doubt, 118, 119, 301

education, 187-188
ego, 228, 305
element, 211, 212, 279
emotion, 76, 161, 162
empiricism, 272, 297, 300-302, 316
end, 44, 46, 101, 105, 156, 163, 172; ultimate, 158, 159
entelechy, 61
Epicureanism, 281
epistemology, 5, 109-120
error, 115, 119
esse, 86, 95, 98, 123-127, 140-143, 328; ipsum esse subsistens, 131, 133, 135, 137, 292
essence, 87, 95-97, 102, 132, 136, 280; divine, 133
ethics, 5, 149-175; Christian, 150, 159; individual, 151; social, 151, 231
eudaemonism, 273
evidence, 117, 118
evil, 143; cause of, 145; kinds of, 144; moral, 144-146; problem of, 143, 324
evolution, 213, 215, 216, 307, 310; human, 219, 220
exemplar, 105, 140
existence, 18, 95, 96, 328; see esse
existentialism, 320-322, 327
explanation, 36, 204; see cause
extension, 51, 196

fact, 117, 204, 205
falsity, 18, 114, 115
family, 243-246
fear, 77, 161
finality, 93; see end; cause, final
force, 47, 161, 208, 248, 258
form, 42, 43, 59, 101-103, 280, 291; subsistent, 125; substantial, 29, 32, 44-46, 61,

81, 102, 124
formalism, 182, 192, 198
fortitude, 153, 159, 170
freedom, 78, 138, 146, 154, 321, 323

genus, 27
God, 97, 121, 122, 272; attributes of, 131-139; existence of, 126-130
good, 74, 76, 143, 157, 280; absolute, 138; common, 166, 167, 231, 235, 240, 248, 251-253, 255, 264; kinds of, 189, supreme, 78, 130
goodness, 91, 92
governance, 139, 147, 216
government, 168, 252-254, 258-261

habit, 29, 82, 152
happiness, 130, 158
hedonism, 274
Hegelianism, 305, 306, 308
hermeneutics, 180, 275, 324
historicism, 307, 310
historicity, 184, 297, 325
historiography, 184; of philosophy, 274-276
history, 183, 268; philosophy of, 183-185
horizon, 320, 325, 330, 331
humanism, 273, 289, 298, 327
humanities, 179, 181
hylomorphism, 211, 214, 291
hypothesis, 204, 223

idea, 106, 280; see concept
idealism, 270, 305, 306, 310, 311
ignorance, 115, 119; kinds of, 162
immanence, 60, 111, 126
immateriality, 64, 73, 74, 81, 82, 111
immortality, 82, 125

implication, 19; material, 199
individuality, 100, 124
individuation, 54, 135, 291, 293
induction, 21, 22, 206
infinity, 51, 52, 134, 135, 147
insight, 107, 330
instrument, 40, 104, 206
intellect, 71, 136; agent, 25, 72, 73; passive or possible, 25, 72
intellection, 71; subsistent, 134, 137
intelligibility, 73, 93
intelligible, 25, 26, 73
intention, 64, 65; first, 28; second, 13, 26, 28, 197, 202
intentionality, 64, 111, 318, 319, 329
intuition, 112, 330, 332

judgment, 17, 114, 328-331
jurisprudence, 261
justice, 153, 159, 171, 172; commutative and distributive, 174; legal, 174, 246; social, 246

Kantianism, 304, 305, 308
knowledge, 63, 111-112, 271, 327, 328, 332; apprehensive, 114; divine, 137; intellectual, 112; practical, 5; preconceptual, 329-330; process of, 71; sense, 66, 112, 113; speculative, 4

language, 179, 204, 294, 316, 317, 323, 324
law, 163, 166; civil, 167, 262, 263; eternal, 168; international, 257; natural, 167-169, 173, 262, 263; philosophy of, 261-264; physical, 206; positive, 173

life, 59, 212-214, 305, 307, 309-311; divine, 136; origin of, 214-215
limitation, 95, 122, 123
linguistics, 179, 221, 317
logic, 4, 39-40, 288, 289; Aristotelian, 13; formal, 14-23; material, 14, 23-29; propositional, 199; symbolic, 197-200, 316
love, 76, 138

man, 80-84, 287, 306, 321
marriage, 240-243
Marxism, 306, 322, 325
mass, 208, 209
materialism, 227, 261, 271, 281, 287, 325
mathematics, 4, 38, 191-194, 290; philosophy of, 4, 191-200
matter, 42, 43, 45; primary, 29, 32, 55, 59, 103, 124, 211, 212, 214; signed, 55; structure of, 211, 212
mean(s), 157, 172, 173
measure, 52, 195
measurement, 52, 205, 206, 223
mechanism, 213, 214, 237, 301
metaethics, 318
metahistory, 184, 276
metaphysics, 4, 38, 58, 85-108, 121
method, hypothetico-deductive, 201, 204; scholastic, 6; scientific, 204; see methodology
methodology, 40, 222, 232, 254, 274
mode, 28, 29, 99, 100
model, 208, 232
morality, 162-165
motion, 49; conditions for, 56; first cause of, 56, 57; kinds of, 50; laws of, 209-210; parts of, 51
motive, 156, 163
mover, 55; first, 156; first unmoved, 55, 57, 142, 143, 156
myth, 185, 322-324

naturalism, 312, 313
nature, 44, 45, 75, 97, 102, 136, 202, 254, 278; human, 82, 234; philosophy of, 41
necessity, 118, 137; natural, 138
negation, 131, 143, 144, 146
Neoplatonism, 282, 290
nominalism, 25, 272, 294
non-being, 144, 321; see privation
number, 53, 54, 194, 195

object, 66, 68, 111
objectivity, 64, 203, 319, 325
occasion, 102
Ockhamism, 294
omnipotence, 139
omnipresence, 135
omniscience, 136, 315
ontologism, 273, 307
ontology, 85, 123
order, 30, 150, 167, 215; social, 234, 235
organism, 61, 213, 237, 313-314
otherness, 91, 93

pain, 76, 144
pantheism, 273, 299, 314, 319
paradigm, 202, 203
part, 62, 63, 227
passion, 30, 51, 56, 60; see emotion; action
participation, 106, 124-126, 132
percept, 70-72; see phantasm
perception, 66, 70, 71, 227, 229, 319
perfection, 131, 143; divine, 135

person, 82, 83, 99, 246; juridical, 236; moral, 174, 236
personality, 84, 229
phantasm, 25, 69-73
phenomenology, 318-322
philosophy, 3, 4, 267; Christian, 5, 6, 123, 127, 141, 151, 187, 283, 285, 328; first, 85, 122; history of, 9, 267-332; moral, 149-175; natural, 4, 38, 41-58; political, 231, 251-264; scholastic, 6, 285, 288-295; social, 231-249
physics, 207-212; mathematical, 48, 192, 294
place, 52, 53
Platonism, 282, 289, 298, 303
pleasure, 76, 281
pluralism, philosophical, 7, 8, 269, 270
poetics, 35, 182
politics, 251, 254
positivism, 227, 306, 307; legal, 262; logical, 315
potency, 49, 94, 95; see act; power
power, 29, 46, 61, 62, 81, 82, 253, 258, 259, 299; cogitative, 69, 70
pragmatism, 116, 117, 312
predicables, 26-27
predicaments, see categories
premise, 20-22
principle, 41, 44, 49, 100, 117; first, 33-35, 93, 110, 118, 168; self-evident, 115; uncertainty, 210
privation, 42, 44, 143
process, 313-315; see change; motion
property, 27, 42, 49; private, 247
proposition, 18; immediate, 33-35

providence, 139, 146, 147, 316
prudence, 153, 159, 169, 171, 172, 181; political, 251, 252
psychology, 4; modern, 222-229; philosophical, 59-84

quality, 29, 205-206
quantity, 29, 194
question, 110, 330
quiddity, 14, 26, 72, 73, 121

rationalism, 272, 297, 301, 303-304
realism, 24, 270-272, 302, 315
reality, 86, 269
reason, 13; right, 163, 169, 172; seminal, 291; sufficient, 93, 303
reasoning, 19, 112
reduction, 213, 214, 319
reflection, 74, 110
relation, 30
religion, 185-187
responsibility, 161, 165, 166
right, 173; human, 175; natural, 174; see justice

scholasticism, 288-295, 299, 327
science, 37-39, 115, 203, 267; behavioral, 219-230; mixed, 38, 48; modern, 7, 201-230, 267; philosophy of, 201-203, 316; political, 254-255; social, 232
Scotism, 293, 295
sense, 67-69; common, 69, 303
sensible, 25, 67; common and proper, 68
separation, 32, 38, 86, 89
sign, 15, 179, 186; formal and instrumental, 15, 66, 72
skepticism, 119, 205, 271, 282, 295, 298, 300, 302
socialism, 261

society, 231, 234-238, 255, 256
solidarity, 235, 248
soul, 60, 145, 281, 287-289; human, 80-82, 125; kinds of, 62
species, 27, 64, 102, 215; expressed and impressed, 65-67; intelligible, 65, 72; intentional, 65
spirit, 81, 305, 306, 311-313, 329; pure, 136
spirituality, 83
state, the, 252, 255-258
Stoicism, 281, 298
structuralism, 226, 323
Suarezianism, 300
subject, 17, 111, 144
subsidiarity, 235, 248
subsistence, 83, 98
substance, 29, 88, 96-100, 302, 303
supposit, 98, 99
syllogism, 21, 22
symbol, 186, 198, 322-324
synderesis, 107, 168-170

technology, 217, 218, 220, 321, 326
teleology, 105; see finality
temperance, 153, 159, 170
term, 15; middle, 21, 22, 36, 38, 48, 127, 128
theism, 216, 273, 304, 331
theodicy, 123
theology, 85, 121; natural, 5, 121, 122, 186

theory, 207; in psychology, 225, 228, 229; quantum, 210, relativity, 211
thing, 83, 91, 93; see person
Thomism, 291-292, 295, 327-332
time, 30, 53, 309
transcendence, 111, 126, 328-330
transcendentals, 90-93
truth, 3, 18, 73, 91, 92, 112-114, 269, 271; double, 292; theories of, 116-117

unconscious, 227, 228
understanding, 107, 115, 168, 233, 310
unity, 91, 92, 195, 235
universal(s), 17, 24-26, 28, 288, 289
utilitarianism, 274, 307

value, 188-189, 312
verification, 117, 180, 204, 315, 316
virtue, 153, 166, 170-172, 252
voluntarity, 169-162; indirect, 164

war, 257-258
whole, 17, 227
will, 77, 136, 145, 323; acts of, 79; freedom of, 78, 80, 146, 155
wisdom, 85, 106, 115, 159, 280, 285-287; practical, 169
work, 246, 306